HQ769.Y59

0 0066 00057992 7

Youniss, James/Parents and peers in so

Whitworth College Library

DISCARD

P9-BJQ-554

Parents and Peers in Social Development

A Sullivan-Piaget Perspective

James Youniss

Parents and Peers
in Social Development

The University of Chicago Press/Chicago and London

JAMES YOUNISS is professor of psychology
and a member of the Boys Town Center for
the Study of Youth Development at the
Catholic University of America. He is married
and is the father of four teenaged children.

The University of Chicago Press, 60637
The University of Chicago Press, Ltd., London

© 1980 by The University of Chicago
All rights reserved. Published 1980
Printed in the United States of America
84 83 82 81 80   5 4 3 2 1

Library of Congress Cataloging in Publication Data

Youniss, James E
  Parents and peers in social development.

  Bibliography: p.
  Includes index.
  1. Child development.   2. Parent and child.
3. Peer groups.   4. Sullivan, Harry Stack,
1893–1949.   5. Piaget, Jean, 1896–
I. Title.
HQ769.Y59   305.2'3   79-25457
ISBN 0-226-96484-1

To my friends, especially Dorothy, and to my parents as well as my children: Carrie, Andy, Emily, and Jessica, who let me experience the parent-child relation from the other side

Contents

Acknowledgments

This book reports the first step of an ongoing research program begun four years ago. Several people have participated in the work and contributed in numerous ways to its progress. The following people helped by conducting library research, interviewing children, scoring protocols, and so on: Gail Cabral, Roger Locker, Barbara Gellert, Douglas Rachford, Diana Martinez, Lois Loew, Michelle Eban, Thomas Granzow, and Alice Lo Cicero. I owe a special debt to three people who worked on this project from its start and contributed directly to this manuscript. Janet Castleman read several chapters and added several clarifications. Jacqueline Volpe was a mutual collaborator in forming ideas which helped to integrate Sullivan's with Piaget's writings. She also designed and conducted study 9 and allowed me to use the data for this book. Margaret Schatzow did all of the above and in addition read and acted as an editorial critic on all drafts of the manuscript. I have benefitted greatly from their professional assistance and personal support.

Two other colleagues have helped me in so many ways for so many years that I can acknowledge their contribution only by the promise of continued friendship. Hans Furth and Bruce Ross have been my mentors, critics, and unfailing friends who have made my professional life most enjoyable. They have helped me understand Piaget's theory and encouraged my explorations for new interpretations of it.

Several people at the Boys Town Center have supported the maintenance of this project. I thank especially Michael Chapman, who taught me much, as well as Sally Ryan and Jim O'Connor. I would like to thank as well my secretaries, Phyllis Brantley, who typed the final manuscript ably, and Marie Weldrick and Catherine Wilmer, who did more to help than I realized at the time with their stabilizing calmness, efficiency, and humor.

This project was supported in part by funds from Boys Town, Nebraska. The ideas and opinions expressed are those of the author and do not necessarily reflect those of Boys Town.

Preface

This is a book about children's understanding of their relations with adults and with peers. These two relations constitute the basic makeup of society as children experience it. In trying to study how children come to know society and become members of society, most social scientists study these two relations. By convention, children's relations with adults are believed to be more important. Children are naïve and adults know what is required for living in society. Adults represent the wisdom of tradition and recognize those patterns of behavior which have been proven useful historically. They are the teachers most beneficial to children's as well as society's long-term welfare. In distinction, peers cannot be expected to know society's norms except insofar as adults have instructed them. It is possible for peers with like training to reinforce each other and, in the process, support adult instruction. Left to their own wits, however, there is no telling what peers would concoct as interesting, right, or practical. We have a glimpse of what they might do through studies of peer pressure which seems to be a potent force in leading to wayward conduct.

The purpose of this book is to suggest a revision of this conventional model. It presents a thesis that children's relations with adults have necessary but only limited roles to play in the path toward social maturity, while peer relations play a more important and more positive part than xi conventional theorists have thought. The argument of the thesis is that were peers left to their own resources, as they often are in friendships, a psychologically healthy and morally principled value system would be the likely product.

This thesis is a synthesis or integration of the writings of Harry Stack Sullivan (1953), a psychiatrist, and Jean Piaget (1965), a philosopher of knowledge and developmental psychologist. They approached the topic of social development independently with different interests in mind. Sullivan was a practicing psychiatrist who observed mainly middle-class clients in Washington, D.C., and New York City in the 1940s (Chapman 1976), whereas Piaget, as a social theorist, dealt primarily with working-class children in Geneva, Switzerland, in the 1920s.

In his lectures and writings, Sullivan evolved a theoretical approach toward the development of the mature personality. This position was controversial with respect to the then predominant view of psychoanalysis. Psychoanalytic theorists emphasized sexual motivation and intrapsychic factors, which, when balanced, constituted adjustment. Sullivan, on the other hand, emphasized interpersonal existence, claiming that adjustment occurs when a person is able to submit his or her personality to the common interest of a relationship with another person.

In seeking the origins of interpersonal adjustment in his clients, Sullivan was struck by the importance of peer relations and friendship in particular. He suggested that the period covering pre- and early adolescence was critical in the path toward maturity. Experience with close friendships during this period plants the seeds and establishes the elements of what becomes love or intimate relations in later life. These elements include interpersonal sensitivity, appreciation of personhood, and mutual understanding. In the intellectual context of the time, Sullivan was aware that he would be attacked for emphasizing peers and diminishing the place of parents. He therefore laid out a theory in which an analysis of relations by structure and function was made prior to statements about parents or friends. Conclusions about the two relations in their developmental effects could then be seen as logical outcomes of the prior analysis. This did not discourage criticism, and perhaps the sharpest critique of all is that contemporary developmental psychologists ignore his theory and give him only historical reference as a figure who added the interpersonal factor to Freud's theory and thought that peers could be positive as well as negative in influence.

The writings of Piaget, on the other hand, are well read by contemporary psychologists. He is frequently referred to and credited with having shown that children are active cognitive agents who participate in the construction of reality. He is also known for his early study of social development through constructs of "egocentrism," "perspective-taking," stages," "heteronomy-autonomy," and "intentionality." These constructs are still topical in the current literature. However, with minor exceptions, Piaget is rarely cited or known as a relational theorist despite the fact that, if he is nothing else, he is that (Furth 1969). In 1932, Piaget produced a study in which his theoretical perspective was applied to social development and the respective roles of children's relations with adults and with peers. His interest was in explaining the origins of principled morality, and his conclusion was that peers were its source.

Piaget was also conscious of the prevailing view that morality was known to society and possessed by adults who communicated it to children. In presenting the counter-case for peers, Piaget, like Sullivan, went back to an analysis of the structure of interpersonal relations. He showed development to be the outcome of structure in the sense that function flows from structure. In Piaget's view, the two relations differ in a number of ways. They expose children to separate views of themselves, other persons, and society in general. These views begin in relations whose development follows distinct paths, at least up to early adolescence. Like Sullivan, Piaget received silent criticism for this proposal. For example, much theoretical controversy surrounds his constructs of "stages" or "egocentrism," while there is hardly any reference to his revision of the roles played by parents and peers in development. While he is recognized for stimulating interest in the child as an active cognitive agent, little has been made of his proposal that children together can construct a mutually understood principled morality which puts common benefit above individual interest.

Upon first reading Sullivan and Piaget, one is struck with the similarity of their conclusions regarding adults and peers. The conclusions stem from rather different data sources; Sullivan observed clients in his psychiatric practice and cast his thoughts in terms such as anxiety and security, the language of his profession. Piaget, in observing working-class children, approached his subject from a theoretical and philosophical perspective. More interesting than their congruent conclusions is the similar mode of analysis they independently selected for the task of explaining development. Both address the child as a member of interpersonal relations rather than as individual or self-contained thinker. Both attribute relational membership to the child's participation in interpersonal interactions. Both propose that interactions can be analyzed through forms of reciprocity and that distinctions among forms provide structural differences among relations. The conclusions they draw about adults and peers are grounded in this type of analysis where different functions or products flow from respective relational structures.

The thesis, which is presented in chapters 1 and 2, is my attempt to show the two levels of agreement in conclusions and underlying rationale. The purpose in presenting the thesis is to offer an innovative perspective on social development, which may be useful to theorists, researchers, and students interested in human development. I have added little to Sullivan's and Piaget's original writings, although the integration makes a logically consistent case which may appear more powerful than either of their individual statements taken alone. In addition to presenting the thesis, I report data from interviews conducted with over 700 children. The topic of all these interviews is interpersonal relations as children understand them and can describe them through their own accounts of interpersonal interactions.

Unlike in other studies of this sort, the data presented here are not offered as tests of theory but are used as means for clarifying constructs and identifying questions worth asking in future research. This is not a defensive disclaimer to fend off methodological criticism. The data are taken seriously as expressions of children's thinking which can give insight into relations as children understand them. Because Sullivan's and Piaget's constructs are complex and have to date been left relatively unattended by researchers and scholars, they demand explication before they can be widely applied. Descriptive empirical data provide a necessary first step toward explication. As will be shown in chapter 3, the predicted outcomes of structure refer to interpersonal behaviors—e.g., interpersonal sensitivity and mutual understanding—for which there are no ready and obvious standards of measurement.

While the Sullivan-Piaget thesis merits study in itself for its potential as a new perspective on development, there are two other reasons which make its presentation at this time especially appropriate. The first pertains to theoretical transitions currently in progress in the field and the second concerns the sociological topicality of peer relations. Any moment in social science is a time of transition. However, currently the main paradigm for the study of social development is undergoing attack and revision. Not very long ago, the study of development of personality, social behavior, and morality was almost synonymous with the study of the mother's influence on her children. Newborns were seen as naïve, totally pliable individuals whose undifferentiated selves were shaped in crucibles of very early existence, in the home dominated by the mother's rearing practices. Countless studies were done to document what mothers actually did, to categorize styles of mothering, and to show the different effects of styles on the child.

These studies and their underlying models have now become open to objections on several grounds. (1) Researchers have come to realize that mothers are not singularly influential even in children's very early years. Fathers also play important roles (Lamb 1976), as do peers (Lewis and Rosenblum 1975) and, more generally, infants may be viewed as existing within broad networks of persons (Weinraub, Brooks, and Lewis 1977). (2) The model of maternal influence implies cause and effect with mothers as cause. It is equally plausible that children themselves not only affect mothers but are essential agents in forming bonds with mothers, fathers, and other persons (Ainsworth 1969; Escalona 1968; Lamb 1977). (3) The warp caused by emphasis on parental influence has never been squared with the fact that children meet, interact with, and are enthusiastic about relations they establish with peers. Upon close inspection, one may find numerous differences between these relations and children's relations with parents. These differences pertain to the content of activity, children's knowledge of the two relations, and differential effects which would logically follow from these distinctions (Hinde 1976 and 1978; Damon 1977). (4) The cause-effect model is based on the assumption that children are individual entities by right who become social through experience and who, upon reaching adolescence, become autonomous but socially informed individuals once again. This assumption contrasts with an equally plausible view that children are social by right, develop through relations they experience, and attain with maturity a full appreciation of their social nature which always precedes their individuality (Macmurray 1961; Riegel 1976; Sampson 1977).

These ideas seem to crystallize in the Sullivan-Piaget thesis, which may serve as an outline and general mode of analysis for development. The thesis integrates these ideas and offers a synthesis which may lead to a new theoretical perspective. The present book may be read as a step in this direction; it at least opens the door to this possibility. It is, however, beyond the present scope to go further than offering a lead which others may pick up and develop.

A second application of this book pertains to social conditions in our society which have provoked serious attention to peer relations (Elder 1975). A number of social commentators have pointed out that our culture seems to be progressively moving toward a greater incidence of "age-mate rearing," unlike in the past when parents and other adults collaborated in rearing children toward a common goal. Breakdowns in this communal process are evident in several sociological changes. Work is now segregated from children's daily experiences. Fathers work outside the home and, increasingly, mothers do also. The normative two-parent family seems to be giving way to single-parent families. Children spend a good deal of their lives in school, and it too is changing. There is a pattern for children to begin schooling at younger and younger ages and to remain in school longer, even through their early twenties. Within school, there is definite segregation by age so that influences between mixed-aged peers are diminished. Age-mate rearing is a trend embracing these and other changes that enhance sheer contact time between peers in replacement of time spent with adults.

For some commentators, these changes portend disturbing consequences for individual development and for society (Lasch 1979). The implicit theory behind their fears is that adults are essential to the cohesion of society since they serve as mediators who pass on mechanisms of stability from one generation to the next. Children themselves lack the experiential wisdom to know this on their own, and the more they are isolated from adult supervision, the further they may move away from tradition. As one commentator puts it: "If children have contact only with their own age-mates, there is no possibility for learning culturally established patterns of cooperation and mutual concern" (Bronfenbrenner 1973, p. 121).

It is important to recognize that peer influences were not always feared by adults or seen as threats to traditional values. In the United States and England, adolescent peer groups were often self-governed and encouraged by parents, church, and the rest of adult society (Gillis 1974, Kett 1977). As for the family, historians of society have identified several patterns of authority from parents to children, each of which may be seen as adapting to social and economic conditions (Shorter 1975). Although a fuller social history needs to be written, the available evidence does not support simplistic views of the two-parent family or sustain pessimism about peers.

Sullivan and Piaget offer a more balanced judgment. They assign to adults proper functions in socialization. At the same time, they argue that when children are left to themselves, as they often are with friends, further positive socialization occurs. When they are together, friends can come to see the need for cooperation and mutual understanding and find the means to put them into practice. The direct intervention of adults may not be needed to teach the advantages of cooperative construction or placement of mutual over personal interest. Children may arrive at these values by working together as equals seeking simply to get along.

Were Sullivan and Piaget merely promoting a Rousseau-like song of praise to childhood, their thesis could be disregarded as idealistic. However, they ground their argument on a logical analysis of interpersonal relations and tie this analysis to empirical facts of everyday interpersonal interactions. The key concept they use is reciprocity, the methods by which children exchange behavior and communicate in action with other people. It is in probing this analysis as a theory and as a perspective from which to understand children's own thinking that Sullivan and Piaget can be seen to provide an optimistic alternative to the more common treatment of peers as specters. This book has been written to give their thesis a full hearing and to encourage others to pursue the positive contributions which peers, especially friends, make in children's social development.

One   The Sullivan-Piaget Thesis

In conventional theories of social development, parents and other adults serve as the link between children and society. Through the efforts of adults children become socialized and their personalities take on characteristics which are socially adaptive. The role of adults serves the dual purposes of promoting children's adjustment and preserving society. In departure from these conventional theories, Sullivan and Piaget propose that peer relations, in particular children's relations with friends, are a major and positive force in development. Through peers and especially friends, children learn to become interpersonally sensitive, how to handle intimacy, and ways to achieve mutual understanding. These achievements are the key to interpersonal adjustment not just in childhood but throughout later life. They are also preserving of society because they are the bases of interpersonal cohesion and stability.

The purpose of this chapter is to present the constructs, definitions, and assumptions that constitute the thesis that relations with adults and peers serve equally important but distinct functions in children's social development. This thesis stems from an integration of the writings of H. S. Sullivan (1953) and Piaget (1965). The chapter begins with an enumerative definition of social maturity derived from their writings. Following this, a general description of social development starting with infancy is given. Commentary on more familiar positions follows so

1

that the thesis may be compared with conventional ideas. The remainder of the chapter is devoted to discussion of development within the spheres of adult-child and peer relations. Two possible courses of development are plotted to give a preliminary glimpse into the progression from infancy to social maturity and to show why Sullivan and Piaget distinguish the two relations by structure and function. The next chapter carries the thesis to the level of interpersonal interactions in an attempt to spell out the basis of relations through the construct of reciprocity. In addition, it ties the thesis to other recently proposed theories and lays the groundwork for an eventual broader synthesis.

A Description of Social Maturity

Sullivan's psychiatric interests led him to think of social maturity in terms of the psychologically adjusted personality. Unlike other theorists working within a psychoanalytic framework, however, he de-emphasized "intrapsychic" balance in favor of *interpersonal* and *mutual* adjustment. Sullivan's (1953) view may be expressed through a set of contrasts between the immature and mature person. Characteristics of immaturity include: an exaggerated sense of one's uniqueness (p. 256); efforts to conceal one's deficiencies (p. 207); emphasis on pleasing others by striving to meet their criteria of approval (p. 209); and inability to merge one's own · personhood with another's in the obligations of intimacy (p. 232). The adjusted, or mature, personality is not focused either on the self or on another but on the relation between self and other persons. The mature self makes "adjustments of behavior to the expressed needs of the other person" (p. 246) and the other person "becomes of practically equal importance in all fields of value" (p. 245). The mature self has a conscious goal which is "the pursuit of increasingly identical [and] more and more mutual satisfactions" (p. 246). Instead of dwelling on the self or giving in to others, the mature person seeks with others "consensual validation of personal worth" (p. 251).

Piaget's interest was also in the mature personality viewed as a principled moral agent. Piaget (1965) describes immaturity in much the same way as Sullivan does, with a stress on feelings of uniqueness (p. 96); striving to please authority figures on their grounds (p.

97); and failure to establish common criteria of worth with others (p. 98). Piaget's conception of the mature moral agent is that of a person who "takes up its stand on norms of reciprocity and objective discussion" (p. 95). This agent "knows how to submit to [norms] in order to make itself understood" (p. 96). In cooperatively constructing norms with others—norms referring to procedures for defining reality—the mature person will ."not only discover the boundaries that separate . . . self from other persons but will learn to understand the other person and be understood by him" (p. 95).

It is evident from this that Sullivan and Piaget perceive social maturity in terms of interpersonal understanding rather than in terms of individual behavior, personality traits, or personal motives. They see the path to maturity as taking a critical turn when persons come to realize the common grounds on which the self and other persons stand. Persons discover that they share similar characteristics and learn the value of building together a conception of what is important in personhood. They jointly establish criteria or norms for nurturing their relationship. In the course of this development, they come to rely on one another for definition and, in the process, evolve the very procedures by which definitions are formed and evaluated. The product of this process is mutual understanding in which the self and the other become progressively articulated, not as "I" and "you," but as *we*.

The Starting Point of Development

Developmental psychologists generally agree that infants are naïve and idiosyncratic with respect to social reality. Infants appear to be bundles of energy and their actions seem controlled by inner biological factors. They will react to strong external stimulation, but once drawn out they quickly return to their private world without missing a step. Lack of connection between inner and outer worlds sets the tone for the major task of social development. Children have to come to know of the existence of persons outside themselves and learn how to situate themselves in thoughts, actions, feelings, and motives of others. Privacy must be converted to sociality.

There are a variety of ways in which theorists describe how this conversion occurs. Theoretical descriptions differ according to assumptions about such matters as infants' natural states, cognitive capacities, and primitive motives. For Sullivan and Piaget, the guiding motive is the infant's natural search for order. Cast into the world, infants face a potentially confusing mixture of actions. They and other persons act simultaneously and sequentially. There is no fixed chronology, nor are there obvious partitions or ready-made stable categories for interaction. Order has to be created, and in analyzing this task, Sullivan and Piaget focus on infants' capacities to act and make sense of actions. Given the sociological fact that other persons coexist as actors in infants' lives, the search for order cannot be centered exclusively on self. It necessarily involves attempts to find linkages between self as actor and other as actor. Infants' actions of crying, sucking, and moving limbs result in contact with other persons and cause them to act in return. Other persons talk back, pick the infants up, or withdraw as they engage infants' actions. Were others wholly passive or simply benign, infants could center solely on their own actions. But others are also active and therefore infants can perceive order only through assessing their own actions in relation to actions of others.

Within the context of interactions, Sullivan and Piaget believe that infants break out of privacy and begin to note contingency between actions sometime during the first year of life. From this point on, social life lived in common with others begins. Actions are no longer viewed as self-contained units which start with an intention and end with their execution. At the very least, the actions of others become continuations of what infants themselves start, and, more properly, the actions of others serve as counterpoints that have to be regarded relative to their own actions. For Sullivan (1953), the study of early development necessarily becomes the study of "a self in interpersonal relations with others" rather than of the "self-contained person" or "individual in inviolable isolation" (pp. 16–20). Piaget (1965) agrees: "There are no . . . such things [as] isolated individuals. There are only relations" (p. 360). Nor is there a self outside relations, "because the self can only know itself in reference to other selves" (p. 393).

This central point of relational existence is sufficiently different from that found in other approaches to warrant elaboration in the next chapter. For the present, it is important to note that theorists who treat the child as individual entity, apart from others, emphasize different aspects of the child and study issues which follow from that premise. For example, they use terms such as *self* and *other* to refer to separate bodies, thoughts, and feelings. These theorists must then be concerned with how individual entities can be brought together to form a bridge between the divided poles. This is why socialization theorists examine mechanisms by which other persons intervene and make themselves known to the child. These theorists stress that other persons instruct, serve as models, or otherwise intrude on the child's privacy. The concern for separate entities also explains why cognitive theorists have to stress the child's developing ability to appraise other persons. If children are wrapped in their own privacy, they must take the initiative to enter the minds of others. Hence, the emphasis on abilities to select cues and make inferences about other persons' behavior. Were children unable to do these things, they would remain locked into their own world and remain separated from others.

By positing early existence as relational, Sullivan and Piaget are able to take development in an interesting direction. The child is said not to concentrate on discrete actions per se but to contend with *interpersonal interactions* for which, from the start, meaning is social rather than private. The child's question is not "What should I do?" but rather "What do you do when I do this or that?" From early in infancy, the question of the meaning of actions is a matter of interpersonal communication which has to be solved through a focus on interaction and joint effort rather than through isolated reflection or the other's imposition. Consequently, following the thesis, the task is "to trace the developmental history of the personality, which as you will see, is actually the developmental history of possibilities of interpersonal relations" (Sullivan 1953, p. 30).

The Thesis and Socialization Theory   In traditional socialization theories, children's original privacy is gradually intruded on from the outside. Step-by-step, other persons add social meaning to children's behavior and consequently bring the child into line with society at large. For example, the young child might strike out in a natural reaction to anger. The child learns from others that aggressive acts may be ineffective means for resolving internal tension and that there are different ways approved of by society to achieve the same end. Socialization theories emphasize the importance of other persons, especially adults, who represent society's agency. These agents monitor children's actions and serve as commentators as well as teachers. Through praise, punishment, direct instruction, and other means at their disposal, agents shape children's actions, thoughts, motives, and feelings and give them social texture.

There is ample evidence that with sufficient exposure, children begin to adopt for themselves social meanings provided by outside agents. For instance, children begin to anticipate how others might react to their overt initiatives, suggesting they may already have learned what others expect of them. Sullivan and Piaget agree on the importance and power of socialization. However, they add to it a distinction most theorists do not make. They propose that there are two, and not one, basic processes by which children acquire social meaning. In the first, another person, who is an agent, operates much as socialization theorists say, by offering a meaning which children will move toward and attempt to adopt for themselves. Sullivan and Piaget see this as a type of conformity which works well especially when the agent is an adult or high-status peer. There is no obvious reason why children, in the long run, would resist this kind of instruction. Conformity has an immediate payoff in rewards and pragmatically facilitates getting along with others.

However, they also see this type of socialization as having limitations. Children are offered meaning which comes from outside their internal frame of reference. It is imposed from an external system constructed by society, but children themselves have a small hand in its making. While children attempt to adopt this system, it is not clear that they are able to do so with assurance of understanding. The risk is poor understanding which, in Sullivan's view, may induce the child to concentrate on the question: "What should I do to get what I want?" (p. 245).

In the second process of socialization proposed by Sullivan and Piaget, the child as well as another person are agents. The child and the other person bring meanings to a situation. Neither person's meaning is "better" or can be singularly imposed. Instead, the persons have to engage in a joint search to discover which meaning—one's own, the other's, or a new meaning—is most workable. The focus shifts from personal interest to the question: "What would be best for both of us?" (Sullivan, p. 245). Piaget sees this as a socialization of "cooperation" in which one child "invents nothing without collaboration of his equals. He is free to create but on the condition of submitting to the norms of reciprocity" (p. 100).

In the first process of socialization, the child and another agent interact with stress on the latter. The child has a meaning for a behavior and acts on it. The agent has a meaning and tries to convey it to the child. When meanings differ, the agent holds to society's meaning, irrespective of the child's. For example, if the child has interrupted a conversation between two adults, one of the adults is likely to point out the violation of a rule of etiquette. The meaning the child may hold is unlikely to alter the rule. It is more likely that children are expected to change their meaning and adopt the adult's view on the matter. This is not to say that agents will not listen to children's views or even solicit them. But when they do, their purpose will usually not be so much to make the children's opinions the basis for new rules as to find out what the children think so that their minds can be changed. Throughout, the rule remains constant and children are expected to move toward it.

In cooperative socialization both the child and the other person are agents and recipients of instruction. The meanings both bring to an event are potentially equally valid. When one expresses meaning, the other may do the same. Neither is free to step outside the interaction and call upon an external system as the final arbiter. Both have to contend with one another's meaning and both are obliged to stay within the interaction to settle the matter. For Sullivan and Piaget, the result is a cooperative production of meaning and a focus on interactive procedures for presenting, listening, and working out compromise. The developmental product of these procedures is meaning which is coconstructed by two agents who, in the process, move toward mutual understanding.

The distinction between these two types of socialization suggests that there may be two social worlds of childhood with two separate lines of development stemming from distinctive forms of interpersonal interaction. When the child is solely a recipient and is asked to adopt preexisting meaning known already to agents, a particular kind of child-society relationship is established which affects a child's conception of self and other as well as his or her understanding of interpersonal relationships. The child's perception of the self as creator of reality will be restricted and his or her opportunities for mutual understanding in relations with others will be limited. When self and other are equally agents and recipients, meaning and order depend on cooperation which, in turn, leads to a different understanding of interpersonal relationships, one marked by the potential for mutuality. Sullivan's *possibilities of relation* may now be seen as a call for the study of the structure of interpersonal interactions and the implications of being a full participant, along with others, in these interactions.

The Thesis and Cognitive Theory   Traditional socialization theories tended to represent the child as a passive and pliable entity. In their evaluations, the theories focused on conformity, attributing most of the impetus for development to external agents rather than to children themselves. Partially as a reaction to these tendencies, theorists, in the 1960s, began to show concern that children were being regarded simply as benign recorders of experience rather than as cognizing individuals. Available evidence from studies of development in the logical sphere indicated that children can and do act on experience, represent it, and organize it conceptually. Based on this evidence, theorists sought a way to show how these cognitive capacities and skills work in the social domain.

They decided to focus on "role-taking" in children, the process by which a child steps out of his or her own perspective (meaning) in a given situation and tries to adopt the perspective of another person in that same situation. When the process works, a result similar to socialization occurs in that another person's meaning is taken up by the child. In distinction from socialization, however, in role-taking the child's perspective is informed by that of the other person through the child's own cognitive initiative. Role-taking is a developmental phenomenon in that it requires the evolution of prerequisite cognitive skills. In general, younger children are said to be limited in their ability to use it, since inherent characteristics such as "centering" and "egocentrism" keep them locked into their own private meanings. With cognitive development, the capacity to move into another's perspective, and the skills for doing so effectively, were found to evolve with age.

Sullivan and Piaget also recognize in children's interactions a process similar to that described above and agree that it plays an important function in social life. However, as with socialization theories, cognitive theories tend to be one-sided, focusing again on the child's obtaining meaning from another person, even though the impetus now comes from the child. What is missing from some cognitive theories is reference to a simultaneous, or symmetrical, process. This occurs when the child and another person each take as well as give perspectives and work toward a mutual perspective. When only the child makes a move toward the other, the result is similar to conformity where there is no assurance of mutual understanding. The child's version of the other person's thoughts or feelings may be purely subjective. In the absence of procedures for gaining mutuality, there is risk of achieving only an illusion of understanding. When both persons give, take, and jointly construct perspectives, uncertainty can be allayed and mutuality becomes a likely product.

Sullivan describes symmetrical sharing of perspectives as emanating from an attitude in which there is a "new necessity for thinking of the other fellow as right and for being thought of as right by the other fellow" (p. 251). Piaget makes a similar suggestion:

> If A respects B, and *vice versa*, this is because A was first respected by B and then placed himself at the same point of view as B . . . . If B simply respects A without the feeling being returned, he will regard as duties all commands laid upon him by A . . . . But as soon as A

identifies himself . . . with B, and thus submits his point of view to the laws of reciprocity, the product of this mutual respect is bound to be something new. [P. 385]

Children's Two Social Worlds

If socialization theories have overemphasized the child's passivity, cognitive theories have drifted too far in the other direction. They place too much importance on the child at the expense of the other person, who functions as the proverbial stoneface which active children puzzle over and have to figure out. Sullivan's and Piaget's addition to both types of theories is the recognition that there are processes in which meanings come to be shared by symmetrical and reciprocal interactions requiring equal work from the child and another person. Meaning may be acquired both unilaterally and bilaterally, or reciprocally. Meaning gained through unilateral means is based on interpersonal differences. Meaning is contained outside the child in a person who knows what the child does not know. The bilateral method of discovering meaning is based on similarities shared by persons and engenders mutual understanding because of joint construction. While the former method implies that persons' minds are separated and its practice tends to keep them apart, the latter implies the possibility of thought in common and its practice tends to bring the persons ever closer together.

Child-Adult Relations

Nature of the Relation

Sullivan bases child-adult relations on "interpersonal situations" (pp. 18–19) which are, specifically, interactions in which children and adults exchange behavior. He characterizes the persons as coming to these interactions with different interests. Children want to find out how social reality is ordered. This means that they want to know what other pepole expect of them and how they might anticipate the actions and reactions of others. Children are, in effect, involved in "the old game of getting hotter or colder in charting a selection of behavioral units" (p. 159). The other side of this relation is filled by adults whom Sullivan characterizes as eager to help children find the order, since they want children to be "adapted or adjusted to living in" society (p. 5). Adults know the order they want children to achieve in the sense of having definite ideas about the social meaning of behavior. They offer social education by not being indifferent and by acting responsively to children's initiatives (pp. 172–77).

Piaget offers a similar analysis. From infancy onward children are said to seek the rules which underlie the regularity of social life. Adults, in turn, are ready to supply children with rules. They do this indirectly by instituting habits pertaining to eating, cleanliness, and the like, and more directly by offering verbal instruction (pp. 51–52). By about 4 years of age children are "saturated with adult rules" and think that they have begun to understand the "Universal Order," of the way things "ought to be" (p. 89). By conforming to adult expectations, children gain a sense of having reached a state of believing that a privileged knowledge of the world has been granted by adults and accepted by themselves (p. 94).

For both Piaget and Sullivan, then, there is a fortuitous match between children's and adults' motivations. One seeks, and the other supplies, order. The arrangement is beneficial to both parties. The child's conformity to adult rules is not only a means of avoiding "interpersonal anxiety" (Sullivan, p. 113), but also a shortcut for what would otherwise be a tedious trial-and-error process on the child's part. From the adult's perspective, the child's conformity helps in simply getting along and avoiding irritation, and in addition, serves as a sign for the prospect of the child's successful long-term socialization.

Limitations   Having noted the obvious advantages of the child-adult arrangement, Sullivan goes on to point out its not so obvious disadvantages. While "the authority-carrying environment" provides children with rules "that are certainly good preparation for life in a social order" (p. 206) the young child "is incapable for a good many years of comprehending" the rules (p. 207). This is true regardless of the techniques adults may use to communicate their views. "Insofar as authority figures are confusing to the child and insofar as authority situations are incongruous from time to time . . . there is no making sense of them" (p. 206). Sullivan suggests that there is an inherent incoherence in the child-adult arrangement. Child and adult bring radically different perspectives and momentary interests to interactions. The child is generally asked to take the adult's perspective, but in fact this is difficult if not impossible to do. The reason is that the adult's perspective typically goes well beyond the behavior of the moment. For example, the adult may abstractly see in any act some long-term prospect pertaining to the child's eventual socialization. The child cannot be expected to conceive of much more than the here and now event.

Nor can the adult easily adopt the child's viewpoint or interest. To exemplify the gap from the adult's side, Sullivan uses the mother-child relation as a case in point. "The mother's personification of the infant is not the infant, but a growing organization ... which includes many factors only remotely pertaining to or dealing with this particular 'real' infant" (p. 112). Remote factors include the mother's future expectations, socially desirable hopes, and similar abstractions which do not necessarily pertain to the moment. If the child has difficulty comprehending the meaning offered by adults, adults have an equal difficulty getting into children's perspectives. Adults approach children encumbered with social expectations which prohibit a focus on the child's behavior as it is or as it is intended. Piaget makes a similar argument.

> The child begins ... to be socialized from the end of its first year. But the very nature of the relations which the child sustains with the adults around him prevents this socialization from reaching the state of equilibrium which is propitious to the development of reason. . . . The very nature of the relation between child and adult places the child apart, so that his thought is isolated, and while he believes himself to be sharing the point of view of the world at large he is still shut up in his own point of view. [P. 36]

Piaget sees the difficulty as occurring from both sides also. Children cannot comprehend adults' reasoning, and adults, because they see children in such complex ways, cannot easily take children's perspectives (e.g., pp. 138, 190–91, 256). Disparity between viewpoints does not result from bad intention or ignorance. It may be attributed to a simple fact of reality. Adults already understand reality. They do not come to children hoping to find new ways of defining it. They communicate as best they are able. Children grasp what they can. They act in accord with rules as they understand them. They even verbalize the rules in terms similar to those adults use. The result is an *illusion* of mutual understanding with a factual disparity in which both persons remain relatively contained in their own subjective perspectives.

Persons Within the System   Within the child-adult relation, children discover that there is a social system into which they and adults fit. The system is known to adults, and it is the children's task to find out what this system is. The system is communicated by unilateral means and as a consequence children can only glimpse it even though they can follow rules which will help them gain adult approval and cover their ignorance. It is not that the system is totally misunderstood but rather that children's versions of it may be subjective and disparate from adults' (and vice versa). Lack of mutuality between adult and child applies with equal force to children's concepts of self and other persons. In conceiving of self and adults, children draw criteria for evaluation from their own subjective understanding of their relation with adults and adults do likewise. Sullivan describes children as coming to appraise themselves in terms of what they should do to meet adults' standards for behavior. Since adults know the social criteria for acceptance, children have to look outside themselves to adults in order to find the standards (p. 154). Children distinguish themselves as the "good-me" and the "bad-me" on the basis of approval or anxiety gained from disapproval of their interactions with adults (p. 161–64).

According to Sullivan, continued experience in this arrangement leads children to conceive of adults more as "authority figures" than as individualized personalities (p. 230). While children get to know familiar adults such as parents well, it is only as they approach adolescence that they can discover adults as "simply people ... with merits ... and demerits" (pp. 230–31). This is not to say that children fail to discriminate among adults. They do make discriminations, for example, on the basis of individual habits. They know that there are cues for doing or avoiding particular behaviors with certain adults. What they do not understand is that adults are persons like themselves. This is the logical consequence of having viewed adults as all-knowing authorities and themselves as having to work through adults to discover the real order of the world. The discovery of a common system which holds for self as well as other and the establishment of mutual criteria for validating self and other cannot easily come from this relation. In Piaget's view, the child-adult arrangement has an inevitable outcome in preadolescence: "Unable to distinguish precisely between what is good in his parents and what is open to criticism, incapable, owing to 'ambivalence' of his feelings toward them, of criticizing his parents objectively, the child ends in moments of attachment by inwardly admitting their right to the authority they wield over him" (p. 192).

Peer Relations

Nature of the Relation

Sullivan and Piaget begin their analysis of peer relations by contrasting them with child-adult relations. Sullivan first:

All of you who have children are sure that your children love you; when you say that you are expressing a pleasant illusion. If you will look closely at one of your childdren when he finally finds a chum—somewhere between eight-and-a-half and ten years—you will discover something very different in the relationship, namely, that your child begins to develop a real sensitivity to what matters to another person . . . not . . . "what should I do to get what I want" but instead "what should I do to contribute to the happiness or to support the prestige and feeling of worthwhileness of my chum." [P. 245]

And Piaget:

In all spheres, two types of relations must be distinguished: constraint and cooperation. The first implies an element of unilateral respect, of authority and prestige; the second is simply the intercourse between two individuals on an equal footing. [P. 61]

Piaget proposes that peers begin to interact with a naïve sense of equality which is gained through the practice of direct reciprocity. One peer is free to behave exactly as the other has behaved in an exchange. If one says, "My older brother is the strongest person in the world"; the other has the right to say, "My brother is the strongest person in the world." Unlike adults, neither peer can step outside the discussion to give the topic a new direction or call on an external judgment. One may try to do so, but then the other is free to do the same. Reciprocity requires that the peers continue to reflect each other's thinking. In contrast to adults, who have already formed ideas which they will not give up easily for children, peers are free to take account of each other's ideas and to formulate new ones in the process. This does not mean that peers must agree. It means, however, that thought is constructed by cooperative presentation and listening and therefore common understanding is reached even in disagreement.

Piaget suggests that "more and more intensive application of the [reciprocal] process of mental interchange" (p. 73) brings peers to mutual understanding. Moreover, reciprocal interaction between equals becomes accepted by them as a *method of verification* (p. 97). Early in development, children understand this method pragmatically; much as they understand a rule for getting along (p. 98). But eventually, as they continue to practice, they come to a mutual agreement on the method as a principle of interaction (p. 98). For example, when playing a game, peers come to agree that "no one has the right to introduce an innovation except by legal channels, i.e., by previously persuading the other players and by submitting in advance to the rule of the majority" (p. 71). Peers come to agree that one "invents nothing without the collaboration of his equals. [Each] is free to create, but on the condition of submitting to the norms of reciprocity" (p. 100).

The Prospect of Rationality   Piaget believes that in child-adult relations, children's constructions tend toward subjective versions of an adult's system of meaning. Subjectivity, for which Piaget also uses the synonym *irrationality* (p. 100; p. 400), applies to understanding which is self-constructed but not honed by counterchecks from other persons' thinking. Piaget traces subjectivity to the manner in which children and adults exchange behavior, since in child-adult interactions, understanding "is imposed from without [and] it leads to a calculation of [individual] interests or remains subordinated to ideas of authority and external rules" (p. 280). In contrast, socially objective, or socially rational, thought follows from the forms of exchange among peers. Piaget sees peers as openly exchanging thoughts, words, deeds, and feelings through direct reciprocity. One peer presents an idea. The second peer is then free to present an idea. In so doing, the second peer reflects the first's idea. When the first child reexpresses the idea, the second child has the benefit of reflection.

Piaget calls this form of reciprocal exchange "mutual engagement" (p. 88). The process of exchange involves "continuous   comparison, . . . opposition, . . . discussion, and mutual control" (p. 393). The prospect is that neither peer leaves the situation with quite the same idea with which he or she entered it. Both peers may affect one another enabling them to achieve understanding which is of the nature of compromise or consent, and, as a result, each child's understanding is "freed from individual caprice and submitted to the control of reciprocity" (p. 88). The resulting system of relation understood by each to describe reality does not preexist as would an external given which one peer might know in a privileged way. Rather, through the practice of reciprocity, each child's tendency toward the subjective is counteracted by the other child. Cooperation yields an "organic solidarity" (p. 320) which is grounded in a system in which peers place themselves voluntarily.

Persons Within the System   A system in which interactions lead to mutual understanding allows children to discover individuals as persons sharing common motives, feelings, and hopes. This is one of the more complex points in the Sullivan-Piaget thesis, and it merits careful exposition. Some psychologists take for granted that even very young children understand the existence of persons. Young children, no doubt do, but not in the sense of being able to locate persons as individual personalities within a range of scales or along broad dimensions of values. Sullivan and Piaget argue that it is only when children jointly construct norms or standards for evaluation of social behavior that they can recognize the reality of the persons involved. This reality includes the personalities of the self and of other persons, understood in terms of what they share as well as how they differ.

For Sullivan, this type of recognition of persons *begins* with peer or friendship relations. Friendship represents "a perfectly novel relationship with the person concerned; he becomes of practically equal importance in all fields of value. Nothing remotely like that has happened before" (p. 245). Sullivan suggests that this innovation develops to the point where, in preadolescence, children discover in themselves and in friends "a need for interpersonal sensitivity" (p. 246). Sullivan unabashedly equates this development with the beginnings of *interpersonal love* (p. 245), when for example, a peer makes "adjustments of [his] behavior to the expressed needs of the other person in the pursuit of increasingly identical [and] more and more mutual satisfactions" (p. 246). Eventually, peers discover in friendship "for the first time . . . consensual validation of personal worth" (p. 251).

It is clear that Sullivan, like Piaget, emphasizes the contrast between preexisting meaning based on unilateral interactions and meaning stemming from bilateral exchanges. The latter give rise to a *necessity* for understanding self and other within a system commonly constructed. For Sullivan, interpersonal sensitivity is not simply an addition to social development. Once peers discover that they have jointly formed a view of social reality, they feel a *need* to be mutually sensitive. They feel that personal worth is not a matter of individual taste but must be founded on *consensual validation* grounded in objective criteria. In the course of friendship, friends "move toward supplying each other with satisfactions and taking on each other's successes" (p. 246). While with adults, children's worth is determined by the adult's criteria for approval, friendship introduces a radical alteration. "In this new necessity for thinking of the other fellow as right and for being thought of as right by the other fellow, much of this uncertainty as to the real worth of the personality" is allayed (p. 251).

Piaget is no less emphatic in his developmental prospectus for peer relations. He asserts that, "Cooperation is really a factor in the creation of the personality" (p. 96). He means by this that criteria for the self's worth cannot be solely subjective or come from outside but depend on an equal application of standards to others as well as self. An agreed upon standard of worth "appears only with reciprocity when mutual respect is strong enough to make the individual feel from within the desire to treat others as he himself would wish to be treated" (p. 196). Piaget proposes that peers agree on the methods by which they should interact—i.e., as equals through reciprocity. This agreement results in a joint construction of a system of social understanding which is marked by mutuality. It is this system which peers look to for establishing criteria of worth for self and for other. And it is by submitting to the system that self and other can be equally worthy (p. 95). It therefore follows that in reflecting on the system children "will not only discover the boundaries that separate... self from the other person, but will learn to understand the other person and be understood by him" (p. 95).

Overview and Summary   Throughout their analyses Sullivan and Piaget hold that children maintain two views of themselves in relation to other persons. They emphasize two lines of development. Within child-adult relations, children come only to glimpse vaguely the order of social reality which adults are presumed to have. Because adults interact as if they knew society well, children believe that it is their job to find out what this system is. Sullivan and Piaget suggest that the procedure by which children and adults interact inherently limits the achievement of mutual understanding. Adults are willing to express the system they know and to help children grasp it. They are not, however, open to making new discoveries or to redefining their system in a collaborative effort with children. They may make modifications of it in light of what children do or say. In the end, however, they expect children to move toward the system pretty much as adults know it.

This is not a negative commentary on child-adult relations. Nor does it imply that children feel oppressed in an atmosphere calling for conformity. Adults are assumed to be well motivated. They want children to have the social benefits that accrue from acting and thinking in socially approved ways. Children in turn derive immediate benefits from adopting whichever parts of the system they can.

The more they act in accord with adults' social expectations, the more they can accomplish through interactions with other persons. Needless to add, there is psychological trust and security in accepting and being accepted in the adult's system.

When children turn to peers, however, they discover something different. They learn that a system can be created with other persons. The system works functionally, is open to modification, and gives a sense of mutual meaning. Particular behaviors are no longer predetermined as right or wrong or better or worse. Behavior can be tested and submitted to mutual definition. The outcome is a set of meanings which give social behaviors new value. As peers move further into this system a different concept of self and other person results. Self is not inferior to other in knowledge or power but self and other are equals in the right to understand and the power to construct knowledge. Unlike the system which children believe adults already know, the one created by collaborating peers has no definite endpoint. It is open to redefinition through a democratic process founded in methods of reciprocity.

The Sullivan-Piaget thesis is based on a conception of the person not as a contained individual but as a member of a broader unit of relationship. Children may view themselves as trusted, believable, and obedient. But these are not characteristics which have absolute existence. Rather, they are constructed from relations with other persons. To be trustworthy, someone else has to ask for your trust and encourage you further when you act accordingly. The same reasoning applies, of course, to definitions of the other person.

The unit of analysis required by the thesis is *interpersonal relation*. Relations are founded in interactions between persons. Sullivan and Piaget believe that children first learn of relations by participating in interactions and conceiving of them in terms of methods and procedures. Children carry this knowledge further by studying how they are bound to procedures with other persons. These relations then become the framework from which meanings of self and other are constructed. The thesis does not deny individuality; instead, it offers a new meaning of individuality. For the person to discover himself or herself as an individual, he or she must be able to place the self into relation with other selves. One does not lose individuality in a relation but gains a sense of self through it. Relationship is prior to individuality since persons must know what they have in common before they can know what makes them unique. The mature and socially adjusted self balances individuality with relationship and grounds individuality on relationship.

In summary, Sullivan and Piaget call for a revision of conventional models in which the self or personality is established through relations with adults and is either supported or counteracted by children's relations with peers. Children's relations with adults provide children with a sense of an ordered social reality and launch them along a relational path. Peer relations enter children's lives to give development an innovative direction. For Piaget: "We must . . . make a vigorous distinction between a social process such as constraint, which simply consecrates the existing order of things, and a social process such as cooperation which essentially imposes a method and thus allows for the emanicipation of what ought to be from what is" (p. 349). And for Sullivan also it is peer relations which introduce children to new "possibilities of interpersonal relations" (p. 30) and carry them beyond the limited views of self and society offered by relations with adults. The two relations give rise to qualitatively distinct worlds, with the world of mutual understanding having its origins in children's relations with peers.

Two Rationale of the Thesis

The key to understanding the thesis lies in Sullivan's and Piaget's analyses of relations. There is a logic behind their challenging conclusions which explains why relational membership preempts treatment of the child as a private individual. It also explains the structure of relations and consequently describes the social functions which follow from structure. Sullivan and Piaget do not argue that children as peers possess inherent capacities for altruism or interpersonal insight which adults have lost or do not possess. Differences between relations are due to differences in structure, when structure refers to the types of interactions which take place between child and other. Children come to see themselves as being able to construct order in society either *through* adults or *with* peers. Not knowing what the rules of order are, children focus on interactions and construct out of them patterns which connect their actions with the actions of others. The result is a discovery of two relationships within which persons can arrive at order.

The goals of this chapter are to expose the logic and mode of analysis which underlie the thesis and to reassess major steps in the developmental chronology proposed by Sullivan and Piaget. The child's first realization that existence is social and not individual is shown to result from participation in interactions with adults who have the child's welfare foremost in their minds. The next step is
21   the establishment of a definite structure by which children

and adults adopt a method for seeking and finding order with one another. This step is achieved early in life and worked out during the preschool years when children attempt to adopt adults' versions of reality and gain approval for their efforts. Once this structure is formed, children live it out by learning to exchange conformity for approval. In the process, they take on a definition of self as learner and of adult as knower, accept the fact that reality is ordered, and gain a sense of achievement by mastering this order with the help of adults. The process involves a continuous line of development beginning in the first year of life and running through early adolescence.

Around the time children enter school and experience peers on a wide scale, another developmental course begins to be charted. School-age children no doubt believe that their views of reality, learned through and endorsed by adults, are shared by society at large. This belief is challenged when children act on their versions of order and run up against contrary viewpoints held by peers. Children most likely initially apply the methods for establishing order which were so effective with adults. When they find these methods do not work, children face a dilemma. Either they must continually run up against one another's viewpoints as barriers or evolve new methods by which consensus versions of reality can be reached. Peer relations proper are established, perhaps selectively with friends, when children discover that viewpoints can be reconciled through cooperative effort. This method of cooperation is innovative because it does not apply to children's relations with adults on the whole. Once discovered, it opens children to a new possibility for interpersonal relationship in which self and other share responsibility in creating order. With this step, Sullivan and Piaget propose that children begin to move toward the mature personality which, as was shown in chapter 1, is characterized by the dominant need for social union and the willingness to place mutual benefit over self-interest.

Establishing the Child-Adult Relation   As shown in chapter 1, Sullivan and Piaget adopt the model of the child as an agent or an actor. They assume further that action is the medium of knowledge. In seeking to find order in reality, children look to their actions in hopes of finding regularity and repeatability. Infants focus on whatever actions they have available such as crying, smiling, and capturing objects with sight. Perhaps very early in life, infants' actions provide a sufficient focus for obtaining order, but in the long run it proves to be inadequate. The reason for its inadequacy is that infants' actions contact other persons who then act on infants. These actions from others spoil any belief infants might have that they can create repeatable results by starting with some intention and executing it in a performance. When other persons react to children's initiatives, they create effects which go beyond the infants' original intention. The meeting of two sources of actions is different from either action alone. For example, the infant might be stimulated interoceptively and cry as a consequence. The act of crying may have as its intended referent the original stimulus. However, it may bring about an entirely different referent which was neither intended nor anticipated when an adult approaches, picks the infant up, and introduces vocal, tactual, and visual stimulation.

Sullivan and Piaget propose that during the first year of life, infants learn that their actions alone cannot produce ordered effects. There are other agents who contribute to effects, and their actions occur in conjunction with infants' own performances. How other persons act becomes crucial to understanding infants' own actions. Other persons are not benign with regard to infants' initiatives. The infant may visually sight a person, but that person can move from view and thereby cancel the object of the original action. In sum, other persons' actions serve to inform infants that there is resistance to what they do. For Sullivan and Piaget this means that infants have to reform their approach to order through actions. They must extend their focus to the *meeting of actions*, which makes interpersonal interactions the medium of social knowledge (see Macmurray 1961, for a discussion of the philosophical implications of this position).

Sullivan and Piaget choose to describe the infant's broadened focus as centering on the reciprocity which occurs in interactions. They pose for the infant the question, "What do you do when I do something"? They argue that it is only in addressing this question that infants can come to find order in reality. They deny to the infant the intellectual tour de force of believing that one's own actions are discrete events, understandable in themselves. They propose instead that the meaning of one's initiatives can be found only in relation to someone else's actions and they suggest that the relation can be comprehended through an understanding of the reciprocity between actions.

This approach to the infant has only recently begun to be explored with seriousness by contemporary theorists (see Lamb 1977). It has important implications for the empirical study of infancy. For example, instead of examining the frequency of particular actions such as crying during the first year of life, researchers have come to examine these behaviors in terms of their reciprocal correlation with actions, such as responsiveness from caretaking adults. Results of studies of crying, for example, demonstrate that the correlation follows an orderly path which, in turn, explains increases and decreases in the frequency of these actions (Bell and Ainsworth 1972; Escalona 1968). By attending to their own actions as parts of interactions, infants come to the central lesson of early life. They are forced out of their view of themselves as completely private entities. The empirical fact of interpersonal interaction brings them naturally to a view of the self as an agent who is reciprocally related to other agents. The insight is not "I exist" but "You *and* I exist" (Lewis and Brooks 1975; Macmurray 1961; Sampson 1977). Thus, from very early in life, the existential fact is clear that the self can be understood through a broader unit, which is the self in relationship to other agents.

Reciprocity of Complement   Having rejected the option of focusing solely on their own actions, children begin to look to interpersonal interactions in hopes of finding order. Sullivan and Piaget suggest that children make two discoveries in their search. First, they find habits and routines in which children and adults play their respective parts. But habits or routines are only restricted activities which hardly cover the fullness of social life. More frequently, interactions are composed on the spot with each succeeding part requiring an optional contribution. Observing and coding specific events is of little help in preparing children for participation in interactions which are to be freely formed. Consequently, Sullivan and Piaget describe a second discovery which is more general in scope and serviceable for the demands of real-life interactions. This is the discovery by the infant of a *method* which is applicable to many different interactions and which invariably leads to the production of orderly results.

Sullivan and Piaget propose that children learn to appraise their own contributions to interactions by identifying how they relate to those contributed by other persons. They argue that there is a general form of reciprocity which tends to characterize children's interactions with adults. It is called *reciprocity of complement* (see Hinde 1976; Watzlawik, Beavin, and Jackson 1967) and refers to a basic asymmetry that exists in children's and adults' contributions to interactions. In this relationship, children's participation is restricted. Rather than asserting initiatives freely or inserting reactions with the aim of directing interactions, children produce initiatives and reactions which meet the directives offered by adults. When they do initiate actions, they look to adults to tell them if those actions are appropriate or acceptable. They build their parts in interactions around adults' parts, following suit rather than taking the lead. The method is asymmetrical because children's contributions are complementary to adults', but the reverse is less true.

At first this seems to be too general a proposal to characterize child-adult interactions. To see its applicability, one has to consider the details of Sullivan's and Piaget's reasoning. They assume that children co-exist with adults who hold to views of an already established society which has rules and values. From this viewpoint, actions are evaluative; not all actions are equally acceptable, and different actions are more fitting for particular situations than others. Children, of course, do not know the societal scheme. Adults, who have lived in the society, do. This disparity in knowledge of societal rules builds a basic asymmetry into child-adult interactions and puts adults in a position of leadership. They know which behaviors are appropriate in which situations. When children restrict their own actions by attempting to follow

adults' leads, they are likely to arrive at orderly and replic-
able results in many different situations. Thus, in adapting to reciprocity of complement with adults, children discover a general method by which they can achieve order
through interactions. By following the method, they are
able to take their part in many interactive situations with
adults as these come up in the future.

Unilateral   Children's discovery of the method of complementariness
Authority   follows from their knowledge of their relational existence
              and leads to establishment of the structure of child-adult
              relations. The process is worked out during the preschool
              period and should be well established by the time children
              enter school. Several questions can be asked about Sulli-
              van's and Piaget's proposal, two of the more important
              being: In which way is reciprocity of complement a gen-
              eral method? and, How specifically is this method pro-
              duced through empirical experiences? Again, one has to
              inspect Sullivan's and Piaget's assumptions and look
              closely at their reasoning to find the answers.

Two assumptions have already been made explicit:
children seek order by searching for methods which will
produce orderly effects in what must be a potentially confusing array of ever-changing interactions; and children
seek order in a context where their lack of knowledge runs
up against adults who are knowledgable. Sullivan and
Piaget also assume that the adults in question are the children's caretakers who are benevolently concerned with the
children's welfare. These caretakers want the children to
be functioning members of society and realize that to do
so they must learn what other persons expect of them in
interactions. These adults, therefore, are attentive to children's actions. They are not disinterested parties who ignore what the children do, nor are they totally open-
minded and accepting of whatever they do. With the children's long-term social adjustment in mind, adults interact with them in an evaluative manner (see Baumrind 1975;
Gadlin 1978).

The term evaluative is charged and requires immediate
clarification. Social scientists have made much of the possibility that parents or other caretakers differ in their approach to children. One of the most important and well-

studied differences is in the degrees of "control" or "permissiveness" adults exercise over children. Controlling adults demand performances from children, while those who are permissive seem to make few demands on them, allowing them to act however they wish, at least up to a point. Sullivan and Piaget were aware of this distinction, which was posed in different terminology when they wrote, but they chose to argue that differences in parental behavior tend to camouflage a broad commonality which holds for most caretaking styles, save rare extremes. Concerned caretakers are alike in treating children's initiatives or reactions discriminatively. Since adults possess well-formed views about society, they cannot help seeing children's actions in terms of being more or less acceptable. Consequently, they must endorse some actions and reject others.

Given the pervasiveness of the literature that emphasizes differences among caretaking styles, Sullivan's and Piaget's point bears repeating. While admitting that adults do differ in how they teach children, Sullivan and Piaget stress that adults, nevertheless, are similar in that they act as evaluators *independent of their particular style*. They do not deny the usefulness of studying differences in style; however, both claim there is more to the parent-child relation. All caretakers give encouragement, discouragement, reinforcement, or otherwise act as arbiters. Specifically, adults have the privilege of endorsing children's parts in interactions or of stopping, interrupting, or demanding changes in these parts. The result is that children learn to look for the order of society through the method of complementariness. By continually modifying their parts in interactions to meet the contributions of adults, children progress toward the viewpoint which they think adults hold about society.

Sullivan and Piaget propose further that reciprocity of complement gives rise to the structure which is known as the child-adult relationship. They call this structure *unilateral authority* or *unilateral constraint*, emphasizing that adults are known to possess evaluative rights which children do not. Two clarifications are helpful at this point. The first is that Sullivan and Piaget do not argue that adults never allow children to set the pace in interactions or to assert initiatives which adults then follow. Indeed, they suggest that adults do make adjustments to children. However, they stress that there are limits which prevent adults from treating children as equals in the task of ordering reality. To treat them equally, adults would theoretically have to enter interactions with an openness to discovering reality afresh. They would have to listen to children and, on that basis, modify their own views accordingly. From Sullivan's and Piaget's perspective, such a prospect is unrealistic. Adults derive their viewpoint toward society through their own experiences which they are not ready to abandon for the inexperienced views of children. They will, however, make adjustments to children, but it is not so much to find new views for themselves as to find out what children think so that the adult's viewpoint can be better communicated.

The second clarification concerns connotations of the terms authority and constraint. Neither is meant to imply authoritarianism or rigidity. On the contrary, authority and constraint can be seen as outcomes of adults' benevolence. Adults want to help children understand and be accepted by society. In the process, adults must communicate their authoritative position. For example, consider the several rules adults express every day which stem from a positive interest in the child. They include: "Wash your hands before you eat"; "It's 8 o'clock and time for you to go to bed"; "Don't eat your candy now, save it for dessert"; "It is not polite to interrupt adults when they are talking"; "Aunt Susanah likes it when you kiss her on the cheek"; or, "Try to play quietly, daddy has a headache from working hard all day". Irrespective of whether children understand these rules, or the reasons behind them, their very existence conveys an undeniable message. Adults know how society is ordered while children do not. Adults approve of children when they act according to this order and disapprove when children do otherwise. If children want to know what this order is, they must work toward it through the minds of adults who are authorities about society.

The structure of unilateral authority may be further understood through the child's definition of the persons within it. Children may see themselves as creative insofar as they are encouraged to figure out society as adults know it. While they are constrained in their constructions by the views which adults hold, children need not feel oppressed. On the contrary, they may see their exchange with adults as fair and legitimate insofar as their attempts to conform are returned by expressions of approval and acceptance (Damon 1977). Adults, in turn, come to be seen as all-knowing figures who have privileged insight into the inner workings of society. The child's road to this insight is through the method of complementariness. Acceptance of this structure allows children to move toward the minds of adults and to become masters of the universal order of society also.

Establishing Relations with Peers   The next major step in this chronology is the establishment of relations with peers, which Sullivan and Piaget consider critical for the period beginning roughly at 5 years of age and continuing through early adolescence. This does not deny that children interact with peers at younger ages. Rather, it stresses the sociological fact of school which enhances contact with peers and extends the scope of contact widely. By convention, this time has been called the "latent" period, but for Sullivan and Piaget it is a time when children discover how to deal with peers, to form friendships, and to derive new definition of self, of other persons, and of relationship. It will be shown also that this period introduces children to a new course of development which is discontinuous with the course established earlier with adults. During this time, children are very active and anything but quiescent.

It was seen in chapter 1 that Sullivan and Piaget propose that peer relations are the source from which critical characteristics of the mature personality come. These include a sense of equality, interpersonal sensitivity, the need for intimacy, and mutual understanding. Reading this proposal, one might guess that the thesis is based on an old theme that children are inherently good, and hence peer relations represent an ideal social unity which eventually gives way to the competitive and self-interested world of adulthood. This is not the thesis at all. In fact Sullivan and Piaget describe the beginnings of peer relations in quite different terms. They assume that children enter the world of peers with confidence that they have mastered the rules of society. Children also believe that their understanding of the order of things, which they learned from adults, is shared by their peers. Thus, children enter interactions with peers expecting their conception of order to be applicable everywhere.

It takes little contact with peers for children to realize that their expectation of a shared view of order is incorrect. Children's games provide direct examples of how this fact is discovered. When children play games like "mothers" or "kickball" they find out that there are as many rules as there are players. They find out further that, when disputes come up, there is no one rule which is better than another. Children think that the rule they hold is right, especially if it has been endorsed previously by an authority figure. However, when one child says, "This is the way you're supposed to play," another child may assert with equal assurance, "No, my way is right." Not only is there no obvious "better" rule, but more importantly, there also is no obvious *method* by which to settle differences of opinion. This is not to ignore the fact that in particular situations one child may be faster or stronger or more authoritative. But across a wide range of situations, children are likely to discover that rules and versions of order are neither shared among peers nor determined by single peer figures.

Instead of offering an idealistic proposal that peer relations begin in agreement, Sullivan and Piaget emphasize that peers are as likely to disagree as to agree. When they disagree, either one peer will give in or both will hold to their own positions and hence reach an impasse. In fact, impasse is the more likely prospect given that each child's opinion may be founded on a sense of mastery of "the way things ought to be." In the case of disputes, each child pits a view against the other so that the two arrive at loggerheads. There is no obvious way out since each believes that he or she is right and that the other is wrong. The two can present and hold to views indefinitely. When one tries to step out of the fray to take charge, the other can do the same. If one calls upon an authority, the other can call on a different authority. Thus, peers reach an impasse and the familiar endpoint when one child says, "If you don't play my way, I'll take my ball and go home."

The Method of Direct (Symmetrical) Reciprocity

Sullivan and Piaget propose that peers quickly discover that their interactions with one another do not follow reciprocity of complement, as did their interactions with adults. Instead, children find that each peer is free to contribute to interactions in similar ways and with acts identical to those of the other contributors. Technically, this form of reciprocity is called *direct* or *symmetrical* (Hinde 1976 and 1978; Watzlawik, Beavin, and Jackson 1967). Like complementary reciprocity, it is a method for achieving order and arriving at a stable form of relationship. However, as shown above, persons who use direct reciprocity do not necessarily arrive at order or stability. When two persons are free to contribute to interactions with like acts, and when neither person can unilaterally constrain the other's contribution, interactions are likely to yield erratic results.

Consider an example which is applicable generally to children's everyday life. Suppose one child were to aggress physically or verbally against a second child. According to direct reciprocity, the second child would be free to offer a symmetrical reaction. Upon this retaliation, the first would be free to aggress again, and so on. In theory, one aggressive act calls forth its symmetrical counterpart in an endless regression. In actuality, of course, one of the children is liable to tire and stop, perhaps by leaving the scene and going home. But the point of this example is that direct reciprocity *on its own* leads in no particular direction and only sporadically results in order.

The Structure of Cooperation

Sullivan and Piaget argue that the experience of interactions based on direct reciprocal methods brings children to a critical realization. Direct reciprocity on its own is an ineffective means to social order. It results in impasse and leaves disputes unsettled. A possible way out is for one of the children to concede to the other, in which case one suppresses self-interest to allow the other's interest to reign. However, as just described, this method replicates reciprocity of complement and contradicts direct reciprocity. There is an alternative solution which Sullivan and Piaget hold is in fact discovered by children. It is to adopt a special usage of direct reciprocity whereby it will be employed, not unilaterally, but *cooperatively*. When one child presents a viewpoint and a second child presents a different opinion, the first child listens to the second and the second listens to the first. Concession occurs on both peers' parts while each also maintains a position. Out of this process, friendship develops.

Sullivan and Piaget propose that this discovery opens children to a form of relationship which they have not experienced previously. It was not evident in relations based on reciprocity of complement and it was not apparent when peers practiced direct reciprocity in a literal tit for tat. The conversion of direct reciprocity from use for self-promotion to use for cooperative purposes is a developmental innovation which has two consequences. First, it allows for the establishment of a new structure of relationship, and second, peers discover that by cooperatively working together they can use the method of direct reciprocity to achieve order. Both of these processes develop gradually over the school-age period and into adolescence.

Sullivan and Piaget suggest that cooperation in the method of direct reciprocity engenders the evolution of new procedures for arriving at ordered results. For example, instead of allowing disputes to keep peers at loggerheads, children learn how to deal with differences of opinion. Specifically, they construct procedures of *discussion, debate, argument, negotiation,* and *compromise.* In each of these procedures, children learn how to present an opinion, listen to another's opinion, and adjust their own opinion in light of the other's view. By the rule of cooperation, adjustment by one child is matched by adjustment in the other child. In the process of evolving and using these procedures, children learn that the order of society is not given, but an understanding of it can be arrived at when two peers work cooperatively to achieve it. One no longer finds order only by turning to an authority. Instead, peers become authorities as well as learners, and by cooperating, they can pool their talents to reach a shared view of order.

As with relations of unilateral authority, the structure of cooperation is explained by a circular process. At first, there is a general form of reciprocity in the interactions between peers. At that point, the interactive method is constitutive of and equivalent to a relation. Later, the peers identify the method and reconstitute it into a known relation. Only then, have they achieved a relation proper which has a known structure. Henceforward, although the same interactions are manifest as before, these inter- actions may be seen as being constructed by the persons with the relational structure as their guiding principle. Using a principle to generate initiatives and reactions, the persons move further toward order with assurance. They can apply the methods of reciprocity to obtain ordered results and, simultaneously, the relation itself yields an order in which the self is known to have a specific position as an agent with regard to other agents, and vice versa.

Adolescence   The further step in this chronology begins presum- ably in early adolescence and continues throughout adolescence and adulthood. For present purposes, only its onset is considered here. Sullivan and Piaget describe young adolescents as having to face a new issue which was not apparent earlier in development. As the structure of cooperative relations comes into being, a contrast be- tween it and relations of unilateral authority becomes ap- parent. The two relations are seen to require distinct forms of reciprocity in which self and other are called on to inter- act in quite different ways. As will be shown below, exer- cise of these forms of reciprocity leads to disparate con- clusions about who the self is and who the self may be within interpersonal existence. Sullivan and Piaget pro- pose that with adolescence, there is a new effort made to reconcile the two relations and to find ways to integrate them. The preferred form for the integrating process is cooperative relations.

Following the thesis, adolescents begin to transform the terms of unilateral authority relations into the terms known from relations of cooperation. The exchange of ap- proval for unquestioning acceptance of another's view- point is no longer adequate as an interpersonal method. The experience of shared authority and its potential to yield mutual understanding is born of cooperation which, in turn, begins to influence adolescents' conceptions of unilateral authority. It is not simply the authority of adults they question. More importantly, it is the adolescents' own capacity to create order through shared authority *that is explored* (see Baumrind 1968; Damon 1977). The transformation of unilateral authority may begin with adolescents' initiatives, but to be effective, it must be accompanied by changes from adults also. That is, having discovered the possibilities of relationship within friendship, adolescents apply cooperative procedures to their relations with adults. To be effective, their initiatives must be met with similar attempts from adults who, of course, understand these same procedures. If, on the other hand, adults resist modifying their parts in procedures and hold to their position as unilateral authorities, adolescents must accommodate themselves to this position as long as they remain dependent on these adults. Psychologically, however, the disparity between the two possibilities of relationship are keenly felt and the problems of irreconcilability probably lead adolescents further away from interest in relations with unchangeable adults and closer to relations with friends as well as with adults who are willing to practice the procedures of cooperation.

Functional Products of Structure
It is now possible to review Sullivan's and Piaget's characterization of the psychologically adjusted and morally mature personality as a logical outgrowth of development from relational structures. The continuity between friendship and the mature personality is not mere supposition. The structure of friendship in cooperation clearly contains the seeds of social union required of adult intimate relations. It is equally clear that the child-adult relation of unilateral authority, founded on reciprocity of complement, is not wholly continuous with the requirements of maturity. The personality as Sullivan and Piaget describe it requires a balance between responsibilities to create order and obligations to respect other persons' versions of order.

The thesis does not hold that adults are incapable of forming cooperative relations with children. Indeed, adults may and probably do form these relations with adolescents. But the likelihood that adults could do the same with young children is small. Adults have experiential histories, sociological positions of responsibility for caretaking, and psychological perceptions of young children as naïve. Given these contextual facts, it is difficult to imagine that adults could enter interactions with young children as equals in the practice of direct reciprocity.

The foregoing chronology identifies the two basic structures of relations and shows how each is established through empirical interactions between children and adults or peers. This is not, however, the whole of the picture. Along with structure, there are functional outcomes which pertain to the psychological conception of persons—self and other—and of relations themselves. In the thesis, persons are not givens which remain constant over time. Relations are developed, and in the process the persons of self and of other become derivatives of these relations. This means, of course, that the child's self changes as it experiences first relational existence itself, then its own place in relations of unilateral authority, and finally its new part in relations of cooperation. While it is proper to speak of the self as a personality, the characterization has to be treated in a relative sense. The personality of early childhood, which is engendered by relations of unilateral authority, has no necessary priority or permanence which dominates the person throughout life. Entirely different requirements are asked of the child in relations of cooperation. The personality which results from experiences of friendship may be more continuous with that required in adulthood than the personality formed by the demands of unilateral authority.

Sullivan and Piaget propose, of course, that the adult personality is a product of all relations but stress relations of cooperation. Cooperation is the reason they identify peer relations as the originating source of interpersonal love and moral maturity. It is not peers per se who know any better than adults how to teach children to suppress self-interest for the sake of long-term social union. The continuity between relations with peers and the mature personality depends on the structure of cooperation and what is learned when the structure gives rise to procedures of direct reciprocity. Simultaneously, the limited contributions which relations of unilateral authority make to the mature personality cannot be attributed to faults in adults. If anything, adults have a clear vision of what this personality is, and, on the whole, adults act with the intention of helping children to develop to this point. The limitation is only indirectly due to adults; it is primarily a function of the structure of the relations which children and adults establish.

With these clarifications, it is possible to review Sullivan's and Piaget's characterization of the psychologically healthy and morally mature personality to see how it derives from relations of cooperation rather than from early-life relations of unilateral authority. This is the topic of the remainder of the chapter. Five characteristics are discussed: mutuality, standards of worth, equality, interpersonal sensitivity, and the primacy of the need for relation. Each is described as it may be seen to derive from cooperative relations and contrasted with characteristics which seem to follow from relations of unilateral authority.

Mutuality   Sullivan and Piaget distinguish mutual understanding by degrees. All relations engender mutuality because the members can draw common meaning from the interactive methods of which they partake. Of the two relations, however, the structure of cooperation yields a higher degree of mutuality than the structure of unilateral authority. Why is this the case? There are two obvious reasons, both of which follow from the procedures which are evolved in making cooperation workable. These include discussion, debate, and compromise. In these procedures, the two persons are expected to act similarly; when one presents an idea, the other is free to express a different idea. The presentation of ideas, feelings, and opinions involves a going back and forth, so that differences are aired and criticism takes place publicly. In this manner, peers work together toward a position which both can accept. The first reason for mutuality is that the procedures encourage peers to reveal their feelings or ideas. While cooperation requires that one listen to another, it also demands that each present a side which the other will consider. The result is exposure of what each feels and thinks.

Relations of unilateral authority engender opposite effects. The method of complementariness has a focal point in the opinions of the person in charge. Interactions are designed around this focus, in part because it represents the true order of things. The person who possesses knowledge of this order distributes approval when the other conforms and disapproval when the other does not conform. Consequently, when differences arise, concealment is encouraged. For instance, should the person seeking approval hold to differing opinions from the person in charge, a dilemma is encountered. If the former expresses the contrary opinion, disapproval is likely. If, on the other hand, the former presents a more acceptable opinion, which the latter wants, approval will be forthcoming. Given the choice, the person might select to conceal rather than risk disapproval. The method also encourages the person in charge to hide opinions. Being looked on as an authority, the person may choose to assert views to cover up gaps in knowledge or other personal weaknesses in a show of strength. The person in charge is under no obligation to tell all and may often find it easier to impose rules rather than to deal candidly with difficult situations.

The second reason for mutuality also stems from procedures. In theory, cooperating peers evolve ideas together, starting with different viewpoints. Ideas are passed back and forth, first for one's criticism, then the other's. In the process of give-and-take, ideas are constructed with each peer's contribution modifying what preceded and leading to a further modification. The result is not necessarily agreement, but it is mutuality insofar as both peers have witnessed the formation of an idea and contributed to its formation. This is the basis for Sullivan's and Piaget's proposal that cooperative relations progressively induce mutual understanding between self and other. Because ideas are constructed jointly and in public, the self's understanding of an idea can be the same as the other person's understanding of the self's idea. Similarly, the self may understand the other in the same terms as the other does.

Relations of unilateral authority have an inherent limitation with regard to mutuality. The person who is the authority has an already well-informed view of reality. He or she presents ideas less as opinions as to be negotiated than as facts to be adopted. While the child may glimpse the meaning which the authority has, it would be difficult for the child to construct (or reconstruct) the full meaning. This would be true even if the authority attempted to break down the idea in simpler pieces so that it might be better grasped. The child still lacks the background to appreciate the authority's position. Sullivan and Piaget suggest therefore that children and adults seek to communicate but frequently end up with each holding only distant versions of what the other is thinking. These versions are adequate to allow the persons to interact smoothly, but mutuality remains more illusion than fact. Further, experiential differences between child and adult make it impossible for the child either to piece together the adult's position or even to know when the adult's position is wrongly understood.

Standards of Worth

In cooperative relations, the order of reality is open to debate. Children realize that they may hold different views and come to believe that together they can work out a common view. Since no one is by right the final authority, authority resides only in a shared consensus. In seeking order, each child is obligated to present ideas to the other for validation. The other cannot simply say yes or no but must present reasons back to the first child. The path to order, therefore, relies entirely on the procedures by which it is achieved. These procedures lead to a new set of criteria for worth which were not appropriate for relations of constraint. In the method of complementariness, the "good" and "bad" child could be judged on the basis of approval and disapproval from adults. The overt criterion is conformity, but the fuller criteria the adult holds are rather mysterious.

The main task of cooperative relations is to evolve procedures which make direct reciprocity a workable method. As with other relations, adherence to the method and derived procedures becomes the overt criterion for judging persons' worth. Children may therefore be judged by their participation in process; for example, how clearly they present ideas, how carefully they listen to counterviews, and how ready they are to work toward consensus. These criteria are not arbitrary but come from the procedures which both peers have an equal hand in making. Two results follow. Criteria of worth are arrived at by interpersonal consensus, and the criteria which apply to one peer's worth, apply without distinction to the other peer. There is not only consensus but mutuality in these relations. In contrast, separate criteria apply to child and adult in unilateral authority. The child is evaluated according to conformity while adults are judged by their benevolence in helping the child to conform.

Similarity between Self and Other   Sullivan suggests that friendship is essential to understanding that one's own personality is similar to that of other persons. A common maladjustment of adulthood is to believe that one is unique and utterly superior or hopelessly inferior to other persons. Such persons do not comprehend that they share views with others and frequently think that their views cannot be understood by others. Friendship, as a primary representative of cooperative relations, stems the construction of exaggerated views of oneself. Its primary mechanism is direct reciprocity which makes manifest the fact that two persons can make identical contributions to interactions. When one friend treats another in a particular way, the other is free to treat the one in the same manner. For younger children, the literal practice of direct reciprocity captures them in a tit for tat. Neither child can unilaterally step out of an ongoing interaction; if one does, the other may also. Once cooperation is understood, treatment of one another as equals is found to work to the advantage of both persons.

The method of reciprocity by complement is asymmetrical in design. Persons do not exchange like actions, and the leader knows more than the child. These facts combine to emphasize inequality between persons. Further, as was shown above, these factors have the effect of separating the persons involved in terms of their thoughts and feelings. Having distinctly different parts to play in interactions, children and adults cannot treat each other alike. Their differences as persons are enhanced. As a consequence, it is difficult for children to see themselves as similar to adults even though they adopt the views of adults. Cooperation, on the other hand, puts emphasis on the similar characteristics which friends have in common. Sullivan and Piaget conclude that friendship engenders a sense of equality which, upon actual practice, is converted into a principle of relationship: children should treat one another as they themselves would wish to be treated.

Interpersonal Sensitivity   The principle of equal treatment is a logical outcome of the practice of cooperation. One's failure to treat others as equals merits unequal treatment from those others. At the same time, the practice of cooperation leads to exposure of individuality in terms of persons' strengths and weaknesses. Friends who spend time together in various situations have to learn that besides their similarity, each is a different individual. One may be more intelligent, another may be a better athlete. One may be more popular, while another may be emotionally more even. How do children reconcile the principle of equality with the facts of inequality? Sullivan and Piaget propose that children learn that they must make adjustments of principle in light of each other's personal makeup. Piaget calls this kind of accommodation *equity* and Sullivan refers to it in terms of the broader concept of *sensitivity*.

According to the thesis, the attainment of equity, or sensitivity, implies that children have already begun to deal with the individual personhood of their peers. Once they are able to do this, children must seek a balance between what they have in common with their peers and how they differ from one another. The task is challenging but its solution allows children to come to know each other in a full grasp of personalities. Consider the contrary results of relations of unilateral authority. Persons remain hidden behind their roles; the child behind the mask of dutiful learner and the adult in the cloud of omniscience. Sullivan and Piaget suggest that children are delayed in coming to know adults as persons who have assets as well as deficiencies. In relations of complement, adults tend to see children as they would like them to be and wish them to become. All persons have deficiences, and it is essential for psychological health to admit one's own weaknesses and be sensitive to those of others. This ability is hindered by the method of complementariness; however, it develops as a natural outcome from relations of cooperation.

Relational
Possibilities

The deeper meaning of continuity between the personality born of peer relations and the mature personality should now be evident. Mutual understanding, consensus in criteria of worth, prizing one's similarity with others, and the need to adjust to one another's personhood have a specific origin in the structure of cooperation. In Sullivan's and Piaget's thinking, psychological and moral health is not achieved by becoming an autonomous individual. Throughout development the young child, the school-age child, and young adolescent seek to find how their own selves fit into relations with others. The structures of two basic relations teach children that individual and interpersonal existence are not contradictory. The former makes sense only in terms of the latter. Further, the existence of the two structures also shows that there are different forms of interpersonal existence. Relations of unilateral authority function to define a self which is different from other, distant in thought, and distinct in role. Benefits accrue when the self unilaterally adjusts to the other and works according to terms set by the other. In the process a clear sense of relationship is established and reality becomes ordered through exchanges of conformity for approval.

The structure of cooperation opens a new path for development. Within its structure, children learn how to present their own views while adjusting to the views of others and how to be heard as well as how to listen. Understanding of self by other, and vice versa, becomes mutual to a high degree. Similarities between self and other are discovered as are differences based on each one's personhood. In being sensitive to others' individuality, while holding to the principle of equality, friends learn to coordinate personal interests with mutual benefits. The worth of self as an individual is founded on the same criteria which apply to the other's worth. As a consequence, the self takes definition in relation *with* other and, when working to enhance a relationship, contributes to the promotion of self and other. In the first realization that "You and I" exist, which occurs in infancy, the child takes a critical step toward maturity. Development then proceeds as the child establishes relational structures and takes from each, new possibilities for interpersonal existence. Of the two basic relations, it is cooperation which brings the child from the primitive "You and I" to the articulated understanding of *we*.

Three   Research Strategy

The aim of this book is to explore the Sulivan-Piaget thesis as a general perspective on social development and as a synthesis for a number of evolving approaches to the study of interpersonal relations. In this vein, it is essential to find out whether Sullivan's and Piaget's ideas correspond to children's actual thinking. Chapters 4 to 7 and 9 to 11 of this text will present empirical data with this end in view. The present chapter will describe the strategy of this research. The chapter is important because this research does not follow the typical model of an hypothetico-deductive test of theory. Rather, because the Sullivan-Piaget thesis deals with complex constructs which are in need of further clarification, and because it addresses outcomes of relational development, such as mutual understanding or interpersonal sensitivity, which are not amenable to simple behavioral measures, this research was undertaken to identify good questions, evolve effective measures, and discover productive leads for subsequent studies.

The present studies were designed to give insights into children's conceptions of interpersonal relations. With this target in mind, children were asked to generate accounts of two-person interactions. In some studies, they were first to generate an action from one person and then describe the probable reaction from the other person. In other studies, they were to describe interactions occurring over long periods of time through a historical chronology.

These accounts put children in the role of storytellers offering a documentation of how people interact in the
everyday social milieu which they know well. Children
were given as much freedom as possible to reveal their
own versions of interactions. The data result neither from
direct observations of naturalistically occurring social behavior nor focused responses checked by carefully controlled laboratory manipulations. Rather, the data were
controlled by the children and are presumed to reflect their
thinking and represent their conceptions of interpersonal
relations (see Damon 1977). While there are limitations to
data of this sort, they provide a necessary first step toward
clarifying the thesis and working toward a scientific
treatment of interpersonal relations which has too long
been left to speculation and avoided by social science researchers (see Hinde 1976).

This chapter describes eleven studies devised to attain
an understanding of children's thinking through their
own accounts of interactions. My major concern, as will be
reiterated throughout the chapter, has been to discover
and evolve measures which meaningfully tap children's
thinking about relations. This problem preempts the use
of standard methods and challenges researchers to find
techniques which fully take account of social life as a process of continuing dialogue (see Riegel 1976).

Rationale of In Studies 1 to 7 children were required to generate simple
Studies 1 to 7 two-person interactions. Both the persons involved and the
outcome, or object, of each interaction were designated by
the interviewer. Each child, as storyteller, was told to consider interactions involving either two children of his or
her own age, or one child of that age and one adult. Children had to describe interactions in which one person did
something kind or unkind for another person. Children
were free to construct whichever interaction they thought
appropriate to these persons and the designated outcome.
It was reasoned that kindness would be a useful means for
getting children to display their knowledge of interactive
methods and relations, since kindness may be construed
as the result of a positive social act whose meaning can be
clearly seen as relational in import. When one person, an
actor, initiates a kindness and the other person, a recip-

ient, accepts it, both persons have before them an overt behavioral account of their relation. The fact that the kindness was directed to someone is already a sign of relation. Its acceptance attests further to the relation. And the way the act is offered and accepted, which is the method of the exchange, adds to these signs by specifying the particular relation to which the actor and recipient belong.

Unkindness may be seen in the same relational sense. To be understood as unkind, an act has to be put into a relational context. It is assumed that actor and recipient come to one another with clear expectations about ways they ought to exchange actions within their relation. Unkindness may result when these expectations are not met. One way to bring about this result is to fail to follow an expected method, in which case a sign is given that the known relation has been interrupted or violated. When enacting a method other than that which ordinarily signifies the relation, a person gives a relational sign— albeit negative—to another. The act is a commentary on the relation in the same sense as is a positive act. Whether the other person accepts the act, and how the other reacts, further attests to the relation and shows equally well what is expected of its method.

The Sullivan-Piaget thesis provides a general outline of the relational systems of meaning children bring to interpersonal interactions. Following the outline, changes within each system of meaning should correlate with development and should be observable in terms of a progression from early school age through entry into adolescence. Even the youngest children should view interactions as following two general methods. Interactions between the child and an adult would signify the child-adult relation when they follow the method of reciprocity by complement which attests to unilateral constraint or unilateral respect. The peer relation should be signified by interactions which follow the method of direct or symmetrical reciprocity. If this translation of the thesis is useful, then we should expect children's accounts of child-adult and peer kindness to be distinguished in terms of these two forms of interactions. Similarly, unkindness should be represented by interactions which do not follow these methods; for example, a child may refuse to accept a unilateral position relative to an adult, or one peer may not treat another as a reciprocating equal.

Sullivan and Piaget suggest that there are certain specific changes in children's perceptions of relations as they develop. Accordingly, we should expect the older children in our studies to bring into their accounts particular features which are either absent or minimally evident in the accounts of the youngest children interviewed. First of all, older children should be able to provide a clear articulation of the persons involved in interactions, and this articulation should be evident in their descriptions of peer interactions chronologically before it appears in their descriptions of interactions with adults. When persons are depicted as individuals, the characteristics chosen for description ought to emphasize the terms of the relation in which the person is being considered. For example, peers ought to be described with an emphasis on equality and reciprocity and adults ought to be described with emphasis on authority and benevolence.

Secondly, as children approach adolescence, the procedures which they have practiced ought to be reconceptualized as principles of relationship. Unilateral constraint and direct reciprocity should no longer be seen simply as practical facts but should be understood as obligatory and essential to relations. A relation can be sustained only if the two persons work toward maintaining the procedures which define their relation. Thus, the older child may find kindness in cases where one of the persons goes out of his or her way to reinstate a procedure when circumstances have made the procedure difficult or unworkable. Similarly, the older child may perceive unkindess as not acting when circumstances provide the opportunity to attest to a relationship.

Third, the thesis suggests that there are separate lines of development for the two relational structures. At the beginning of school age, children should understand the method by which peers interact reciprocally as equals. As children approach adolescence, mutuality should be heightened, interpersonal sensitivity should become a need, and peers should consciously seek intimacy in their relation. The child-adult relation follows a different developmental course. Beginning school-age children should understand the method of unilateral constraint and see themselves as beholden to adults who know what the social order is and who have the duty to teach it to children. Unilateral constraint, and the unilateral respect resulting from it, should be heightened during middle childhood. At this period of development, children can accept inequality between themselves and adults and feel confident that they have come close to acquiring adults' knowledge of the social order. The next developmental step according to the thesis is not, however, the ability to extrapolate this interpersonal understanding. Instead, young adolescents should transform conceptually the child-adult relation into terms more similar to those already discovered in peer relations. Young adolescents should begin to bring procedures of direct reciprocity to their interactions with adults and view themselves more as equals with adults. This new direction is no doubt stimulated in part by actual changes in the way adults interact with children and how they reconceptualize their relations with children. But what is important is that young adolescents reconceptualize these changes using the terms they already have discovered within their peer experiences.

Studies   In study 1, 126 children were to give accounts of interactions in which a child did something kind for a peer or an adult or an adult did something kind for a child. These accounts were designed to reflect the children's understanding of the differences between peer relations and child-adult relations, particularly in terms of applying the two general methods Sullivan and Piaget consider appropriate to these interactions—the methods of complementary and direct reciprocity. The accounts were also expected to show differences in understanding of relations, based on the age of the storyteller. Following Sullivan and Piaget, as children approach adolescence, they should show an increasing ability to distinguish and articulate personalities in a relation. It was expected that younger children would perceive the two types of relations as clearly distinct from one another, while older children, in

their perceptions of the child-adult relation, would show
movement toward equality between participants as in
peer relations.

In study 2, 48 children were to give accounts of kindness. The terms child and adult were changed to friend
and parent, respectively. The purpose of this change was
to see whether the results would be similar to those obtained in study 1 if the interactants were designated as
specific individuals rather than members of a general
class.

Study 3 was designed to check the validity of the accounts generated in studies 1 and 2. An independent sample of 66 children was presented with a set of stories that
had been generated by other children of the same ages.
The children in the study were asked to judge whether
these stories were kind and to say why they were or were
not so. For those they judged unkind, children were to
modify the stories so that they would become kind. If the
original stories represented children's interpersonal
understanding, then it was expected that other children
would agree that these accounts were in fact kind per relation. Specifically, we anticipated that there would be
agreement between stories and judgments by same-age
but independent groups of children. On the other hand,
we expected that adolescents would probably find stories
of 6-year-old children to be in need of modification so that
they would properly represent their own distinctive perceptions of kindness.

In study 4, 74 children were asked to generate accounts
of unkindness, and in study 5, 66 other children were
asked to judge and give reasons for their reactions to a set
of the original unkind stories. These two studies provide a
validity check on one another in the same way as do
studies 1 and 3. In addition, they provide a means to compare kindness to unkindness and to find out whether, as
the thesis suggests, they ought to represent two sides of
the same methods and relational structures.

For study 6, 120 children were asked first to generate a
kind act and then describe how the recipient might reciprocate. This approach was expected to illustrate clearly
the two methods of reciprocity corresponding to the two
basic relations. Peers were expected to reciprocate directly

and to draw closer together upon being offered a positive sign of relation, while children were expected to reciprocate indirectly adults' kindness by acting in complement to their initiatives. In study 7, 60 of the children from study 6 were asked to describe unkind acts and reciprocations to them. In addition, the first actor was to react to the recipient's reaction and next the original recipient was to react to that last action. Again it was anticipated that sequences of exchanges would reveal differences between methods as well as conceptual changes in each method with the increasing age of the storyteller.

Results of Studies 1 to 7   The results of the first seven studies correspond to the Sullivan-Piaget thesis in that the children's descriptions of peer relations showed a definite progression from a point at which children naïvely treat each other as equals to a relation in which children with like personalities attend in an intimate way to one another's needs and interests. The results show also that a developmental change takes place in child-adult relations, with a move toward more equality as children approach adolescence. However, the results do not show the corresponding move toward intimacy or sensitivity to the same degree suggested by the thesis. In the adolescents' accounts, child and adult were still different persons operating from complementary positions. While they appeared to be moving toward mutuality, they still perceived themselves in relation to adults as distinct persons with different interests, needs, and identities. These results imply that children not only distinguish the two relations but gain two quite different understandings of social reality from them. In one, self and other form a known identity which is the *we* of mutual worth. In the second, the *we* of self and other is less mutual and less intimate. It is divided by differences in the viewpoints from which self and other are operating and which they respectively prize as important.

Rationale of Studies 8–11   The potential significance of the distinction between the two relations and its developmental implications suggested the need for a new line of investigation which would help sharpen focus more closely on the growth of interpersonal understanding in peer relations. A look to social reality and a careful reading of Sullivan and Piaget brought this new line of work into sight. If a merging of identities and enhanced sensitivity resulted from peer experiences, the best way to inspect details of the process was to study *friendship*. Everyday facts suggest that children differentiate from among peers in general those whom they like and want to associate with in a special way and those in whom they have no interest. Even casual observation suggests that, during school age, children devote inexorable energy to friends, almost excluding other peers and adults from the sphere of their attention. Thus, we decided that a closer look at friendship might help uncover more of the process which leads to self-identity and interpersonal understanding.

According to the thesis, sometime after 8 years of age children reconceptualize the practices of peer procedures into principles of relationship. When they do this, the relation becomes a means for seeing particular interactions as integrated with one another. While the performance of one interaction produces an immediate effect on the persons involved, it also produces a second effect, which is on the relation itself. When the participants are able to articulate the relation as an object of thought, interactions become understandable to them in terms of the relation. Piaget gives several interesting examples of this development. For example, suppose one peer were to aggress against another peer. According to the practical rule of reciprocity, the second peer has the right to retaliate. Then the first can aggress again, and so on in continuing battle. However, were the second peer to have the relation clearly in mind, his or her original reaction would be altered. Were the second peer not to return the aggression but instead offer a positive gesture of friendship, reciprocity would require the original aggressor to return a positive sign of friendship. This possible sequence of events illustrates the difference between practice of a method and conceptualization of principles by which persons should proceed in order to maintain their relation. It also shows how a concept of relation can be used to interconnect actions to give them a purpose. That is, an aggressive initiative seen in isolation is antirelational. When, however, it is coupled with a positive sign in a reciprocal pairing, the pair serves an opposite purpose which is, in this case, an attempt to bring the two persons back together again.

Sullivan and Piaget carry their analysis of friendship further to allow children to come to a consciousness of themselves within the relation. For Sullivan, friendship is more than a matter of taste or preference. Peers move closer together as they consensually validate one another's worth. Piaget argues similarly; solidarity and mutual respect result because two friends subjugate themselves to the same norms of relationship. There are two expectations in these proposals. One is that young adolescents should be more conscious of the friendship relation, what it is and how interactions affect it. The second is that the self and the other in a friendship will be able to articulate the similarities of their personalities which are mutually defined and understood.

Studies   In study 8, 120 children were asked to describe interactions which would be characteristic of *friends* and *best friends*. The children involved had already participated in some of the foregoing studies. We expected these accounts to be consistent with one another in their emphases on reciprocity and equality as principles. However, we expected to observe changes as storytellers increased in age. For example, while beginning school-age children might focus on the method of direct reciprocity per se, older children, and especially young adolescents, would not only emphasize principles, but would also articulate similarities between personalities involved in interactions. They would begin to show an understanding of the mechanisms underlying the principles.

In study 9, 84 children were asked to think about friendship as a relation with a natural history over time. They were asked to describe what two peers might do to get a friendship started. Once started, they were asked how the two friends might become *best friends*. Then they were asked to describe interactions which might lead to the end of the friendship. It was expected that adolescents would be better able than younger children to give coherent accounts of these aspects of friendship and the transitions leading from one to another state of the relation.

They should be in the best conceptual position to view particular interactions as subordinate to the relation itself.

Study 10 reviews results from the same 60 children who participated in study 7. Their descriptions of unkind acts toward friends and subsequent reactions were reanalyzed with an eye toward identifying ways friends resolved conflict. In study 11, 36 new children were asked to describe conflicts between friends and then describe interactions which occur over time to resolve the conflicts and bring the friends back together. It was assumed that conflicts would be understood as violations of norms of conduct expected of friends and that the nature of violations would change in accordance with the age of the storyteller as would the sequence of interactions required to bring the interactants back to their normative state of friendship.

Interactions as a Source of Data

The purpose of having children give accounts of interactions was to gain insight into children's conceptions of the relations among procedures, methods, and persons. Children's accounts were bounded by specifications of persons in terms of class names (e.g., "a child your age") and of the intended outcome of interactions (e.g., "unkindness"). Within these boundaries, children were free to supply details of persons and acts. All situations involved two persons while interactions involved single acts, single exchanges of an initiative and a reaction, multiple exchanges, or an indefinite number of exchanges occurring over long time spans.

The rationale was that story tellers would choose details appropriate to the implied relations. In describing an act, such as obedience, in order to describe how a child was kind to an adult, children were most likely to say that the actor was meeting the recipient's expectation. It would be unlikely that children would supply acts which only one or neither of the parties understood. In positive terms, story tellers were assumed to be filling in details which fit their conception of the way actors and recipients understood their interpersonal relation and the interactive behavior attesting to it.

If this approach is plausible, then the accounts may be read as representing the several levels of relationship addressed by the Sullivan-Piaget thesis. The behavior described in interactions may be taken to signify methods of reciprocity and the specific procedures they include. These methods should also be reflective of structures of complementariness or symmetrical reciprocity. Furthermore, depictions of the actors and recipients may signify relations from still another angle, for example, through treatment of persons as similar personalities or by emphasis on the persons' intimate understanding of one another. In sum, the conceptions of the relations children bring to interviews ought to be the basis of the stories they generate with these accounts, which shed light, in turn, on children's understanding of relations.

Approaches to Analysis   We approached our analysis of the data from two perspectives. The first was to examine children's accounts in the light of the Sullivan-Piaget thesis that children distinguish two general methods of interactions and understand relations as conceptual structures of these methods. These methods are, again, those of reciprocity by complement, usually characterizing child-adult relations, and direct reciprocity, more characteristic of peer relations. By itself, this approach presents several problems. The principal one is that, because of the general nature of the descriptions of the two methods of relation as given by Sullivan and Piaget, distinctions of behavior within each method are inexplicit. For example, when an adult punishes a child, the act may constitute unilateral constraint. However, this same constraint may be exercised by an adult when he or she lovingly tells a child he or she has done something wrong and explains why. This may, of course, influence whether a child perceives an act as kind or unkind. Another problem is that accounts might also describe behavior which is ambiguous in relation to characteristics of the methods.

For these and other reasons, we also chose to analyze accounts following a descriptive approach. For most of our studies, accounts are classified by descriptive labels. They are then grouped according to their apparent similarity and reported together as a group. This is a conservative approach which discourages the forcing of data to fit preexisting theoretical categories. This approach also may help clarify the meaning of such terms as constraint and cooperation. As will be shown, children were quite individualistic in generating the content of interactive behavior. At the same time, they were quite similar in generating themes which bear on constraint, reciprocity, and unilateral respect. When examined closely, seemingly unique creations turn out to be versions of common themes, stemming from shared understanding of social reality.

There are three ways to assess the utility of classifications. One is to examine the consistency of accounts among children within given age levels. In many studies, 80% or more of the accounts generated within an age level were classified as variations of common general themes. The second is to seek out agreement between stories told by one group of children in one study and judgments of these stories by an independent group in a second study. The third means comes from finding consistent trends across studies. When themes recur in freely generated stories from several independent samples of children, one has to look on the recurrence itself as an important piece of evidence. This form of consistency cuts across samples of children, each of which is focused on different aspects of social interaction.

Perhaps the most challenging problem of measurement pertains to the assessment of the functional products of relational structures. Recall that Sullivan and Piaget propose that persons become known through the structure of their parts in interactive methods. Thus, the child in a unilateral relation is seen to possess different characteristics from the same child in cooperative relations with peers or friends. One way we chose to measure this proposal was to note the terms children used to describe the persons participating in their accounts. To discourage children from focusing on adjectival states rather than persons' activities, interviewers explicitly avoided asking children to describe persons. Thus, some children produced accounts only of interactions while others couched interactions in descriptive explanations of how the persons were feeling or thinking. How children chose to describe participants clearly corresponded to their ages. As with accounts of interactions, these descriptions of persons are grouped for analysis in seemingly like categories.

Other functional outcomes are not so readily amenable to descriptive measurement. We have no standards for measuring the core constructs of the thesis, particularly, degress of mutual understanding, interpersonal sensitivity, intimacy, and the principle of equality. This point, more than any other, emphasizes the exploratory nature of the present research. For this reason, we thought it best to let possible measures for these constructs evolve from the data rather than to force results toward desired outcomes on the basis of a priori definitions. If these constructs represent children's actual ways of viewing society, then children ought to bring them out spontaneously in their descriptions. As it turned out, children did emit several interesting versions bearing on these constructs. They are reportedly fully and seem to suggest ways of approaching functional aspects of relation more directly in future research.

Statistical Treatment   To some readers, the present studies may appear to violate conventional norms for treating data. As stated above, children's accounts of interactions were recorded and classified into categories on the basis of descriptive similarities. Aside from obtaining some measures of reliability of classification, which are reported below, no other formal treatment of data was done. This was judged to be in keeping with the stated exploratory goals of the research. There is, at present, no consensus on ways by which to analyze interactions as fitting one or another method of reciprocity. Further, there are no definite ways to identify particular procedures of interactions as instances of general methods. Needless to add, measures of functional outcomes of relational structures are optional at present. Readers should regard the failure to submit the data to statistical computation as a conservative approach rather than a violation of conventional canons. The measures reported are tentative and meant to be taken for their heuristic value.

There is an equally valid reason for adopting this cautious attitude toward the data. At present the field of social development is overcrowded with efforts to impose a sort of quantification on children which distinguishes them by "stages." There are as many schemes for stages as there are theorists looking at their own results. The thesis, of course, points to changes in structures and functions which should be evident with increasing age. Sullivan even goes so far as to specify the period of 8½ to 10 years as the time when children should begin to articulate the individual personhood of their peers. If there are stages or sharp age discontinuities, the present studies are unprepared to identify them. Instead, three separate age groups are observed in each of the eleven studies; these groups correspond to the beginning of school age (6 to 8 years), middle childhood (9 to 11 years), and early adolescence (12 to 14 years). Some of the developmental differences proposed by the thesis ought to be evident in the differential accounting manifested by children in these three groups. For the present work, it will be satisfactory if children in these age groups or levels are consistent across studies in the ways they describe relations. Consistency of themes will then be considered in terms of developmental differences which can be pursued in subsequent research.

The search for consistency bears repeating at this point. In the absence of statistical tests, performance in any one study may appear uninformative. It will be shown in the concluding chapters, however, that children within three age levels produced recurrent themes in describing kindness, unkindness, and friendship in its several aspects. This spontaneously generated consistency across independent samples, which approached relations from quite different angles, suggests that themes may represent common conceptions children at various ages hold about relations. In some ways, this sort of evidence is strong and merits further consideration. If it leads to questions that seem worth pursuing further, and if the themes help to clarify Sullivan's and Piaget's constructs, the present studies will have proven profitable. They will also have shown that the thesis is more than another interesting statement and that it addresses development of relations as children themselves understand their parts in them with respect to adults and to peers.

Use of Verbal Data   There is deserved skepticism regarding the value of verbal data. In the present studies two questions stand out: In what way do verbal accounts of interactions represent children's social knowledge? To what degree do verbal accounts correspond to children's actual social behavior? In answer to the first question, verbal accounts fit within a historical tradition in developmental psychology. Piaget's own research is a representative example. It is too simplistic to argue merely that to find out what children know, one should go and ask them. On the other hand, by going directly to children, one puts a theory in their hands and faces the possibility of their rejecting it. Children's verbal statements represent something of their thinking and whether it represents the whole of their thinking is open to debate. What is important to recognize is that the use of these statements is only one of several avenues available to uncover children's knowledge, and it should be treated with caution and ultimately be reconciled with other sources of data.

In the present studies, statements are narrow in scope, limited to children's descriptions of interactive events. We assume children can easily understand interactions, since they have reference to them in their everyday life. This contrasts with asking children for abstract definitions of relations or forcing them to convert feelings about persons into verbal summaries. As a side effect, the focus on inter- actions also may deter children from concocting statements for the sake of providing socially desirable impressions. This possibility, of course, can never be ruled out. In studies 1, 2, 3, and 6, children were asked to describe socially desirable and positive events involving acts of kindness. Studies 4 and 5 required descriptions of inter- actions involving unkindness and violations and conflict. Children were also asked in these latter studies to de- scribe the less desirable sides of social life. While there is no definite way to determine whether or not accounts reflect life as it is known or life as children think the interviewers wanted to hear it, there are means to make judgments about the degree to which it entered accounts.

Accounts will be presented here in full so that readers may square them with their own observations of children in naturalistic or laboratory settings. As will be argued later, we found the accounts obtained could not have been overly determined by children's efforts to make good im- pressions. The nature of the differences based on age level which were observed could not have been foreseen by the storytellers. Quite specific changes in themes were found from one age level to another, and it does not seem plausible to argue that children knew when or what changes the interviewers were expecting. The preliminary conclusions presented in chapter 8 make a strong case that changes seem more in keeping with development of relational conceptions, as proposed by Sullivan and Piaget, than with attempts to create impressions. That is, positive impressions could have been made if children would have adopted a single posture toward interviewers, and they did not. Children at the three age levels focused on disparate themes, and, within any age level, children described interactions with content sufficiently diverse as to suggest that their focus was on relations as they knew them more than as they thought interviewers wanted them to be.

As to the correspondence between accounts and actual behavior, two points are important. There is no assurance that children's accounts of interactions represent the exact ways they would act were they put into these situations. Most accounts, however, appear believable. For example, acts of kindness seem to be of an everyday observable sort, neither heroic nor fantastical. Acts of unkindness were similarly realistic reflecting competition, efforts to dominate or attempts to aggress. They did not express unusual cruelty. And, interactions within friendship, which touched on both positive and negative sides of the relation, seem to square with those everyday performances one sees in children's making, keeping, and losing of friends.

Verbal accounts are not always the best substitute for naturalistic observations. They represent children's thinking, but they don't necessarily indicate that children would act thusly in real life. Nevertheless, the types of questions raised by the thesis preempt naturalistic study at this time. Consider first, studies 6 to 11. They deal with interactions occurring over days or months. One would have practical difficulties following friends over the history of their relation (see study 9) or even knowing which of the uncountable interactions that take place between the friends are relevant to the relation and which are incidental. We assume here that children's concise summaries differentiate among events and provide a context for subsequent observations. More importantly, the very constructs with which the thesis deals, make verbal summaries the most convenient data source at present. Consider the construct of reciprocity and its presumed developmental course from literal practice to principle which is used to guide practice. When direct reciprocity is literal, one should see like exchanges occurring in sequence; for instance, A hits B, then B hits A; or A shares with B, then B shares with A. Once converted into a principle, however, the exchange may not occur immediately in time, and it may require different currencies which only the participants understand as equivalent. Both of these points have been emphasized by sociologists who have submitted reciprocity to close inspection (see Gouldner 1960). Indeed, Sahlins (1965) has even argued that the closer the relation between parties, the less obvious reciprocity is to outside observers. Only the participants know what to exchange for what, and when an initiative has to be returned in time. In this context, verbal accounts are useful for uncovering reciprocity, especially as children conceive of it within their close relations to parents and friends where the equivalence of items exchanged or temporal boundaries are known only to the participants.

Samples of Children Our studies were limited to children living in affluent modern suburban society of the mid-1970s. Most of the children were students in private schools, with about 75% coming from Catholic parochial schools. As judged by geographic location, most of the children came from families in which parents were highly educated and had incomes above the national median. Ethical practice prevented direct entry to school records, but it is assumed that most children came from intact families in which the father was the major wage earner, employed as a government official, business executive, self-employed businessman, professional, or skilled technician.

There were 628 individual children who participated in these studies. Approximately half were males and half were females. Differences between this total and the numbers reported for each study result from some children's participation in two studies. The overlaps occurred with studies 2 and 5, 3 and 4, 7 and 10, and 8 with several other studies. In every study, three age levels were sampled: grades 1 and 2 in which children were 6 to 8 years of age; grades 4 and 5 in which children were 9 to 11 years old; and grades 7 and 8, in which children ranged from 12 to 14 years. These levels correspond to three important points of transition which have already been described in the chronology outlined in the previous chapter. They do not cover the whole of the developmental process for relations which clearly begins earlier and continues well beyond early adolescence. They specifically match the period which Sullivan and Piaget consider normative for the establishment of friendship and the beginnings of transformation in child-adult relations.

Interviews   All interviews were conducted in the several schools during school hours on an individual basis. Ten different adult interviewers were used; all were graduate students and two were males while eight were females. Except in three studies, at least two interviewers collected data for each study. They worked independently under the coordination of the author. Children's accounts were at first tape-recorded and written down by the interviewers. However, tape recording was abandoned as a distraction to the children, and thereafter the interviewers were instructed to record faithfully what children said while they were speaking. In most cases, accounts were brief and easily captured. When difficulties arose, interviewers repeated what they thought they had heard or asked children to repeat what they had previously said.

Scoring   All protocols were scored by the author, based on classifying children's accounts according to the created categories. In all cases, interviewers also participated in scoring protocols in all phases. The goal of scoring was to reach agreement and not to see whether independent scorers could separately classify protocols similarly. The scoring process consequently began with two or three persons reading each protocol of a study. This was followed by discussion and comparison of categories thought to cover most protocols. Once categories were constructed and criteria stated, the protocols of individual children were read again and each was assigned appropriately. When disputes arose, categorization was determined through discussion.

In any study, no more than about 15% of the accounts caused dispute. This was in part due to the general criteria used for scoring and that accounts were scored primarily in terms of the actions which children described. In most cases, this allowed immediate identification through the verb which children used. In addition, other features were scored separately. These included any description children might have given of the persons (actors and recipients) or of particular outcomes of interactions, either material or psychological. Again, differences of opinion were submitted to discussion. If differences could not be resolved, protocols were not assigned to a category. Use of the null category, equivalent to a "miscellaneous" class, accounts for differences between the number of children who participated in a study and the totals which appear in the tables describing frequencies. The number interviewed minus the totals of columns in the tables shows exactly how many protocols did not readily fit the categories.

Several standard checks were made to determine whether categories could be reliably reconstructed. These checks consisted of having two persons—the author and someone else—reclassify protocols after the categories were defined and criteria stated. Results were as follows. For study 1, there was independent agreement in 92% of the 126 cases for the category of interaction and whether or not children qualified the interaction as an example of peer kindness. There was 83% agreement regarding kindness of child actors toward adult recipients. Corresponding results for study 2 were 85% and 93%, respectively. For study 5, where children judged accounts of unkindness, there was 90% agreement on the reasons children gave for peer unkindness and 93% agreement on their reasons for children's unkindness toward adults.

As a final note, in preparing this manuscript, the author reread all the protocols which had previously been classified as belonging to particular categories. This was done study-by-study, one category at a time. This procedure occurred after the original categorization process with the gap in time being up to eighteen months in some cases. The object was to check the sense of the original classification and to remove those cases which appeared ambiguous. This process resulted in the elimination of several protocols from reportable to the "miscellaneous" category. In no study did this result in more than a 5% removal rate.

Four   Kindness in Two Relations

This chapter is a report of 126 children's ideas about child-child and child-adult relations. Seventy-two children told stories in which one person did something *kind* for another person. Fifty-four children told stories in which one person showed another that he *liked* him. It was assumed, and results confirmed, that the two types of stories reflected the same process. The common process is called relational *acknowledgment,* meaning that the interactions serve as overt signs to let actor and recipient know that they belong to a particular relation. The sign is conveyed by the content of the interaction and especially by the method followed.

There were 42 storytellers from each of three age groups: 6 to 8 years (youngest), 9 to 11 years (middle), and 12 to 14 years (oldest). Children came from grades 1 and 2, 4 and 5, and 7 and 8, respectively. The children were sampled from three parochial elementary schools of similar socioeconomic composition.

There were three adult interviewers, two females and one male. Each interviewed children individually during class hours on several questions pertaining to their social understanding. The part of the interview of present interest consisted of three questions about kindness or two questions concerning one person's liking of another. All questions were posed by asking children to tell a story as follows: (*a*) "Tell me a story in which a child your age does something kind for another child your age." (*a*₁) "Tell me a story in which a child your age shows another child your age that they like them." The focus of these stories was *child-child* relations. (*b*) "Tell me a story in which a child your age does domething kind for an adult, a grown-up." (*b*₁) "Tell me a story in which a child your age shows an adult, a grown-up, that they like them." And (*c*) "Tell me a story in which an adult, a grown-up, does something kind for a child your age." These stories dealt with *child-adult* relations with (*b*) and (*c*) pertaining to both sides of the relation.

In the description of results that follows, stories are reported in groupings that correspond to aspects of the Sullivan-Piaget thesis. Actual stories are presented verbatim with occasional deletion of words that have no substantive bearing on meaning. The sex and age in years of the storyteller is given in parentheses before each story. The appearance of "?" in a protocol refers to a question or comment from the interviewer which was typically: "Why is that kind?" or "Tell me more about it." Stories are reported in italics.

Child-Child Results   The overall results are summarized in table 1. Stories were categorized into five areas of content determined by the verb describing how the actor performed kindness or liking toward the recipient. The content areas, with the number of stories for each, are as follows: "giving/ sharing" (46 stories), "playing" (39 stories), "physical assistance" (15 stories), "teaching" (11 stories), and "understanding" (13 stories). Two stories did not fit into these areas of content. Stories were also categorized according to whether or not circumstances surrounding actions were stated. In 69 stories, actions were explicitly *qualified* by descriptions of either recipients, actors, or both; while in 55 stories actions were not accompanied by descriptions, and are hence called *unqualified*. These two types of categorizations were combined to yield an overall classification which is reported in table 1 where frequencies are given for the age and sex of children and the type of story recounted.

Two general age trends are obvious. Frequencies of unqualified stories decreased while qualified stories increased as the age level of the storytellers increased. Second, the youngest storytellers focused almost exclusively on content areas of sharing and playing while the middle age and oldest story tellers used all of the content areas. A subsidiary finding is that sex seems to have no bearing on the type of story recounted at any of the age levels. Stories are now presented in detail as they bear on points of the thesis.

Table 1   Child-Child Stories: Frequencies for Males and Females

Content and	Ages 6–8		Ages 9–11		Ages 12–14	
	Male	Female	Male	Female	Male	Female
Giving/sharing, unqualified	12	12	1	2	2	2
Giving/sharing, qualified	1	3	2	1	6	2
Playing, unqualified	3	4	4	4	3	6
Playing, qualified	2	2	4	5	1	1
Giving physical assistance, qualified	2	1	3	4	3	2
Teaching, qualified	—	—	2	4	2	3
Understanding, qualified	—	—	4	2	2	5

Stories
*Unqualified
giving/sharing*

All the stories comprising the "unqualified giving/ sharing" category contain variations of the verbs "give" or "share." Actions were stated with minimal reference to context, actors, or recipients. These stories appear to represent the children's idea that method of direct reciprocity alone acknowledges a relation between peers.

Examples of stories based on the verb "give" follow each preceded by the abbreviation for sex and age of the storyteller:

(M,8) *Like I have lots of candy. I give a lot of it away.*

(F,6) *Give them flowers.*

(M,7) *Give him some candy or ice cream. (?) Because that was their friend.*

(M,7) *They give everything to the person. (?) A book or a pencil. (?) To be nice.*

(F,6) *Give them stuff. (?) Some of their snacks.*

(F,7) *If you're going to get something to eat, you could give them some.*

(F,7)   *Give them something. (?) Because it's just nice.*

(F, 9)   *Give presents to him.*

(M,11)   *Give them things.*

Examples of stories containing the verb "share" are as follows:

(F,7)   *By sharing stuff with them.*

(M,6)   *They were kind because they were sharing candy because they were the same age.*

(M,6)   *Share gum. (?) It would be nice.*

(M,7)   *Share; trade. (?) It's being nice to one another.*

(F,6)   *Sharing. (?) Because they like it.*

(F,7)   *Susie is kind to me by sharing erasers . . . she'll trade a lot.*

(F,12)   *Sharing with them.*

Examples of variants of giving or sharing include the following stories:

(M,6)   *He let one play with his toys and look at his books. (?) He probably likes him.*

(F,10)   *She let her neighbor use her trampoline for a Hershey bar.*

(M,13)   *Offer him some gum.*

(F,12)   *Let someone borrow a pen.*

Qualified giving/sharing   The stories making up the "qualified giving/sharing" category contain the verbs "share," "give," or variants thereof. They differ from the unqualified stories exemplified above in that the actions described here are predicated on explicit statements of material descrepancies between the actors who give and the recipients who accept some material object. If unqualified sharing represents acknowledgment between peers applying a method, then sharing qualified by actor-recipient discrepancies may represent this method as it is adjusted to actual persons and the circumstances they are in.

One set of these stories contains descriptions of actor-recipient differences in material possessions; one peer has something the other peer does not have. Some examples are:

(F,6)   *One kid has a bike and one didn't. The one who has would take turns.*

(M,9)   *In class somebody doesn't have a pencil or a book. You let them borrow it.*

(M,13)   *He doesn't have any money. You take him to a movie.*

(M,12)   *A bunch of kids are out at the Hot Shoppes . . . and you don't have any money. They give you some so you can buy a coke or something.*

(F,12)   *If you don't have a pen, someone lends you one.*

(M,13)   *One shared candy with the other one who didn't have any.*

A second subgroup of these stories involves giving to recipients who do not have something because they have forgotten or lost it. Examples are:

(F,7)   *If they forgot their lunch, you could share your lunch with them.*

(M,10)   *One gives up some of his money . . . to the one who forgot his money.*

(F,10)   *Michelle forgot money yesterday for lunch and I let her borrow some.*

(M,12)   *One loses his pen; the other one lends him one so he can do a test.*

(F,12)   *One drops a book . . . the other one finds it and gives it to him.*

The common element among these stories is that actors and recipients were said to be in unequal material circumstances. With inequality as context, actors' initiatives operated to put recipients into new positions. The outcome of actions was to bring recipients into similar material circumstances as actors. As a consequence, actors and recipients were materially more equal after than before the initiatives were exerted.

Unqualified play   Most stories constituting "unqualified play" contain the verb "play" or particular examples of play. Examples are:

(M,6)   *Play with them nice and don't fight.*

(F,7)   *When you play with them.*

(M,6)   *Play with him. (?) Because he's nice.*

(M,14)   *Play; do something with them.*

A subset of stories differs slightly in that actors were said to invite recipients to play. Examples include:

(M,7)   *By asking them to play.*

(M,9)   *Ask him to play baseball with him.*

(M,10)   *Ask him if you want to be friends.*

(M,13)   *Invite them to your house.*

(F,12)   *Ask them to do stuff with you.*

As with unqualified stories of giving, these stories were based on no obvious circumstance. Actions of play were presented in themselves as acknowledgments of peer relations. In other words, the method alone accounts for acknowledgment.

Qualified play   In each of the stories of "qualified play," an actor's initiative was directed to the social condition of the recipient. One subset of stories deals with the quality of play between two peers which was improved by the initiative of the actor. Examples are:

(M,6)   *If you're swinging and that one wants to, you let them take turns.*

(M,7)   *Like if they ask you a question, answer them instead of saying, "Never mind."*

(F,9)   *Your best friend is in the back of the line . . . you're in front. You give her fronts.*

(F,10)   *Like if I wanted to play baseball and they want to play tennis . . . go along with them.*

The remainder of the qualified stories of play, all deal with invitations to play extended to recipients who had no friends or were lonely. In each instance, the actor's initiative gave the recipient social opportunities to have friends. Stories are:

(M,10)   *If they're a new kid in school, you could show them around.*

(F,9)   *If they're new and move in, you can introduce them.*

(M,9)   *When a new student comes in, don't make fun of him. Play with him.*

(M,10)   *Like a new girl . . . other people poke fun. You make friends with her.*

(M,12)   *Say one is playing in a group. A kid wants to get in . . . . He might be jealous and feel bad. You let him in.*

(F,12)   *One is left out; you go over and talk with her . . . . Make her feel like somebody likes her.*

It is clear that the general form of these stories begins with social inequality. After the actor's initiative, actor and recipient are brought closer to social equality. In the first subset of stories, the initiative seems to solidify ongoing play. In the latter subset, the initiative is the beginning of a social relation which had not previously existed. One child (the actor) presumably had friends while the other (the recipient) did not. The actor's initiative changes that inequality so that the recipient now has at least one social equal, the actor.

Qualified assistance   Most of the stories in the category of "qualified assistance" (meaning physical help) follow a general framework. A recipient had an accident and was physically hurt. An actor then offered assistance so that the recipient's pain could be relieved.

(M,6)   *He's stuck on a swing . . . . He's going to get his mother.*

(F,7)   *One fell down. The other one could help him up.*

(M,9)   *They were playing and she fell off a swing. The other girl rushed over and got help.*

(F,9)   *They were riding their bikes and one fell off. The other boy came over and helped him.*

(F,12)   *When someone's hurt, don't just walk away. Help them.*

The remaining stories were also of physical assistance but did not involve bodily harm. Examples include:

(M,10)   *If your sister had a lot of books, you could help her carry some.*

(M,12)   *When the chain fell off his bike, you go over and fix it . . . . He doesn't know how.*

Qualified teaching   In all but one story, accounts of actions categorized as "qualified teaching" deal with assistance in schoolwork when recipients were having difficulty learning. Examples are:

(M,9)   *Bob would help Tim with homework . . . . He has low grades [and Tim would reciprocate].*

(F,9)   *Someone was absent from school and asks help with work . . . . Her friend helps.*

(M,10)   *Like someone's stuck on their math. Just help . . . . And they would help you with spelling.*

(F,13)   *If he's slow in a subject, you can help him.*

(M,13)   *He's smart in school and he's not as smart. One can help the other.*

(F,12)   *If a boy in class doesn't know how to divide, I can teach him.*

(F,12)   *If they don't understand their homework, you could help them in school.*

These stories are quite explicit in showing that recipients are not equal to actors, who are knowledgeable about schoolwork. Actors then become teachers. Recipients, because of the teaching, do better in their schoolwork. The result is not so much a matter of equality, as was the case with giving or playing, but represents more an achievement of *equity*. After teaching, a recipient may not be so smart as an actor, but recipients will be doing better relative to their capacities for school success.

Qualified   Those stories showing "qualified understanding" in
understanding   clude the widest variety of content. There are, however, elements common to all of them. Recipients were always described as being in states of emotional upset. (The closest description to this in previously described categories is of instances where recipients felt socially alone or excluded.) Secondly, the initiative on the part of the actor was always the show of concern for or understanding of these emotional states. Examples include the following stories:

(M,10)   *Take up for him if someone's picking on him.*

(F,10)   *If somebody's being mean to that person, and can tell them not to and ask why.*

(M,10)   *You're playing and one of them cheats. [They argue.] The other one said, OK. He let it go. They were friends again.*

(M,10)   *I sort of got in trouble and sort of blamed it on my friend. He would let it stay.*

(F,10)   *When someone found out they were adopted . . . try to cheer them up. Make them feel better.*

(M,13)   *Joe's dog died. John was his best friend. He takes time out to really understand him.*

(F,12)   *One girl is really insecure. The other girl tries to understand her.*

(F,13)   *Someone messes up in diagramming. Instead of laughing, she helps out. Help him as an equal and don't look down at him.*

(F,13)   *Jane gets in trouble with her parents. Jill tries to comfort her . . . gives her advice.*

(F,13)   *Two kids are on vacation . . . . One is homesick. Keep her*
          company. Try to distract her.
(M,13)   *He's a loner . . . . Help him to make friendship [and] learn to*
          get along.

As with teaching, stories of understanding began with inequality, moved toward equality, and ended in achievement of a sort of equity. It is not obvious that actors' initiatives could fully remove the emotionally troubled states of recipients or place them in the presumed untroubled states of the actors. The result of understanding was then a sort of equity which is nothing other than an attempt to acknowledge equality and to work toward it as much as possible under the circumstances.

Interpretation of Child-Child Stories

The majority of stories generated by 6 to 8 year old children described two peers sharing or playing nicely together. Sharing and playing may be seen as two procedures which exemplify the general method of direct reciprocity. These procedures contain elements of equality and reciprocity as the thesis suggests. Both elements are presented literally. Equality is expressed as: Whatever one peer possesses, the other peer should also possess. And, whatever one peer is doing, the other should also be doing.Reciprocity is evident by implication. The actor initiates sharing, but if material possession were reversed, the peer who is the recipient would then become the actor. Reciprocity is expressed in play by the adverb "together." One peer takes the first step to start play and the other peer takes the next step so that the peers are playing together. Without reciprocity there could be no play.

As Sullivan and Piaget suggest, between about 8 and 10 years of age, children add two things to their concept of peer relations. First, equality and direct reciprocity are reconstituted as principles of relation. Earlier they were understood as pragmatic rules for getting along, now they are principles to be worked toward. Second, the principles of the peer relation are now coupled with an understanding that individualized persons are involved. Previously, peers were seen more as classes of persons, almost as if one peer could be substituted for another. Now peers are specific persons who present themselves to one another in different states of their individuality.

Both changes are seen to occur simultaneously beginning with the middle age group of storytellers. The articulation of this new understanding is explicit. The majority of the stories told by children older than 9 years were predicated on differences between actors and recipients. The peers were described as being factually unequal. One had something the other did not. One was hurt, the other was physically sound. One had friends, the other did not. One was successful in school, the other was doing less well. One was emotionally troubled, the other was not. If equality is a principle, then inequality is an occasion for testifying to a peer relation: actors took steps to undo inequality and to bring about equality or equity. In cases of material possession, equality results when the actor gives the recipient the thing which the recipient does not have. The consequence of giving is that actor and recipient share the same material possession.

Evidence that children in the middle age range regard equality as a principle of relation and perceive peers as individualized persons is shown by the fact that most of their accounts were based on a disparity between the actor and the recipient, such that a single initiative could not produce literal equality. For example, offering assistance to a peer who is physically in pain does not remove the pain. Similarly, teaching does not make the two peers equally smart; and understanding or sympathizing does not erase an emotional problem. What the initiatives do is to present an overt sign that both peers are entitled to treatment as equals. When this principle is applied to the facts that the peers are different persons who are now in different states, equity results. That is, the principle of equality is acknowledged as adjustments are made to the individual circumstances of the peers. Because both peers recognize the fact of individuality, their interaction achieves the end they both understand. The material result of the interaction may be secondary to the attestation that the peers are entitled to equal treatment and equal states of existence.

The data bear on the thesis in more specific terms also. Sullivan proposes that at about 10 years of age children relate to peers with a "need for interpersonal sensitivity," adjust their behavior to one another's "expressed needs," and pursue "mutual satisfactions" in validating each other's "personal worth" (p. 246). After about 9 years of age, our children's stories did, in fact, show a turn in each of these directions. Sharing and playing provide a clear demonstration. For the youngest storytellers, sharing and playing were kind as acts in themselves. But after about 9 years, sharing was only considered kind when it was qualified by one peer's compensating another's lack of material possession, and playing was kind when it was directed by one peer toward another's need for companionship. Stories concerning teaching and understanding showed the same point from a different angle. Children seemed to be saying that one peer's problems should be taken on by the other peer so that both can work toward a solution. The impetus may be the assumption that recipients are worth being concerned about. It is in working toward a problem's solution that peers can validate each other's worth and attain mutual satisfaction.

It is important to recognize that older storytellers freely chose to describe actors and recipients as being in disparate positions as the qualification for kindness. Interviewers did not direct children's focus toward inequality. Rather, children spontaneously generated inequality as the test of relationship. They also chose the content which ranged from material deprivation to emotional difficulties. The impression one gets from these choices is that in peer relations both parties share interest in the full personality of one another. Any deviation from well-being can be an occasion for concern. Actors then put forth effort and recipients accept it. Thereby, both peers present their personalities for mutual validation and simultaneously solidify their special relation.

Child-Adult Results

Child (Actor)- Adult (Recipient) Results

Of the stories dealing with child-adult relations, the stories in which children are actors and adults recipients will be considered first. These stories were classified into four areas of content: "obeying" (33 stories), "being good/ polite" (46 stories), "doing chores" (35 stories), and "showing concern" (12 stories). As with stories between peers, some were unqualified in that actions alone were described, while some were qualified on explicit descriptions of the persons involved.

An overall view of results is given in table 2. There were no obvious male-female differences, but there were clear trends corresponding to age. Unqualified obedience and being good/polite accounted for most of the youngest group's stories (36), declined a bit in the middle group (26 stories), and declined further in the oldest group (17 stories). Qualified stories of doing chores and showing concern had the opposite age effect. Frequencies increased from the youngest (6 stories) to the middle (16 stories) to the oldest group (25 stories).

Table 2   Child (Actor)-Adult (Recipient) Stories:Frequencies for Males and Females

Content and Conditions	Ages 6–8		Ages 9–11		Ages 12–14	
	Male	Female	Male	Female	Male	Female
Obeying, unqualified	7	7	4	8	4	3
Being good, polite, unqualified	13	9	8	6	7	3
Doing chores, qualified	1	5	8	6	6	9
Showing concern, qualified	—	—	1	1	4	6

Obeying   Two variants of the story type categorized as "obeying" were observed. In one, storytellers asserted a general rule that children were obeying or should obey adults. In the other, they said that child actors were doing something specific which adults had asked them to do. The latter type of story borders on being qualified since it includes a statement about the (adult) recipient. But all such statements referred only to the adult's wanting something without reference to personal circumstances.

Examples of the first variant are the following:

(M,6)   *Do what it says. (?) Because it's a grown-up.*

(M,7)   *By doing what they say.*

(M,6)   *Obey him. (?) Because your dad wants you to do what he says.*

(F,6)   *Obeying him. (?) They're your parents.*

(F,7)   *By doing whatever they tell you to do.*

(F,7)   *When you obey them.*

(M,11)   *Don't disobey them.*

(F,10)   *Do what they tell me and not talk back.*

(F,10)   *If an adult says to do something, you could do it.*

(F,10)   *Trying not to disobey.*

(M,11)   *You don't disobey.*

(M,13)   *Do what they say. (?) Don't neglect chores.*

(F,14)   *Obeying them. (?) Respect them.*

(F, 12)   *Listen when you're being told to do something.*

Examples of the second variant include the following:

(M,7)   *When his father asks him to get his shoes for him and he gets them.*

(F,11)   *Run errands if they ask.*

(F,10)   *You're anxious to play. Your mother tells you to go to the store. You should do what she says.*

(F,10)   *I'd clean up my room and do anything she told me to.*

(M,13)   *When his mother asks him to do an errand, he does it.*

These stories seem to be self-explanatory. Child actors show kindness, or that they like adults, by obeying adults. They do whatever adults ask with no specification as to why adults might ask them to do it. Only the method seems important.

Being good/polite   We observed three subtypes among stories in the "being good/polite" category. In the first, child actors acted pleasantly toward adults; in the second, child actors did not act badly; and in the third, child actors acted with politeness.

Examples of pleasantness included the following:

(F,7)   *Give them a present (?) Say you love them.*

(M,7)   *Play games with him.*

(M,7)   *Play with him.*

(F,6)   *By talking.*

(M,7)   *Love them and be nice.*

(F,7)   *She could say, 'I love you.'*

(F,7)   *Bring them flowers.*

(M,9)   *Putting the dishes away after dinner.*

(F,9)   *Tell them you like them.*

(M,9)   *Do something he likes.*

(F,10)   *On Mother's Day, buy a present.*

(M,13)   *Be friendly. (?) Talk to them.*

(F,13)   *Doing extra chores without being asked.*

(F,13)   *Giving them a good comment. Go out of your way to be nice.*

(M,12)   *Offer to do something for him.*

Examples of not being bad include the following stories:

(M,6)   *Don't fight with them.*

(M,6)   *Not fight him.*

(M,6)   *Because he never lies.*

(F,7)   *By not being bad.*

(F,7)   *When she [mother] took a nap, he didn't cry.*

(F,9)   *Don't be rude.*

(M,14)   *Don't talk back to them.*

Examples of politeness were:

(F,7)   *If you're having a party, take their hat and coat.*

(M,6)   *Picking up something for him.*

(F,7)   *Being polite. (?) Saying, 'Please.'*

(F,11)   *Be polite.*

(M,9)   *When they come for a visit, don't ask stupid questions.*

(F,9)   *A child could open the door for an adult.*

(M,13)   *Open doors for them.*

Being nice, not being bad, or acting politely may represent a rule parallel to the aforementioned rule of obedience. Since no conditions accompany the actions, it may
be assumed that the actions are self-explanatory to the
actors and the recipients. Their very enactment is a communication which both actors and recipients understand
as an acknowledgment of their relation. The constitutive
rule is *act nicely* and *do not act badly*. The method is for the
child to build behavior to meet adults' wishes, in short, for
the child to act in complement to the adult.

Qualified   Stories characterized as "qualified doing chores" were of
doing chores   a unitary type. In each, an adult was depicted as being
in need of physical assistance. Child actors were kind, or

showed adults that they liked them, by performing the appropriate physical labor. Most often the labor pertained to chores around the house. Needs of adults varied widely.

Examples of house chores when needs of adults were based on old age or sickness include:

(M,11)   *Like somebody's really old; you could mow their lawn.*

(M,10)   *If they're old and sick, you could run errands for them.*

(M,9)   *Doing an errand for a sick grown-up.*

(F,10)   *When her mother was in the hospital . . . she cooked and did the housework.*

(F,9)   *An adult could be sick. I could fix them something to eat and make beds.*

(F,10)   *If they were sick, you could clean up the house or vacuum.*

(F,14)   *Pick up boxes that are too heavy for real old people . . . . Do it freely.*

(M,12)   *He helped chop down a tree for this old man . . . . He was too weak to do it.*

(M,13)   *There is this old man, who is a neighbor . . . . The kid works around his house.*

Children also depicted adults as needing help when they are physically overburdened or busy. The child's chore was then done in lieu of the adult being able to do it himself at that time. Examples are:

(M,9)   *A woman's grocery bag tears [in the shopping center]. He can help her pick things up.*

(F,10)   *Babysit if they have lots of kids . . . Do it freely.*

(F,9)   *If my mother asked me to get something and she's having a party, I'd get it for her.*

(F,9)   *Maybe a mother has to work very much and can't do things for her baby. You could take him for a walk when he's crying.*

(F,13)   *Doing things to help them (?) Like babysitting . . . do it for no money.*

(M,13)   *He might not have time to do something. You can work around the house.*

(M,13)   *A lady is carrying lots of bags. You help her . . . . She's having trouble.*

(F,12)   *Mothers have a lot of things to do. You can help her wash dishes.*

(F,12)   *If they have a big family, they can help out mother.*

(F,12)   *Help parents around the house . . . maybe it's too much work for them.*

It is clear that initiatives from child actors stem in part from the need for help which is attributed to adult recipients. In each case the need is for some physical labor, usually house chores. Needs, in turn, are described in terms of old age, sickness, being physically overburdened, or having too many things to do. All of these needs put adults in positions of being unable to do the work they could ordinarily do themselves. Child actors then take on the role of substitute laborers who can do the work which the adults cannot.

Showing concern   The last group of stories, those showing "qualified concern," also deals with adults in need, when need went beyond the immediate requirement for chores.
Examples are the following:

(F,9)   *A clerk in a store gives you too much change . . . . Instead of keeping it, you give it back . . . . Don't take a reward.*

(M,10)   *They're in the hospital and you write them letters . . . . Make sure they don't get sad.*

(M,13)   *When you're delivering newspapers you put it where the old man won't have to bend down to get it . . . . He's got arthritis.*

(M,12)   *Lots of kids hassle old people . . . . They're lonely . . . . Cheer them up.*

(M,12)   *One day a person with eye trouble dropped something in the grass . . . . Instead of laughing . . . the child helps them find it.*

(F,12)   *You don't like this friend of your mother. She's always mean . . . . When she visits try to be polite . . . . She's unhappy.*

(F,13)   *Sometimes when the teacher makes a mistake all the kids let her know . . . . She's embarrassed. You don't make a big deal of it.*

(F,13)   *When the class is being mean to a teacher . . . Go after class and let her know that not everybody hates her . . . Go and help her out.*

(M,13)   *Like when a bunch of guys go to a nursing home . . . . We visit old people . . . . Sing for them . . . . No one visits them.*

(F,13)   *When an adult is sick in the hospital, go visit him. Try to distract him. Entertain him.*

(F,13)   *Our neighbor's a real old lady . . . with no family . . . . Go over to keep her company . . . . Be with her.*

These stories are similar to those told when child actors showed understanding of emotional states of child recipients. In the present stories adult recipients are presented as being in emotionally troubled circumstances. Child actors show kindness, or that they like adults, by offering signs which indicate that they are concerned about their emotional states. The results are generally that adults feel better because some other person has let them know that they are not alone in their difficulty.

Adult (Actor)-
Child (Recipient)
Results

There were 71 stories in which adult actors did something kind for child recipients. Stories were classified into six content areas: "playing/being nice" (7 stories), "granting a favor" (27 stories), "offering assistance (5 stories), "giving" (9 stories), "teaching" (8 stories), and "understanding" (15 stories). Thirty-four stories were unqualified and 37 stories were qualified by recipients' needs. Age differences can be seen in the data of table 3. Most stories from the youngest group were unqualified (20 of 24) and about playing and being nice or granting a favor (18 of 24). By contrast, only 5 stories from the oldest group were unqualified and in addition the oldest group's stories covered five of the six possible content areas.

Table 3   Adult (Actor)- Child (Recipient) Stories:Frequencies for Males and Females

Contents and Conditions	Ages 6–8		Ages 9–11		Ages 12–14	
	Male	Female	Male	Female	Male	Female
Playing/being nice, unqualified	5	2	—	—	—	—
Granting favors, unqualified	7	6	6	3	1	4
Giving, qualified	—	—	1	2	2	—
Giving physical assistance, qualified	—	3	1	2	2	1
Teaching, qualified	—	1	1	1	2	3
Understanding, qualified	—	—	3	4	5	3

Playing/being nice

All stories about playing and being nice were about adults who were doing something pleasant with children. Examples are:

(M,7)   *Plays ball with him. (?) Because they like kids and kids like grown-ups.*

(M,6)   *Because he goes with him all the time. Like watching TV and playing with him. (?) Because he likes it.*

(M,7)   *Because he likes you.*

(F,6)   *Eating together. (?) 'Cause they like it.*

Granting a favor   The "granting" a favor category contains stories in which adults went out of their way to do things which children liked. In one subtype of these stories adults gave material goods to children. There were 14 such stories:

(M,6)   *By buying him candy. (?) Because it's really nice.*

(F,7)   *If your daddy gave you a whole bag of candy to share with your friends.*

(F,6)   *Your mother buys Twinkies and other things the kids like. (?) That makes the kid happy.*

(M,10)   *A boy asked his dad if he would take him to MacDonalds ... and his dad said OK.*

(F,10)   *Maybe the kid wanted candy. The mother or father could buy it for you.*

(F,9)   *Taking him out shopping. (?) Because they let you get anything you want.*

(F,12)   *My parents give you what you like. (?) If you want to go to a movie, they let you go.*

In a second subtype, adults granted permission for some activity children wanted (13 stories). Examples are:

(M,6)   *Let him stay out late at night. (?) Because he could play.*

(M,6)   *Take them where they want to go.*

(F,6)   *Parents let your friends stay overnight. Your parents like you.*

(M,10)   *She [your mother] could drive you to baseball practice. (?) She takes time out to do it.*

(M,9)   *Let 9 year old go to a movie.*

(F,12)   *The grown-up could give you a ride somewhere.*

(F,12)   *Taking them someplace they want to go; like the movies.*

(M,12)   *People on the street are having a party ... but they allow the kids to make noise on the street ... to have fun.*

In none of these stories was the need of the recipients specified. In all cases, adults appeared to have the right to grant or not grant the desires of the recipients. In fact, they always granted them, and the children were pleased.

All the remaining types of stories with an adult actor and child recipient contained actions predicated on children's needs and are hence considered qualified. Stories differed by content of actions and needs.

Giving   All stories of "giving" dealt with the transfer of material items:

(M,9)   *A boy lost his tennis balls. A neighbor saw this and gave his to the boy.*

(F,9)   *I needed something for school and told my mother at the last minute. She got it for me.*

(M, 12)   *He was buying a present for his mother and was ten cents short. The adult gave him ten cents.*

Offering assistance   Stories dealing with physical assistance described children who were hurt, sick, or unable to perform some deed and thus required physical assistance. For example:

(F,7)   *The child fell down and started to bleed . . . . The grown-up could put a Band-Aid on it.*

(F,7)   *When he was sick . . . his father drove him to the hospital and stayed overnight with him.*

(F,10)   *Maybe she's sick and her mother works. The neighbor takes care of you . . . gets you medicine and stuff.*

(F,6)   *If they can't do something, the grown-up could do it for them . . . Put on their shirt or something like that.*

Teaching   "Teaching" stories all dealt with help adults gave children needing assistance with schoolwork.

(F,10)   *If you have homework you don't understand, your mother would try to make you understand it.*

(F,12)   *When you don't understand something, the teacher could tell you about it.*

(F,12)   *He's doing poorly in school. Parents go out of the way to help.*

(F,13)   *When it's a hard test, they explain it to you.*

Understanding   Stories concerned with understanding invariably referred to children's emotional states. Adults recognized children's difficulties and responded to them with understanding. All 7 stories told by 9 to 10 year olds dealt with children's emotional states of loneliness. Examples are:

(M,10) *Maybe the parents are always going out . . . . The child is unhappy by himself. His parents let him join the boy scouts.*

(M,9) *If you don't have any friends, he might play cards or chess with with you.*

(F,9) *When they're lonely, they play and eat with them. And you'd be with them as much time as you can.*

(F,10) *A child has nothing to do. They take her to a circus. They didn't want to leave her alone.*

The remaining 8 stories of understanding, told by the oldest group, referred primarily to problems other than loneliness. Adults responded by offering advice or treating child recipients "like adults." Examples are:

(M,12) *You're having trouble with friendship . . . . Grown-ups could give you hints on how to make friends better.*

(M,13) *A boy was caught stealing . . . . The owner, instead of calling the police, gives him advice . . . lets him work for it.*

(F,13) *A kid did something bad in class. The teacher didn't embarrass him in front of class . . . . She talked to him afterwards.*

(F,12) *Helping you out with a problem. Talking it out and trying to solve it . . . It helps you face things better.*

(M,13) *The adult might trust you with responsibility . . . letting a kid have the feeling that he's doing something for people.*

Interpretation of Child-Adult Stories
The child-adult stories discussed above contrast sharply with stories told by the same children regarding peers. Two differences are notable. The method underlying most child-adult interactions is based on complementary rather than symmetrical reciprocity. And, the recognition that adults are individualized personalities does not enter stories until about age 12 years, whereas the treatment of peers as individuals occurs at around age 9.

Reciprocity of complement is represented by the storytellers in two ways. In the first, child actors are generally characterized as doing what adults ask them to do. The impetus for actors' initiatives comes from adults' wishes. Actors then try to meet adult demands. In the second, children are recipients, and adults, as actors, may or may not meet children's desires. When they do, it is in the form of granting a favor or privilege. It seems evident that storytellers view children and adults as nonequals. Children have to obey, act as adults want them to act, and do chores which adults designate as important. The reverse is not true. Adults may act to meet children's wishes but they have the right not to do so. And there is little indication that adults act with the goal of making their own behavior conform to children's standards.

Recalling that these stories were intended to indicate a response to shows of kindness or liking, one can gain some insight into children's thinking. Children do not necessarily see themselves as oppressed, or adults as authoritarian ogres. They see unilateral control as a procedural fact. When they obey, they are being kind or showing adults that they adhere to the terms of their relation. By conforming to adults' standards, children act their part in complement and positively acknowledge their relation to adults. While control is unilateral, obedience is seen to have its rewards. Adults do reciprocate by doing favors for and granting privileges to children. They also help children who are experiencing problems. This method of reciprocity involves the exchange of unlike acts and implies an adjustment to the fact that children and adults are not equals. Adults know more, possess more resources, and have rights which children do not have.

Sullivan and Piaget suggest that children's understanding of adults as persons is relatively late in developing. They also suggest that this understanding occurs after the discovery that peers are individual personalities. Our data indicate that the gap corresponds roughly to age 9 for peers and age 12 for adults. It is only in the stories of 12 to 14 year olds that there is a coupling of the complementary procedures with an adjustment to personal needs. Kindness or liking is still represented by doing chores and other labor, but the child's work is predicated on adults' inabilities to do it for themselves. Adult needs are based on old age or being momentarily overburdened. In all cases, then, the procedure is adjusted to the adult who is seen not as an authority figure but as a person in momentary need of another's assistance.

It is also only with the oldest group that results show

children actors able to establish emotional closeness between child and adult as was amply evident between peers
already at 9 years of age. It was the young adolescents who
introduced emotional states of loneliness, sadness, and
embarrassment in adults and had children respond to
these needs with sensitivity to the persons. And it was
these same young adolescents who saw children bringing
their emotional problems to adults with adults accepting
the request to offer advice and sympathy. Thus, although
the recognition of the personality of adults is comparatively delayed, the indication is that young adolescents
begin to understand themselves more as equals with
adults or as persons who are concerned with one another's
personhood and, by implication, as persons who can
understand one another's emotional problems and have
the initiative to operate on them.

Five   Additional Studies of Kindness

The data reported in this chapter were collected in order to answer two general questions. The results of study 1 show that children at all three age levels told stories which distinguished child-child from child-adult interactions. The ways in which these stories differed correspond with major points of the Sullivan-Piaget thesis. In study 2 an attempt is made to determine the generality of the differences between peer and child-adult relations. Designations of persons were changed from "a child your age" to *friend* in child-child stories and from "an adult" to *parent* in child-adult stories. The latter modification is important. It was observed in study 1 that storytellers tended to describe "adults" as classes of persons and as authority figures rather than as individualized personalities. This type of description persisted up to about 12 years of age. Study 2 was designed to find out whether children also tend to depict parents more as authority figures than as individual persons.

Study 3 has a different focus. It was designed to validate some of the findings of studies 1 and 2 and to determine whether the differences in descriptions of interactions corresponding to the ages of the storytellers were based on actual differences in perception or, in part, simply on differences in verbal ability. For example, studies 1 and 2 revealed that younger children tend to produce accounts of unqualified acts, while older children frequently add qualifications such as depictions of persons involved in interactions. Although these tendencies fit the Sullivan-Piaget thesis, we devised study 3 to check these results. To do so, we presented qualified and unqualified stories to children so that they could judge whether or not both types of stories represented kindness. For example, kindness between peers was presented in one story as an interaction of *sharing* alone and in another story as an interaction in which sharing was qualified by a *recipient's need*. If 6 to 8 year old children think that need, and its implication of inequality, is important, they ought to identify it when given the explicit example. Conversely, if 12 to 14 year olds think that need or inequality are essential components of kindness then the story with unqualified sharing alone ought not to be judged as kind.

Study 2: Kindness with Friends and Parents

Forty-eight new children were interviewed. There were 23 males and 25 females, with 16 children in each of three age groups: 6 to 7 years, 9 to 10 years, and 12 to 13 years. Each child was interviewed individually by either a male or female adult and asked to generate two stories about kindness. In one story children were to describe an interaction in which "a child your age does something kind for a friend," and in the second story an interaction in which "a child your age does something kind for their parent."

Results for Friend

The content of interactions and the proportions of unqualified to qualified stories were similar to those found in study 1 when "peers" were the interacting parties. The younger the storytellers, the more likely they were to produce interactions of unqualified sharing or playing. The older storytellers were more likely to describe acts of aid predicated on need or actor-recipient inequality. An overall picture of these results is given in the top half of table 4.

Unqualified stories

All of the unqualified stories deal with sharing, giving, or playing. Storytellers did not describe circumstances leading to the interactions but focused on the acts themselves.

Sharing. There were eleven stories of "sharing" or "giving." Here are some examples.

(M,6)   *Share.*
(F,6)   *If she gives you something, say 'Thank you.'*
(F,6)   *I would give her all these pictures.*
(M,7)   *I bought something for him when I found some money.*
(F,9)   *I give her some candy.*
(M,10) *Share; give him pencils you don't need.*
(M,10) *On the way home, buy him a candy bar.*
(F,10) *I give her some candy.*
(M,12) *Sharing candy.*

Table 4   Kindness Stories Between Friends and Child and Parent: Frequencies at Each of Three Ages

	Age		
	6–7	9–10	12–13
Friends			
Unqualified Stories			
Sharing	5	5	1
Playing	9	3	1
Qualified Stories			
Material giving	1	0	5
Giving physical assistance	0	5	3
Teaching	1	0	4
Understanding	0	3	2
Child-Parent			
Giving	1	1	1
Obeying	11	7	7
Doing chores	4	8	8

Playing. There were thirteen stories of "playing." Examples follow:

(M,6)   *Playing with him.*
(M,7)   *Play with him a lot.*
(M,6)   *When he calls up to come over, he comes over.*
(F,7)   *Let her play jump rope at recess time.*
(F,7)   *Being nice.*
(F,7)   *When they go to their house and play with them.*
(M,10) *Play a lot together. Let him swim in his pool.*

(M,10)   *Bring him to the beach with his family.*

(F,10)   *Invite them over to my house.*

(F,13)   *Playing with them fair.*

Qualified stories   As before, qualified stories were defined as interactions which included statements of the circumstances
persons were in which may have induced the kind initiatives. The content areas covered were, as in study 1, sharing, playing, assisting when hurt, teaching, and understanding. Social inclusion, in which a peer on the outside
was invited in, was not a story told for friends. This makes
sense insofar as friends do not lack friendships whereas
other peers might need friends.

Examples by content area follow:

(M,7)   *Give him something to drink when he's thirsty.* (Material
need)

(M,12)   *When they don't have lunch, I give them part of mine.*
(Material need)

(F,12)   *If they don't have something, share it with them.* (Material
need)

(M,10)   *If he gets hurt, help him.* (Physical assistance)

(F,10)   *She fell and hurt herself riding bikes. I took her home
washed her knee and gave her a bandaid.* (Physical assistance)

(F,6)   *If they don't know how to do work right, help him with it.*
(Teaching)

(F,13)   *She helped her when she needed help for a test.* (Teaching)

(M,9)   *When he fractured his finger, I comforted him and made him
feel at home.* (Understanding)

(F,10)   *Everyone was being mean to her. I thought she was sad so I
went and played with her.* (Understanding)

(M,9)   *If he was lonely, I could go to him and play with him.*
(Understanding)

(F,12)   *Help when they're in trouble.* (Understanding)

(F,13)   *Trusting them. Not lying to them.* (Understanding)

Results for   The overall results of child-parent descriptions are shown
Parent   at the bottom of table 4. Of the entire 48 stories, there was 1
in wihch need was explicitly stated. In all other stories
kind initiatives were unqualified descriptions of self-
apparent acts. There were 3 stories of giving, 25 stories

of obeying, and 20 stories of doing chores. Examples of stories are now presented by content area.

Giving   One child from each level told a story about giving or being good. The stories are:

(F,6)   *Give them something.*
(M,10)   *Buying them a gift on their birthday.*
(M,13)   *Give their mother a good present or something.*

Obeying   As in study 1, stories describing obeying were statements that children should do what adults tell them. Examples include:

(M,6)   *Obey them.*
(M,6)   *Do what they tell me.*
(F,6)   *By obeying them.*
(F,6)   *Doing what they ask you to do.*
(M,7)   *Do what they're told.*
(M,7)   *By obeying (?) He asked me to do it.*
(F,7)   *Do what they say.*
(F,7)   *Obey what they say.*
(M,9)   *When mother asks you to do something, do it right away.*
(F,9)   *If a parent asked them to clean their room and they obey them. Usually they wouldn't want to.*
(M,10)   *If you're watching TV and they ask you to go to bed, you should do it right away.*
(M,10)   *Telling them the truth.*
(F,10)   *If they asked you to do something, don't talk back. Just do it. Ask if you can do anything else.*
(M,12)   *Obey them.*
(F,12)   *If they asked you to do something and you are ready to leave, you did it without making a big deal about it. Even if it would take the whole day.*
(M,13)   *When they ask you to do something, do it and not argue.*
(F,13)   *If they tell you to do a job, do it right away.*

Although all these stories fit the category of obedience, there appear to be subtle variations based on the ages of the storytellers. In the 6 to 7 year range, children simply asserted obedience. From age 9 years and up, children described child actors as not just obeying but as obeying immediately or without complaining. This addition to stories may represent an understanding that children do not always obey or that they obey sometimes under coercion. In either case, the addition is congruent with results found for judgments and reasons (studies 3 and 5) in which the child's attitude is a deciding qualification as to whether an interaction with an adult is kind or unkind. Emphasis on attitude contrasts with the 6 to 7 year olds' seeming focus on unqualified acts of obedience per se.

Doing chores   Stories of doing chores, as in study 1, described a child actor doing physical labor for the parent without specification of the parent's need. Examples include the following stories.

(M,6)   *Clear the dishes. Help clean the house.*

(M,6)   *Cleaning the bedroom. (?) You're supposed to do it.*

(F, 6)   *Helping mother do the housework.*

(M,9)   *Keep your room neat and make your bed. In other words, by helping.*

(F,9)   *Helping them washing the dishes.*

(M,10)   *Clean up after the dogs.*

(M,10)   *Helping them clear the table after dinner.*

(F,10)   *Helping clean up the house.*

(F,10)   *Help them clean dishes, make beds, put clothes in the dryer.*

(M,12)   *Doing chores for them.*

(F,12)   *Help around the house. Do little things for mother and father.*

(M,13)   *Not talking back. (?) Give a little more help.*

(F,13)   *Help do housework.*

The single qualified story was the following:

(M,13)   *If they were doing something, you could help. It would save a lot of time for fun.*

Summary of   Differences between stories about peers and adults,
Study 2   obtained in study 1, were replicated in the present findings for friends and parents. Kindness between friends involved sharing, playing with, and helping in time of need. Needs ranged from material goods to psychological under-

standing.The younger the storyteller, the more likely the story was about unqualified sharing or play. The older the storyteller, the more likely the story involved recognition of an inequality in well-being which the kind initiative then counteracted. The switch from "peer" to friend did not change the content or form of stories. Introduction of *parent* as the recipient of kindness did not substantially change the content of stories from when "adults" were recipients. Children still said that obedience and doing chores were acts of kindness. The youngest children emphasized obedience and the older children gave equal weight to doing chores.

If there was any surprise in these findings, it was the absence of qualified stories from the oldest group when parents were recipients. It was expected that some proportion of their descriptions of chores would be predicated on stated needs of parents. Instead these children described what appear to be unqualified acts of complementariness: obey and do chores which parents expect you to do. These findings support the earlier result that children look on one another as individualized persons before they see adults as individuals. In the present study, this age differential is exaggerated. Even at 12 years of age, children were described as acting toward parents as if parents were authority figures. The relation appears to involve the same form as in study 1: adults/parents tell children how to act and children meet these expectations. And, as in study 1, peers/friends are kind when they join *with* each other in play, sharing material possessions, schoolwork, or physical or emotional problem-solving. In contrast, children are kind to adults/parents when children act properly or do work *for* them.

Study 3: Judgments of Kindness   In this study, 6 stories told by children regarding kindness were presented to a new sample of children for judgment. Children were asked whether the stories represented kindness and, if so, why. The goal was to determine the following: (1) Would 6 to 8 year olds judge unqualified interactions of sharing between peers and obedience by children to adults as kind? And how would 12 to 14 year old children judge these same stories? (2) While 6 to 8 year olds, in our earlier studies, did not spontaneously predicate kindness on actor-recipient inequality, would they recognize it as a condition of kindness if it were presented explicitly for inspection? (3) Although 9 to 10 year olds in our studies showed a gap between recognizing peers as persons and treating adults as constraining "figures," the disparity may be an artifact of spontaneous storytelling. Would children of this age recognize states of need in adults if these states were presented for inspection? (4) Finally, and more generally, would an independent sample of children judge as kind stories told by other children describing sharing for peer relations and obeying for child-adult relations? This question pertains to the validity of storytelling as a method. Before proceeding further in interpreting stories, we considered it necessary to rule out the possibility that the samples of children in our first studies or the storytelling method itself might have produced biased accounts.

Sixty-six new children were interviewed by two adults, one of whom had participated in the first two studies, the other of whom knew nothing of the prior results. There were 22 children each from the 6 to 8 year, 9 to 11 year, and 12 to 14 year old ranges. Half were boys, half were girls. The children came from two Catholic parochial schools serving similar socioeconomic populations as the schools respresented in studies 1 and 2.

The part of the interview germaine to present interests consists of six stories presented to this new group of children. Three stories were about sharing between peers. The first story was about unqualified sharing for example, "Sam shares his snack with Bob." The second story added the component of recipient's need, for example, "Pat forgot to bring her lunch to school. Sally shares her lunch with Pat." The third story introduced a factor which, while rarely presented in accounts, may have been implied in spontaneous stories. It may be regarded as the actor's attitude and refers to such factors as whether a kind act is performed voluntarily or represents a sacrifice for the actor. The example we presented was: "Even though Jack wanted to ride his bike, he let Michael ride it."

The three examples we gave of stories about a child's obedience with an adult were: "Jim does what his mother tells him to do" (unqualified obedience). "Mother is busy cleaning the house. She tells Ellen to babysit for her brother so Ellen does it" (adult's need). And, "Even though Lisa wanted to go to her friend's house, she worked with her father in the yard" (voluntarism or sacrifice).

After each story that child was asked: "Is that story kind, unkind, or can't you tell?" If the child said, "Kind," the interviewer asked, "Why?" If the child said, "Can't tell," the interviewer told the child to change the story so that it would be kind. No child said that any story was unkind.

Child-Child Results — An overview of results is reported in table 5. All of the youngest children judged each story as "kind." Only children in the middle and oldest groups said they could not tell whether stories were kind. "Can't tell" judgments occurred 11 times when sharing was presented as an unqualified act, 8 times when sacrifice qualified sharing, but only twice when sharing was predicated on need.

Table 5   Child-Child Sharing: Frequencies of Judgments of Reasons

	Sharing Alone Age			Sharing Plus Need Age			Sharing Plus Sacrifice Age		
	7	10	13	7	10	13	7	10	13
Judgments									
Kind	22	18	15	22	22	20	22	19	17
Can't tell	—	4	7	—	—	2	—	3	5
Reasons									
Sharing	20	12	10	12	4	5	15	6	3
Need	2	5	8	10	17	12	2	4	5
Sacrifice	—	5	4	—	1	5	5	12	14

Reasons for judgments, which included modifications to make neutral stories kind, appear in the bottom part of the table. Reasons for judgments were classified into three types. The category "sharing" refers to reasons focused on the unqualified act, as if it were self-apparently kind. Generally this reason was given most by the youngest and least by the oldest children. The second category, "need," included specific references to the recipient's need for or lack of the item which was shared. The last category, "sacrifice," was used almost exclusively by children from the middle and oldest groups and referred to the actor's attitude as the basis of kindness. Reasons will now be analyzed in greater detail with the aim of finding out how children in these three age groups differentially conceive of kindness between peers. Each story is analyzed separately.

Unqualified *Sharing Story*   In this story only the act of sharing was presented. Children could say that the act itself was kind, or they could read into the act other factors, such as need or sacrifice. It can be seen in table 5 that children interpreted the story differently depending on age. Almost all of the youngest children attributed kindness to the act per se. This tendency declined with increasing age. About half of the middle and oldest age children brought in need or sacrifice in order to make the story kind.

Examples of each type of reasoning are now reported. Cases of reasons which focused on sharing itself were as follows:

(M,6)   *Because you're sharing.*
(M,7)   *Because when he shares, that's being kind.*
(F,6)   *Because you're sharing something.*
(F,7)   *Because it's nice to share your food with people.*
(M,9)   *He's sharing with someone else.*
(F,9)   *Because it's really nice to share.*
(M,13) *'Cause you're sharing.*
(F,12) *It's nice to the person.*

These answers imply that children understand sharing as a practical rule fitting the normal procedures by which peers show one another that they are related. It is interesting to note that 20 of the 22, 6 to 7-year-old children reasoned that enactment of this procedure was de facto evidence of kindness.

Fifteen children, only 2 of whom were from the youngest group, brought need into the story to make it a case of kindness. Examples are:

(M,7)   *Because if the other person forgot his lunch.*
(M,9)   *If he didn't have a snack.*
(F,9)   *She forgot her lunch.*

(F,9)   *Because she'd be hungry.*

(M,12)   *If Bill has nothing to eat.*

(M,12)   *If he was really hungry.*

(F,13)   *She didn't have a lunch that day.*

It is clear that in each case the recipient's lack of food, or the actor-recipient disparity in having food, was the basis for kindness.

Finally, 9 children brought the factor of sacrifice to the story. Examples are:

(M,9)   *If he made the lunch himself [rather than his mother] and gave it up.*

(M,9)   *John really likes what he has and has only one. And he breaks it in half and shares.*

(M,11)   *If he really liked it, he'd be sacrificing.*

(F,12)   *Because you don't have to do it.*

(M,13)   *He didn't have to give it up but he did.*

Sharing qualified by need story   One sees in table 5 that when the story of sharing included specific mention that the recipient had forgotten his or her lunch, 39 children recognized this as a condition for kindness. Still, 21 children ignored need and attributed kindness to the act of sharing. Twelve, or half of the youngest group, did this indicating that need is not necessarily essential to kindness. Examples where children did identify need are as follows:

(M,6)   *Bill doesn't have any lunch.*

(M,7)   *He'd be hungry.*

(F,6)   *When Mary left hers at home.*

(M,10)   *He could be really hungry.*

(M,9)   *They don't have something to eat.*

(F,10)   *She could starve.*

(M,12)   *He would probably be hungry.*

(F,13)   *She had nothing to eat.*

Although this story presented need, 6 children passed over this potential condition and introduced the factor of sacrifice. Examples are:

(M,10)   *John [the actor] might be real hungry.*

(M,13)   *He was sacrificing half his lunch.*

(F,13)   *She sacrifices part of her own meal.*

(F,12)   *She didn't have to do it.*

(F,13)   *She could have had it all for herself.*

Sacrificing Story   The explicit presentation of sacrifice enhanced its selection as the reason for kindness. A total of 31 children identified this factor with 5 of them coming from the youngest group. Importantly, 15 of the 22 children in the youngest group still focused on the unqualified act of sharing indicating that they either did not notice sacrifice or did not think it to be a condition for kindness. Finally, 9 children stated that the recipient's need made sharing kind, even though need was not mentioned in this story.

Examples of reasons which focused on sacrifice are as follows:

(M,6)   *He was giving up part of his fun time for him.*

(M,7)   *[The actor] wanted to ride it . . . but since Mike wanted to ride it, he let him ride.*

(F,6)   *When you have something you want and you let somebody else play with it.*

(F,7)   *If she lets her use it and she [the actor] doesn't use it.*

(M,9)   *He wanted to ride it and so did the other one and he let him use it.*

(M,10)   *He wants to do something but he lets his friend do it.*

(F,9)   *Because she gave up something she wanted to do.*

(F,10)   *If she wanted to go somewhere very much, she could wait a little longer and let her friend use it.*

(M,12)   *He gave it up so his friend could ride it.*

(M,12)   *Doing something for somebody else instead of yourself.*

(F,12)   *Letting somebody else use it even though she wanted it.*

(F,12)   *Doing it on free will.*

Interpretation of Child-Child Results   In spontaneous stories of studies 1 and 2, children from the 6 to 8 year groups described acts of sharing alone as kind. In the present study, children of this same age level judged the story which had only the unqualified act of sharing as kind. Twenty of these 22 children specified that sharing was in itself kind. When these same children were given the story containing need, 12 also said that sharing was the reason for kindness. When sacrifice was presented, 15 of these children still said that sharing was in itself kind. These results are congruent with the findings of studies 1 and 2. They show that younger children tend to understand the peer relation in terms of a simple reciprocal method; "I give, then you give." They also tend not to take account of the persons in the method either from the point of view of need or sacrifice. In summary on this point, the age trend with judgments is congruent with the age trend obtained with freely generated stories.

Secondly, in studies 1 and 2 children introduced the factor of persons into kind interactions most notably at about 9 years of age. This same age level served as the differentiating point in the present study. It is at about this age that need or sacrifice was read into the given unqualified story by about half the children and that need or sacrifice was recognized in stories where they were stated, by a majority of children. This is not to say that 6 to 8 year olds did not understand need, sacrifice, or person. Some proportion of these children did. But the age trends observed in all three stories were the same. Six to 8 year olds in the main focused on acts per se. A sharp refocusing on acts in conjunction with states of persons appeared in the 9 to 10 year old group. And the continuance of this trend shows only a slight change at ages 12 to 14 years. Thus, it appears that somewhere between 8 and 10 years the importance of the personalities in interactions becomes crucial.

Child-Adult Results   Frequencies of judgments of "kind" or "can't tell" are reported in table 6. The story of unqualified obedience was judged as "kind" by all of the youngest and all but two of the middle age children. It was judged as "kind" by less than half of the oldest children. The story of obedience plus need produced similar results. Four more of the oldest children said the story with need was "kind" than said so of the unqualified story. The story with sacrifice resulted in a different pattern since no clear age trend was observed.

Reasons for judgments varied with age and with story. Reasons will now be inspected in detail to clarify how children interpreted a child's kindness to an adult and which factors children of different ages considered central to the relation.

Table 6   Child-Adult Obedience: Frequencies of Judgments of Reasons

	Obey Age			Obey Plus Need Age			Obey Plus Sacrifice Age		
	7	10	13	7	10	13	7	10	13
Judgment									
Kind	22	20	10	22	20	14	21	17	17
Can't tell	—	2	12	—	2	8	1	5	5
Reasons									
Obeying/Helping	21	19	10	16	8	5	13	8	5
Parent's Need	1	2	3	5	7	4	1	1	5
Actor's Sacrifice	—	1	9	—	7	13	8	13	12

Story of Unqualified Obedience   All but one of the youngest and all but three of the middle age children identified obedience as kind in and of itself.Some of the children used the term obedience in their reasons while others used the term helping. Examples in which obedience was emphasized are:

(M,6)   *He should obey his mother and father.*

(M,7)   *'Cause he's listening to his mother.*

(F,6)   *When you do what your mother says for you to do.*

(F,6)   *If she did what her mother told her.*

(M,9)   *He's doing what his mother tells him to and is not disobeying.*

(M,10)   *You're suppose to do what your mother says.*

(F,9)   *When she's asked, she does it.*

(F,10)   *She obeys whatever her mother says to do.*

(M,13)   *Because he's obeying mother.*

(F,12)   *She's obeying her mother.*

Examples of helping, which is considered a subclass of obedience, were the following:

(M,7)   *'Cause he's loving his mother.*

(F,6)   *Because she helps her mother.*

(M,10)   *He helps his mother.*

(M,10)   *Helping his mother.*

(M,14)   *He helps his mother.*

(M,12)   *He does it for his mother.*

While these reasons introduce the term help, no reference is made to a need for help. These statements may be interpreted to mean that children are supposed to do what their mother tells them to. Hence, they may be considered to be versions of obedience.

In contrast, 6 children spontaneously introduced need into the story. This was done by depicting the mother in the following ways:

(M,7)   *Because his mother had something to do and had no one to help her.*

(F,10) *She needed help making a party.*

(F,10) *If her mother is sick and the laundry has to be done.*

(M,12) *If his mother was senile.*

(F,12) *If her mother was sick.*

(F,12) *If her mother was sick or something.*

Finally, 10 children, 9 from the oldest group, spontaneously qualified the act of obedience by introducing sacrifice, which includes voluntarism, on the part of the actor. Examples are:

(F,10) *If she did it when she wasn't asked to do it.*

(M,13) *Doing it willfully.*

(M,13) *If he offered to do it and she didn't tell him.*

(F,13) *She did it without being told.*

(F,12) *Doing it without being asked.*

Obedience With Need Story   When the act of obedience was coupled with the mother's need, 29 children reasoned that the story was kind because the child was obedient. Sixteen of these children were in the youngest group. Examples of this reasoning are:

(M,7)   *Everytime her mother told her to, she would.*

(M,13) *He should obey.*

Sixteen children reasoned that the story was kind because of the mother's need. There was no clear age pattern to this answer. Examples are:

(M,7)   *Because she's working.*

(F,6)   *When she's doing something and can't take care of the baby.*

(M,9) *His mother can't do everything.*

(F,9) *Because his mother is busy cleaning.*

(M,12) *She needed help; she couldn't do it by herself.*

(F,12) *Mother can't do it with kids around.*

Twenty children heard the story about need but said that the child who was asked to do babysitting was kind because he or she was sacrificing or acting freely. This reason was used by 7 of the middle age and 13 of the oldest children; none of the youngest children gave this reason. Examples of sacrifice are:

(M,9) *If he wanted to do something else.*

(F,9) *It takes up part of her playtime.*

(F,10) *She gave up something she was watching or doing.*

(M,14) *Maybe he didn't like his brother and still helped his mother out.*

(M,13) *He might have wanted to do something else.*

(F,13) *She babysits instead of going out.*

(F,14) *If she had something else to do.*

Examples of sacrifice with emphasis on voluntarism include:

(M,10) *Because you could say "no."*

(F,10) *If she doesn't want to do it and does it without complaining.*

(F,13) *She just went ahead and didn't say anything.*

It is clear that the story with the mother's need explicitly stated was not equivalent to the comparable story in which a peer's need was given. The majority of the youngest children passed over the mother's need to focus on the act of obedience. The middle age group was split evenly among the act, the need, and the actor's sacrifice. And, over half of the oldest children introduced the element of sacrifice while only 4 made reference to the stated need. In other words, need was the least used reason (16 children). The act was cited by 29 children, and sacrifice was cited by 20 children.

Sacrifice Story   Twenty-six children, 13 from the youngest group, heard the story with sacrifice but said that obedience per se was the reason for kindness. Seven children introduced the father's need for help with yardwork as the reason for kindness. And, a total of 33 children identified sacrifice, the factor which was presented, as the basis for kindness. Of these 33, 8 were from youngest group, 13 from the middle, and 12 from the oldest group.

Examples of sacrifice were:

(M,7)   *He wants to go to his friend's, but he works instead.*
(M,7)   *He helped instead of playing.*
(F,6)   *If you want to go to your friend's.*
(M,9)   *Giving up play to work.*
(F,10) *If she really didn't want to do it.*
(F,9)   *She cares more about what her father has to do than what she has to do.*
(M,12) *He sacrifices.*
(M,13) *He's taking off his time to help the family.*
(F,13) *She gave up something.*

Examples in which voluntarism was stressed include the following:

(M,7)   *If his dad didn't have to ask.*
(M,10) *He did it on his own.*
(F,12) *She did it on her own free will.*
(F,13) *She helped without being asked.*

Interpretation of Child–Adult Results   In all three stories half or more of the youngest children identified the act of obedience as kind in itself. This was true when need or sacrifice had been presented as a possible reason. The result conforms with the data obtained from spontaneous stories in which 6 to 8-year-old children said that obedience was kind without specifying need or sacrifice as a necessary qualification. Secondly, in spontaneous stories few children outside the 12 to 14-year-old group mentioned the adult's need as a condition for kindness. This result was sustained in judgments of the story which explicitly contained need. Out of 66 children, only 16 recognized need of the mother when it was presented. This small number contrasts with the total of 39 children who recognized a peer's need when it was given in the story. It also contrasts with the 20 children who spontaneously introduced sacrifice into the story which presented need. Apparently, children do not readily view adults as individuals with needs that children can service. These same children were able to recognize need when it applied to a peer.

Thirdly, sacrifice, which includes voluntary action, appeared infrequently in stories from studies 1 and 2, yet it appeared forcefully in the present study, especially within the child-adult context. Ten children introduced it into the unqualified story. Twenty children brought it into the story with need. And 33 children recognized it when it was presented as a choice. Like need, actor's sacrifice was a minimal factor for children in the youngest group. It was more significant at the 9 to 11-year-old level and was strongest for the oldest children.

Conclusion   Results of studies of judgments with reasons conform with the those of spontaneously generated stories. Children within the age range of interest differentiate child-child from child-adult relations. Children in the 6 to 8-year-old level describe peers as being kind when they share or play together. They describe children as being kind when they obey adults. Neither form of interaction has to be conditioned; the methods in themselves define kindness. The method governing peer relations is a literal representation of equality and implies reciprocity, while that governing child-adult relations shows children acting in complement to and under the constraint of adults.

Children in the 9 to 11-year-old level introduce and identify another peer's need or the two peers' inequality as a condition for kindness. Sharing is judged to be kind when one peer needs or lacks something which the other peer possesses. A few children consider the actor's initiative of sharing kind because it represents sacrifice. These same children say that obedience represents kindness of a child to an adult. About one-third of the children of this age level identified the adult's need as a condition for kindness, while approximately two-thirds identified the child's sacrifice as an important factor when it was offered as an alternative.

The oldest age level, of 12 to 14 year olds, rarely say that sharing between peers or obedience toward adults are kind. They introduce either need or sacrifice as a necessary qualification. Need is more likely to be applied to a peer, as person, than to a parent. If sacrifice is freely brought in as a factor, it is more likely to be applied to the child acting toward a parent rather than in relation to a peer. However, if sacrifice is explicitly stated, it is equally identified in both relations.

Six Unkindness in Two Relations

Studies 1 to 3 were designed as approaches to children's concepts of interpersonal relations. We assumed that interactions of kindness would represent, in part, children's understanding of peer and child-adult relations. Because the action assigned to an actor was to be performed in relation to a recipient, its enactment would represent an overt acknowledgment that two people are in one rather than another relation. Thus, results show, sharing is a sign of peer relations for 6-year-old children while obedience signifies a 6 year old's relation to adults. Similarly, sharing in time of need and working for an enfeebled adult constitute signs of peer and child-adult relations, respectively, for young adolescents.

In the following studies, children's concepts of relations were approached from a new angle. In study 4, children were to generate stories of *unkindness* and in study 5 another group of children was to judge a sample of these stories. These stories and judgments were expected to provide further insights into relational conceptions. Instead of showing how relations are acknowledged, children's assessment of unkindness should reveal how two persons show each other that they are not, for some reason, in relation.

In real life there are innumerable acts which people recognize as unkind. They usually take a negative form, such as actions which harm another person. In the present

104

model, the definition of "negative" acts is assumed to be relationally determined. Acts which constitute unkindness in a relation ought to acquire this meaning because of the relation in which they occur. For instance, if sharing between peers is kind because it acknowledges equality between the peers, then not sharing may be unkind because it denies equality between the peers. Failure to share is not a negative act in an absolute sense, but in the context of a relation which is based on a principle of equality it takes on a specific meaning. It becomes a failure to acknowledge the relationship and, therefore, is considered unkind. Put differently, if sharing represents one child's fulfillment of the method of direct reciprocity, then not sharing may represent failure to meet the terms of direct reciprocity.

Study 4: Stories of Unkindness A total of 60 children told stories of unkindness. There were 10 males and 10 females from each of grades 1, 4, and 7, making up three age levels: 6 to 7 years; 9 to 10 years; and 12 to 13 years. The interviewers were the same adults who had served in study 1. The children told three stories corresponding to the following instructions: "Tell me a story in which a child your age does something unkind to another child your age;" "Tell me a story in which a child your age does something unkind to an adult, a grown-up;" and "Tell me a story in which an adult, a grown-up, does something unkind to a child your age." (Only 12 of the 20 children from each age level were asked to tell this last story.)

Child-Child Results A general picture of results is shown in table 7. The youngest children tended to tell unqualified stories about not sharing or aggression. The oldest children tended to tell qualified stories in which actors recognized but failed to assist peer recipients in need. The middle level children fell midway between the youngest and oldest groups.

Unqualified Stories *Taking, breaking, or not sharing.* There are 9 instances of stories involving unqualified taking, breaking, or not sharing, 7 of which came from 6 and 7-year-old children. The model story involved not giving a material thing to a

Table 7   Child-Child Unkindness: Frequencies for Males and Females

	Age					
	6–7		9–10		12–13	
	Male	Female	Male	Female	Male	Female
Unqualified *Interactions*						
Not sharing; taking; breaking	4	3	2	—	—	—
Hitting; fighting	5	5	2	3	1	3
Other	—	—	1	1	2	—
Qualified Interactions						
Not sharing	—	1	2	1	1	1
Hitting	—	1	1	2	—	—
Social exclusion	1	—	2	—	1	1
not sympathizing	—	—	—	3	5	5

peer, or taking something from a peer when not explicitly provoked. The following examples represent versions of this type of story:

(M,7)   *Breaking their toys on purpose.*

(F,6)   *Take things from them. (?) Maybe it was new and their mother and father wouldn't buy them a new one.*

(F,6)   *They wouldn't share their things with me. (?) Because if I share with them, they don't share with me. I was kind and they weren't.*

(M,6)   *They don't share candy and they don't watch TV together.*

(M,6)   *He doesn't let the friend play with his toys.*

(F,7)   *By not giving him something.*

(M.9)   *I'm unkind to my sister. I take things away from her. (?) She's bratty too. (?) I'm not nice to her.*

(M,10)   *He's not nice. (?) Like steal something from him.*

These stories appear to reflect the converse of peer sharing as exhibited in studies 1 and 2. In those stories, one peer shared whatever he or she possessed with another peer. In the present stories, unkind actors either did not share or took a material thing which the other peer possessed. In both cases, the occasion for acting was material possession with no other condition being stated. One can see that interviewers' questions, such as "Why was that unkind?" did not evoke statements of qualifications, but rather, children generally elaborated on the act they had just described. The lone exception was the 6-year-old female who mentioned in her own terms that reciprocity may have been at stake.

Hitting or fighting. Acts of unqualified hitting or fighting were described by half of the youngest group and occurred with decreasing frequency as storytellers grew older. It was represented by the following examples.

(M,6)   *He hits a person—then the other person hits him back.*

(M,6)   *Fight. (?) Because they can get hurt.*

(F,6)   *They can hit each other. (?) Because they can hurt each other.*

(F,7)   *When they slap them.*

(M,10) *Throwing rocks at each other.*

(F,9)   *Harold picks on kids. He took a gun, filled it with dirt, and shot it in my face. He threatens you. (?) Says, 'I'm gonna beat you up.'*

(M,13) *Pushes him around (?) Putting him down, saying he's better than he is. (?) You're supposed to treat him like everyone else.*

(M,6)   *Like if someone kicked you.*

(M,7)   *My friend bothers me sometimes and hits me in the face. (?) Because he's being bad.*

(F,12) *When they get upset about a game and start a fight.*

As with stories of not sharing, these stories were marked by a lack of qualifications and a focus on the act itself. Questions did not yield provoking circumstances, although in the case of the 13-year-old male, the interviewer's query did bring out a statement about the principle of equal treatment.

Qualified Stories   The remaining 28 stories all contained explicit conditions surrounding the unkind initiative. They are classified in table 7 and presented here by the content of the unkind act.

Not sharing. The 6 stories of not sharing were the following:

(F,7)   *Like one child didn't have a bike and they asked the other person and they said no. That would be unkind to one another.*

(M,10) *One has the swing and the other one comes along. If he doesn't let him use the swing. (?) It's not being nice to other people.*

(M,9)   *One guy has candy and the other doesn't. He doesn't share.*

(F,10) *My friend and I were going down the street and we saw the Good Humor man. I didn't have any money. She said, "Want some ice cream? That's your tough luck." She got herself some.*

(M,12) *He wants to borrow a pice of paper and the other won't let him. One needs it and the other one has it.*

(F,13) *One dropped their meal ticket. The other one picked it up and used it.*

The common element in these stories is the difference between two peers—one possesses something and the other does not. Except in the one case where there was a verbal insult, unkindness resulted from a failure to share on the part of the possessor.

Hitting. There were 4 stories of physical aggression in which qualifications were stated. These stories were:

(F,7)   *You're playing with someone and they push you. Maybe you don't mean to do it so they push you.*

(F,10) *Some kids are playing kickball and someone makes an out. The other kids hit him and pick on him. (?) He couldn't help making an out.*

(M,10) *The kind kid threw a ball at the other kid by mistake and the unkind kid got real mad and grouchy. He threw the ball back at him . . . and hit him.*

(F,9)   *A boy beats up a girl. (?) He's stronger.*

The theme of the first three stories is that aggression is an unwarranted retaliatory act. The recipient did something which another peer did not like and reacted to it physically. But the original act was not intended to cause harm, and thus a negative reciprocation was unkind. In the last story, the stronger boy took advantage of the weaker girl, the violation having to do with their physical inequality.

Social exclusion. The 5 stories describing social exclusion follow:

(M,7)   *Someone's playing a game. You say, "Can I play?" And they say, "No, you can't play."*

(M,9)   *Another kid wants to play kickball. A kid says, "No, You're not good enough." (?) Because they don't let him play because he can't run fast.*

(M,10) *Two boys, every recess one would have a lot of friends and they wouldn't let the other one play. Never let him play.*

(M,13) *Somebody wanted to play on a kickball team but the other kid wouldn't let him.*

(F,13) *When you're choosing sides, sometime the captain won't pick a person who's a lousy player.*

In 3 of the stories, children stated that the excluded peer was in a one-down position either by not being as good a player or not having as many friends. In all cases, unkindness resulted from excluding the peer from the group.

Not sympathizing. The remaining 13 stories center on one peer's failure to sympathize with another peer's feelings. The specific content areas covered are broad and do not fit into a simple categorization. Examples of the stories are as follows:

(F,9)   *My brother and me were building a fort. He accidentally hit his thumb. I said, "I'm sorry," but he said, "Shut up."*

(F,9)   *One girl is sick and asked a friend to bring her her homework. She refused.*

(M,12) *Someone wins a game. They would say, "We creamed you." Rubbing it in.*

(M,12) *Someone who's crossing the street gets hit by a car. A boy who's watching just walks away . . . just ignores the fact.*

(F,12) *If he's in trouble, you could help him get out of it. But you don't talk to him. Leave him there.*

(F,12) *Maybe she's not as pretty as the one doing it and she's teasing her about the way she looks. (?) She can't help the way she looks.*

(M,13) *This person, a really good friend, knows his friend is really bad in school or has a problem in the house. The boy could be unkind by not caring about the person . . . . Just ignoring him.*

(M,13) *One had to take a test and didn't have all the outlines. If one rejected the person and didn't want to give him the outlines.*

(F,13) *If they don't understand something in school and you understand it, you don't help them. Say you don't have time (?) It's deliberately not helping . . . turning them away.*

(F,13) *A girl is not liked by anyone in class. No one would play with her. You make no effort to let them know you want to be friends. Go along with everyone else. Make her feel awful.*

Interpretation of Child-Child Unkindness

As with kindness, 6 to 7 year old children told stories with singular focus on acts. Seventeen of the 20 children of this age identified unkindness with not sharing, which included taking or breaking material possessions, and hitting or fighting, which are cases of not playing nicely. This emphasis compares with accounts of peer kindness which involved sharing and playing. If kindness requires procedure in which equality is literally enacted through positive reciprocations, then unkindness involves opposite procedures or failures to reciprocate. The child who possesses something keeps it to himself or herself. Or, the child who does not possess something takes or breaks another child's possessions. Or, instead of playing together, children initiate physically aggressive behavior in which one child hurts the other and sets the two peers apart. In these stories, unkindness is constituted by interactions in which inequality is literally enacted through nonreciprocity.

After about 9 years of age children began to express equality differently. Accounts of unkindness were less bound to direct negative initiatives. Instead, unkindness was described through acts of *omission*. One peer did not have to harm another physically to show unkindness. All the peer had to do was not act when the other peer would have expected a positive sign of relationship. Thus, not choosing someone to join a game, not helping another with schoolwork, or not empathizing with another's problems indicated unkindness. The theme of older children's stories, especially in the 12 to 13-year-old group, was to leave or ignore a peer in need. To leave someone alone is not to act. And not to act can be unkind only if there is an expectation or obligation to act. In other words, failure to act is unkind if the child is obligated to reciprocate some previous act which had been initiated by the recipient in the story.

For the majority of the oldest children, the context for unkindness was a stated inequality between actor and recipient. Inequality covered a variety of content: One was a winner, the other a loser; one knew how to do a school assignment, the other did not; one had friends, the other

was unpopular; one was pretty, the other was not. Unkindness ensued when these inequalities were left unattended. To leave a peer in a state of deficiency is to fail to
act in accordance with the principle of equality. It is in this
sense that omission can be viewed as unkind.

Stories of unkindness reflect the age shift from focusing
on method alone to focusing on principle pretty much as
did stories of kindness in studies 1 to 3. Younger children
seem to understand the peer relation by direct reciprocity,
in either positive acts which bring peers together or negative acts which separate them. From about age 9 onward,
the literal methods are reconceptualized as principles in
which equality becomes a point of concern. At the same
time, the idea of the individual person is brought in so
that individual differences become occasions for asserting
the principle of equality. Older children see individual
differences in comparative terms. Actors in one-up positions are better off than recipients in one-down positions.
To leave peers in these unequal positions is equivalent to
denying the principle of equality. As with kindness, older
children do not demand that equality be expressed in literal, material form. Their concern is more for equality of
treatment, or reciprocal treatment. For example, in their
accounts, no act could undo a peer's having lost a game,
being unpopular, or not being pretty. Nevertheless, the
one-down peer was entitled to being treated as an equal
and with respect in the same sense that the one-up peer
was so entitled. Since they deserved equal treatment, recipients could expect to be empathized with, or at the very
least, not to be demeaned. Actors' failures to act on these
principles became, therefore, failures to acknowledge peer
relationship, and were thus unkind.

Child- Adult
Results

Forty-six of 60 stories with child actors were accounts of
unqualified initiatives. The content of these stories is
described generally in table 8 where it is seen that children
focused on disobedience, misbehavior, and disrespect.
Disobedience and misbehavior decreased in usage with
increasing age while disrespect, most often represented by
"talking back," was used almost exclusively by the oldest
group. Qualified stories occurred with some frequency

only in the middle and oldest groups. However, compared with stories of *peer* unkindness, the incidence of stories qualified by description of adults as individuals declined by about one-half.

Table 8   Child (actor)-Adult (recipient) Unkindness: Frequencies for Males and Females

	Age					
	6–7		9–10		12–13	
	Male	Female	Male	Female	Male	Female
Unqualified Stories						
Disobeying	6	5	6	4	4	—
Misbehaving	3	4	2	2	1	1
Talking back	—	—	1	—	4	3
Qualified Stories						
Not helping	—	1	—	3	—	5
Insulting	—	—	1	1	1	1

Unqualified Stories   *Disobeying.* Twenty-five children described unkindness simply with stories of disobedience. Examples are:

(M,6)   *When someone doesn't do what their mother says to do.*

(M,7)   *Not doing what he's told.*

(M,6)   *Being disobedient.*

(M,7)   *Arguing with your mother. (?) Because when your mother says something, you can't argue with her. You have to obey her.*

(F,7)   *You're not doing what your mother tells you. Your mother knows more than you do and you got to learn to do what your mother tells you to do.*

(F,6)   *They don't listen to their mother or father. (?) Because they're not listening to what they're supposed to do.*

(F,6)   *They don't listen to her when she says, "Wash the dishes."*

(F,6)   *Not do what they say.*

(M,9)   *He doesn't listen to what the grown-up says.*

(M,10)   *Disobey elders. (?) You have to do it.*

(M,10)   *His mother wants him to take out the trash. He tells his mother, "No, I'm too tired."*

(M,9)   *I take piano lessons. When my mother goes out she asks me to play the piano. After she leaves, I go out and start playing outside.*

(F,9)   *Your mother asks you to do the dishes but you go out and play.*

(F,9)   *The child won't listen to what the adult said.*

(F,10)   *She asked me to go out and dump the trash. I said, "This is a good TV program. Wait until it's over." You should do what they say.*

(F,9)   *Not doing what the adult says. (?) If she doesn't do it, making them shout and shout and shout.*

(M,13)   *Parents ask you to do something. You don't want to do it and say you're doing all the work in the house and being picked on when actually you're not doing anything.*

Misbehaving. Thirteen stories pertained to misbehavior, direct aggression, or impoliteness. Examples are:

(M,7)   *Calling them names.*

(F,7)   *When you wreck something of theirs.*

(M,6)   *Not sharing with adults.*

(M,7)   *Saying, "I hate you." I'd get a spanking if I said that.*

(F,7)   *Hit him.*

(M,10)   *Call him names; like if they're ugly.*

(F,9)   *The parent is talking on the phone. The child says, "I'm hungry. Get me this. Get me that."*

(F,10)   *If two grown-ups are talking and the kid butts in. (?) You're not supposed to.*

(M,9)   *Stamp all over their flowers. (?) Do something bad. (?) Or break a window with a baseball.*

(M,13)   *Somebody knew this grown-up liked his tool set very much and the kid stole it.*

(F,12)   *Do something to their house, like throwing eggs.*

Talking back. There were 8 stories in which unkindness was described by the child as "talking back" to an adult. Here is what children said:

(M,10)   *Talk back to them.*

(M,12)   *Talk back to him. (?) Because you're not supposed to talk back to adults.*

(M,13)   *Talking back. (?) Everyone has to work so you might as well do it and get it over with.*

(M,12)   *Unnecessarily talking back. (?) Not treating them with respect.*

(F,12)   *Make rude remarks to something they say.*

(F,12)   *They talk back unkindly.*

(M,12)   *Not listening; mocking.*

(F,13)   *If you're told to do something, talk back to them. (?) Because you're defying what they said.*

Qualified Stories   *Not helping.* There were 9 stories in which child actors saw adults in need but failed to offer assistance; all 9 stories were told by females. This is the first time in these studies that a substantial difference is noticed between males and females. Here are the stories:

(F,7)   *If the grown-up needed something the kid said no.*

(F,9)   *The doctor asked the girl to help her father get exercise. She said she was too busy, when she hardly had anything to do.*

(F,9)   *When a grown-up asks you to get pills or something when they're sick. The child says, "No, I'm doing something else," when they're just standing there.*

(F,9)   *An old lady's in a wheel chair trying to open a door. The 9 year old walks on by. Laughs at her. (?) Leaving her when she needs help.*

(F,13)   *Mother tells her to hang out clothes and the kid doesn't feel like doing it. (?) Mother does cooking and everything so you should give her a hand.*

(F,13)   *If there's a teacher no one liked . . . give her more trouble. Give her more grief.*

(F,13)   *If a lady had lots of packages in the elevator. She was dropping them. Don't help her. Pick up (take) one of the things.*

(F,12)   *If there's an old lady crossing the street, let her go by herself instead of helping.*

(F,13)   *If you knew they had a lot of work you'd stay out of the way so they wouldn't make you do some of it.*

Insulting. The last 4 stories presented a context in which adults were in a position of doing things for children. Unkindness came when children failed to show appreciation and instead insulted the adults. The stories are:

(M,10)   *His mother was baking dinner. The kid didn't like what she was making and was real grouchy and said he wanted something else.*

(F,9)   *A grown-up goes out to the store to buy a younger person a game. The child just throws it down and says, "I don't like games."*

(M,13) *If your parents are real old and you're supposed to have them drive you somewhere but you're too embarrassed to be with them. So you don't.*

(F,12) *It could be a rich person who has a maid. The child is always degrading them . . . always bossing them around.*

Interpretation of Child-Adult Stories

Child-adult kindness in 6 to 11 year olds was mainly represented by obedience and good behavior. In the present study, unkindness was, for children in this age range, primarily a matter of disobedience and misbehavior. As with kindness, the stories were unqualified. This implies that children approached this relation through procedural rules emphasizing complementariness. Unkindness was described by violations of this method of reciprocity. The oldest children of 12 to 13 years followed a similar approach, but they were less focused on disobedience and misbehavior. The procedure they described as a violation was talking back to parents in what were presumably face-to-face verbal defiances of adults' requests and other shows of disrespect. Seven children from the oldest group (35% of the sample) were able to depict adults as persons who needed children's assistance. In 5 cases, unkindness was expressed by acts of not helping and in 2 instances by forms of insult. As with kindness, this result suggests a developmental lag in children's regard of adults as individual persons compared with their regard of peers as individuals. By about 9 years of age, peers are described as individuals, and children see themselves as free actors in that they can choose how they will behave toward them. They can adjust or not adjust their actions in light of individual conditions. However, at this same age, adults are described more as figures to whom children are bound by rules of constraint. Adults are not seen as individual persons, and children are not seen as free to behave as they choose toward adults or as free not to adjust actions to adults' wishes.

Adult-Child Results

There were 36 stories in which adults were unkind to children. The following results are of interest. Eleven of the 12 children 6 to 7 years old told unqualified stories in which adults were mean or refused to grant favors to child recipients. In contrast, 11 of the 12 stories in this general category told by 12 to 13 year olds were qualified. These stories pertained to failures by adults to assist children in need (6 stories) or by adults' failure to attend to children's feelings. The performance of the 9 to 10-year-old group was split. Six of their stories showed the same content as those of the 6 to 7-year-old group. The other 6 stories resembled those told by 12 to 13 year olds. Examples are given here of stories in each of the general categories.

Unqualified meanness

(M,7) *A man doesn't like a boy. He might punch him and stuff.*

(F,6) *Send her to bed without dinner.*

(F,10) *A grown-up hit the child every time she tried to say something.*

Unqualified not granting favors

(M,7) *Not let him do anything he wants. (?) Being bad to the child.*

(F,6) *Not doing them a favor. (?) Being mean to them.*

(M,9) *It's the last day of a fair. The child wants to go. The parent just wants to sit down . . . . They're too lazy to take him.*

Qualified Failure to Assist

(M,9) *You can't get cereal in the cabinet because you can't reach it. You ask him and he doesn't do it . . . . He doesn't want to get it for you.*

(M,9) *A 9 year old doesn't play tennis well. A lady who's real good doesn't bother to help teach her.*

(M,12) *If it was a teacher and you were messing up and the teacher wouldn't let you do it over again.*

(F,13) *If a kid didn't understand math. If the kid keeps asking for help and the adult says, "I don't have time," every time they ask.*

*Qualified Failure
to Attend to
Feelings*

(F,9)   *We went and helped a man deliver papers and accidentally
dropped some in the mud yesterday. He said he'd never let you
help again.*

(M,12)   *Your dad promises to take you fishing on the next trip. On the
next trip he tells you at the last minute he doesn't want to go.*

(M,13)   *If everyone is going to a baseball game you've been nice and
your mother says no.*

(F,13)   *If they didn't get along with their parents, and they punished
them for no reason.*

Conclusions
from Stories of
Unkindness
Stories of unkindness show similar patterns to stories of
kindness. Children of all ages distinguished peer from
child-adult relations with interactions expressing equality
and unilateral constraint, respectively. Peer interactions
showed a developmental change from accounts of unqualified reciprocity to accounts in which actions were conditioned by individual states of peers. Younger children
described procedures in which one peer physically ag-
gressed against or took something from another peer.
Older children described one peer in need compared to
another peer who was better off. Given this inequality,
unkindness followed when the latter peer did not offer
to help the peer in need.

Child-adult interactions also showed a developmental
pattern similar to that obtained for kindness. When children were asked to describe unkindness toward an adult,
younger children emphasized disobedience and misbehavior. Similar stories were told by 9 and 10 year olds.
Some older children introduced the notion that adults
were individual persons in need who could be helped by
children. Unkindness resulted when children failed to
offer assistance and left adults in states of trouble. The
same picture was obtained when children were asked to
describe unkindness by an adult toward a child. Younger
children described adult actors as unkind when they
either did not grant child recipients favors or misused
their power to hurt child recipients. Older children pre-

sented children in need and said adults were unkind when they did not offer the assistance which would put child recipients in better positions.

The data which emphasize that acts of *omission* constitute unkindness provide compelling evidence that older children have reconceptualized procedures of interactions into principles of relationship. In everyday life, circumstances are such that a person is often not attending to the needs or interests of other persons. Obviously, children do not think that persons live in a state of continuing unkindness. If omission is unkind it must be understood within a context of obligation. Thus, when one person is supposed to take an action toward another but does not, unkindness results. Stories of older children show what the conditions of obligation are. For peers, actors are supposed to take initiatives when presented with clear inequalities. Young adolescents see similar obligations when adults appear in one-down states to child actors or vice versa. In other words, omission is unkind when circumstances present occasions to act on the principle of equal treatment. This principle appears first in peer relations at about 9 years of age and later enters child-adult relations at around early adolescence. In both cases, the principle becomes evident at about the same time that children stop seeing persons as simply filling roles in a method and begin to recognize their individuality. This individuality is expressed most clearly in actor-recipient comparisons when the latter is in material or emotional need and the former is in a position to better the recipient's condition.

Study 5: Judgments and Reasons for Unkindness   The goal of this study was similar to that of study 3. Four types of stories about unkindness were presented to new groups of children who were asked to give judgments and reasons about these stories. The issue was whether younger children would agree that not sharing and disobedience were unkind because of a violation of method and whether older children would require that not sharing and disobedience be qualified by actor-recipient inequality. The new sample consisted of 66 children, 22 each from the three age levels: 6 to 8 years, 9 to 11 years, and 12 to 14 years. The children came from the same school as those in study 1 and 18 of these children served in that study as well. All 4 stories were told as acts of omission. Two stories pertained to peers and two involved child actors and adult recipients. In each relation, one story was unqualified and the other was qualified on a stated need of the recipient. Examples of the stories were:

"Sam doesn't share his snack with Bob."

"Bob forgot to bring his lunch to school. Sam doesn't share his lunch with Bob."

"Mother tells Jim to do something. Jim doesn't do it."

"Jim's mother is busy cleaning the house. The mother asks Jim to babysit for his brother. He doesn't do it."

After each story was presented, the interviewer asked the child: "Is this story kind, unkind, or can't you tell?" If the child said it was unkind, the interviewer asked for the reason. If the child couldn't tell, the interviewer told him or her to change the story so that it would be unkind.

Child-Child Results
No child judged stories as kind. Children either said the stories were unkind or that they could not tell. An overview of the results is shown in table 9. Unqualified not sharing was judged unkind by all of the 6 to 8 year olds, by 14 of the 9 to 11 year olds, and by only 7 of the oldest children. Judgments for the qualified story showed 21, 17, and 13 agreements, respectively, by age group as to unkindness. Thus, there was a decrease in judgments of unkindness with increasing age for both stories. Addition of the qualification of recipient's need produced slight increases in the unkind category in the older groups.

Table 9   Peer Unkindness: Judgments of Stories about not sharing between Peers

	Not Sharing			Not Sharing Plus Need		
Judgment	Ages 6–8	Ages 9–11	Ages 12–14	Ages 6–8	Ages 9–11	Ages 12–14
Unkind	22	14	7	21	17	13
Can't tell	—	8	15	1	5	9
Reasons						
Action Itself	15	9	4	13	8	4
Recipient's Need	4	5	7	7	11	7
Actor's Attitude	3	8	11	2	3	11

Reasons for judgements were classified in three general categories: the action itself, the recipient's need, and the actor's attitude. Table 9 reports how children's reasoning changed as a function of their age. It is clear that the younger the child, the more likely the reason given would be the act itself. Conversely, the older the child, the more likely the reason would refer to the recipient or the actor, citing the recipient's need or the actor's attitude.

Not Sharing per se. Judgments based on the act of not sharing per se follow:

(M,7)   *He's not going to share it.*

(M,7)   *Because he wouldn't share*

(F,6)   *Because she doesn't share.*

(F,7)   *She's not sharing.*

(F,8)   *She wasn't being very nice. (?) Because she wouldn't share her lunch with her.*

(F,7)   *Because she wouldn't share her snack with her friend.*

(F,9)   *She didn't share.*

(F,10) *She should share things with others.*

(M,10) *Because he doesn't share with his friend.*

(M,12) *You should share things.*

(F,12) *Because she doesn't share.*

There were 28 cases of this type of reasoning. In all of these, children did not refer to persons but focused on the act itself or gave a general statement about the act of not sharing. These are considered clear cases of stress on procedure instead of person.

Recipient's need. Sixteen children heard the unqualified story and read into it that the recipient was in need of food or did not have food. Examples include:

(M,6)   *Maybe they're poor.*

(M,8)   *Because if he has lots of things and the other boy doesn't have anything.*

(M,8)   *Because somebody forgot their lunch.*

(F,7)   *If someone else doesn't have a lunch and someone has a big lunch.*

(M,10) *If he was hungry.*

(M,10) *He might not have anything.*

(F,9)   *It depends if she didn't have any food.*

(M,10)   *If he has a big, big lunch and if he [recipient] forgot a lunch.*

(M,13)   *If he had forgotten lunch or had given things to Sam.*

(M,13)   *If you have something and they don't.*

(F,12)   *If she didn't have any lunch.*

(M,14)   *He may have nothing else and may be really hungry.*

(F,14)   *If Ann didn't have anything, Mary should have offered.*

In each of these explanations, reference was made to the recipient's lack of, or need for, food. In sum, children made a direct comparison between the actor's possession and the recipient's nonpossession. It appears that children who used this reason were operating from the premise that the actor-recipient differential was an occasion for sharing and were saying therefore that the act of omission was unkind.

Actor's attitude. Twenty-two children heard the un-qualified story and attributed unkindness to the actor's attitude. Examples of this type of reason were:

(M,6)   *He's being mean to him.*

(F,6)   *She's being mean.*

(M,9)   *Because Bob shared with Sam, and if Sam didn't share he wouldn't be like his friend.*

(F,10)   *If she asked if she could please have some and Betty said, "No, I don't want you to have any."*

(M,13)   *If Sam passed to everyone else and said," "You can't have any."*

(M,14)   *He's more selfish than anything else.*

(F,13)   *It depends on her [the actor's] feelings.*

(F,13)   *If she really doesn't like her.*

The condition implied by these reasons is the actor's intention not to be nice. It is expressed in various forms ranging from meanness to exclusion of the recipient. In all cases children seem to be saying that the actor should have treated the recipient differently and should have shared.

Reasons for judgments of qualified story   Table 9 shows that children in some age groups changed while in other age groups they did not change their reasoning when presented with the explicit statement of need. In the youngest group, an additional 3 children made need

the source of unkindness. Reference to need nearly dou-
bled from 5 to 11 in the middle age group. The oldest
group did not change at all in the reasons given here compared to those given in the previous story. This is understandable, since these children, when responding to the
qualified story, had already referred to need or attitude
when they heard the unqualified story. They did not require an explicit statement of need since they were not
focusing only on the act of not sharing, but viewed it
conditionally from the start.

Child-Adult
Results

An overview of results of judgments of child-adult stories
appears in table 10. Almost all children judged both stories
of disobedience as unkind. There were, however, sharp differences in the reasons given by children of different ages.
Most of the youngest children attributed unkindness to
the act of disobedience per se; use of this reason declined
with increasing age in both stories. A total of 12 children,
only 2 from the youngest group, mentioned the adult's
need in judgments of the unqualified story. When the second story contained a statement of need, 25 children referred to it as the basis for unkindness. Actor's attitude
was mentioned by 15 children in judging the unqualified
story and by 14 in the qualified story. The majority of
children who used this reason came from the oldest group.

*Reasons for
judgments of
unqualified story*

Examples of the three types of reasons are now presented
for the story in which the act of disobedience was
described.

Disobedience per se. Thirty-eight children judged as unkind
the act of disobedience per se, which was in effect equivalent to saying that children ought to obey adults. Actual
statements include the following:

(M,6) *He's not obeying his mother.*

(F,6) *She's disobeying.*

(M,6) *Because he's not doing what his mother says.*

(F,7) *She won't do what her mother says for her to do.*

(F,8) *Because she won't do what her mother wants her to do.*

These examples characterize the 6 to 8-year-old group's
emphasis on the act which violated the method of rec-

Table 10   Child-Adult Unkindness: Judgments of Stories About Disobedience Between Child (actors) and Adult (recipients)

Judgments	Disobedience			Disobedience Plus Need		
	Ages 6–8	Ages 9–11	Ages 12–14	Ages 6–8	Ages 9–11	Ages 12–14
Unkind	21	19	17	21	20	19
Can't Tell	1	3	5	1	2	3
Reasons						
Action Itself	19	12	7	14	8	4
Recipient's Need	2	6	4	5	11	9
Actor's Attitude	—	4	11	3	2	9

iprocity by complement. Some older children gave similar reasons but introduced a new element—that the child actor *should* or was *supposed* to obey. Here are ways they said this:

(M,10) *You're supposed to listen to your mother.*

(F,10) *You're supposed to do what your mother says . . . she loves you a lot.*

(M,11) *If his mother tells him to do something, he should do it.*

(M,12) *You should do things that parents tell you to do.*

(F,13) *If her mother asks her to do it, she should do it.*

(M,13) *You're supposed to obey parents.*

Parent's (recipient's) need. Twelve children who heard the unqualified story spontaneously read into it that the mother needed help. Unkindness was thus attributed to not obeying in the face of need. Examples are:

(M,8) *Because maybe she has lots of things to do and he just goes and plays instead of helping his mother.*

(M,9) *If mother had a rough day; he knows it and still doesn't help.*

(F,10) *If she was going to have a party and she didn't help . . . mother may not be ready for the party.*

(F,13) *Maybe the mother is tired from doing lots of work and is busy doing something else.*

In this type of reasoning, children were attributing need to the adult and assigning unkindness to need coupled with an implied belief that the child actor should help out.

Child's (actor's) attitude. Fifteen children said that unkindness was due to the child's attitude rather than to the act of disobedience itself. They said the following:

(M,10) *If he's just being lazy.*

(F,10) *If her mother asked her to do something and gave her an allowance and she doesn't do it. It would be unfair.*

(F,11) *She should do it for her mother because her mother is so nice to her.*

(M,12) *He's being inconsiderate.*

(F,12) *Her mother does a lot of things for her.*

(M,13) *They give him everything. I don't see why he can't be a little kind back.*

(M,13) *Parents do enough for you. You should give some of yourself.*

These reasons reflect something akin to a conception that children and adults are in a direct reciprocal relation. Children seem to be saying that parents do things for children and children should do other things in return for parents. This type of reasoning goes beyond the belief that children are expected to obey. They should help out because parents help children and fairness requires reciprocity.

Reasons for judgments of qualified story

The reasons given for this story, which contained an explicit statement of need, were generally similar to reasons used for the previous story. One new reason was observed. Of the 25 children who focused on the recipient's need, 9 chose to attribute need to the baby in the story. For example:

(M,10) *It's unkind to the baby. The baby wants to play.*

(F,13) *The baby might be a troublemaker. Give the baby something to do.*

In all other respects, reasons mirrored those stated for the previous story. The youngest children emphasized disobedience as an act which was unkind. The middle group stressed need. And the oldest group mentioned need as well as attitude. As to the latter, children referred to the child's obligation to reciprocate for what parents do for children. For example:

(F,12) *She's selfish; doesn't take time to help out the family.*

(M,13) *You're part of the family. You have to give of yourself.*

(M,13)   *It's his mother. She does stuff for him and he should try to help her.*

(M,14)   *She has to give for him so he should show consideration.*

Conclusions   Results from this study of judgments and reasons concur with findings from the stories themselves. Six to 8-year-old children generally see unkindness as failing to follow a normative method. This view takes little account of the persons involved. With peers, sharing is expected; not sharing is therefore unkind. With parents, obedience is the rule. The rule is violated and unkindness results when the child does not obey. Some few children at this age level, 7 with peer stories and 5 with child-adult stories, attributed unkindness to need when need was stated in the story. The majority, however, dealt exclusively with acts as unconditionally representative of what should occur in these two relations.

As with stories about kindness, the 9 to 11-year-old group was transitional between focusing on method alone and having a clear view of relational principles. Some referred to not sharing and disobedience as unkind in themselves. Others were able to introduce need spontaneously or to identify it when it was presented. Still others referred to the actor's attitude as the source of unkindness.

The oldest group also showed a new insight into the child-adult relation which few of the children in the other groups showed. These young adolescents saw disobedience as a failure to reciprocate for the good things parents do for children. They spoke of fairness, giving back, considerateness, and the like, indicating that there is more equality in the relation. This is the age at which children also view adults as individual persons and clearly see parents as having needs. For example, a mother can be busy, tired, harrassed, sick or otherwise in a momentary state of needing assitance. Given these insights, child actors are no longer simply bound by unilateral constraint. Rather, they are more like equals to adults as persons and obligated more by the principle of reciprocity to offer assistance when circumstances call for it.

Seven Reciprocity in Kindness and Unkindness

In the studies reported up to this point, children described single initiatives within interactions. The results of these studies have allowed us to make certain inferences concerning reciprocal methods. For example, the acts most often described for peers appear to imply direct reciprocity in that deeds assigned to actors could easily have been assigned also to recipients. In the two studies reported in this chapter, children were required to describe initiatives as well as reactions, so that the original recipient became an actor and the first actor then took the role of recipient. The Sullivan-Piaget thesis suggests that there ought to be two forms of action-reaction sequences. Peers are said to function within a general form of direct reciprocity: whatever one peer does, the other is also free to do in return. The predominant form of child-adult exchanges should be different. It should follow the method of reciprocity by complement. A child's initiative or reaction should be designed to fit with an adult's expectation or initiative since complementariness means that the adult's part in the interaction determines what the child can do.

In study 6, the two methods of reciprocity were submitted to observation by having children generate acts of kindness and likely reactions to them. Actors and recipients were varied so that the original actions came from a child or an adult and subsequent reactions came from a child or an adult. The expectation was that there would be greater frequency of direct reciprocity between peers and a high incidence of reciprocity by complement between children and adults. In study 7, reciprocity in unkindness was studied and longer action-reaction sequences were obtained. Reciprocity by peers to unkind acts should show a special pattern. According to the literal application of direct reciprocity, one unkindness can be met with another and that, in turn, with another, and so on. Were this to happen, in fact, peers would be caught in an endless series of retaliations once one peer initiated an untoward act. It would be in keeping with the principle of reciprocity, however, if one of the peers voluntarily stopped the negative series instead of reciprocating exactly as he or she had been treated. Only then could the general principle of reciprocity serve to put the peers in a positive relation toward one another once the principle was threatened.

Study 6: Reciprocity in Kindness   One-hundred twenty children, 40 each from ages 6 to 8, 9 to 11, and 12 to 14 years, were interviewed. The children came from two schools; half were interviewed by one female adult and the other half were interviewed by another female adult. Neither interviewer was familiar with the results of the previous studies, the content of stories other children had given, or the expected results of the present study. All children told one story in which a child actor did something kind for another child. After the child told a story, the interviewer asked for a further description in terms of what the recipient was likely to do either next in sequence or the next time the actor and recipient met. All children also told another story in which a child did something kind for an adult. They then had to say what the adult might do next in reacting to the child's kindness. Finally, one-half of the children told a third story in which an adult did something kind for a child and the child reacted to it.

Results when Children Respond to Peer's Initiatives   Children's descriptions of peer kindness were similar to those obtained in studies 1 and 2. Younger children told stories of unqualified sharing and playing while older children told stories of assistance qualified by need.

Content covered the familiar range of assistance with schoolwork to understanding of emotional problems. These results indicate that the present groups of children were operating with conceptions of the peer relation comparable to those of children in previous samples.

Descriptions of reactions to kindness by a peer were classified into three categories. One category pertained to *gratitude* and was most frequently represented by children saying that the peer would say "thank you" to the actor. In the second category, children said that the recipient would react with a different, but approximate, act to the actor's initiative. *Approximate reciprocity* was characterized, for example, by an actor's sharing followed by a recipient's offering of an invitation to play. The third category was *direct reciprocity*. Children using it said that the recipient would next do the same act that the original actor had done. Frequencies of children using each of these categories are reported in table 11. In no category did the storyteller's age appear to be a determining factor. A majority of children in each group described direct reciprocity; gratitude ranked second but was followed closely by approximate reciprocity. Taking approximate and direct reciprocity together as representing the same form, it occurred at a 3:1 rate over gratitude. Detailed descriptions of the three categories are now presented.

Gratitude. Thirty-two children described reciprocity with gratitude. Examples include the following statements. The original kind act is summarized first and is followed by the child's actual description of the reciprocal act in italics. A question mark in parentheses stands for the interviewer's question, "Does she do anything else?"

(M,7) Share lunch with a peer who forgot theirs: She says, *"Thank you."* (?) *I don't know.*

(M,7) Share lunch with a peer who forgot theirs: Say, *"Thank you."* (?) *Say, "You're very kind."* (?) *No.*

(F,8) A friend lets you play in a game: *Play the game.* (?) *'Cause she says, "Thank you."*

(M,10) A friend gave him something: *Tell them, "Thank you."*

(F,10) Her brother stopped someone who was picking on her: *Thank him.*

Table 11   Reciprocity in Kindness: Frequencies of Children Describing Different Types of Reciprocity

Types of Reciprocity	Age		
	6–8	9–11	12–14
Child to child			
Gratitude	13	10	9
Approximate reciprocity	6	10	7
Direct reciprocity	21	18	23
Child to adult			
Gratitude	15	8	7
Approximate reciprocity	3	10	11
Direct reciprocity	0	2	2
Adult to child			
Gratitude	15	18	16
Reward	21	17	16
Direct reciprocity	4	4	2
No reciprocity	0	0	4

NOTE: N does not always equal total numbers of children, because one or two children gave answers which did not fit our categories.

(F,11)   Friends let her play: *They're happy.*

(M,12)   Someone helped another with mathematics: *Ask for more help.* (?) *They thank you.*

(M,14)   A friend explained to another how to play basketball: *Thank me and is glad someone'll take time to show 'em.*

(F,13)   She put books away for a friend who got sick in class: *Thank me.*

(F,14)   She shared a lunch with someone who did not have one: *They're happy and say, "Thank you."* (?) *They just say, "Thank you," and now they're happy because they have lunch.*

Apparently, these answers represent a belief that a verbal expression of gratitude is an adequate reciprocation to a peer's kind initiative. Most of the children who gave this answer were probed, indicated by (?), and encouraged to say more. The interviewer asked, for instance, "How would they show they were happy?", "What else would they do?" or "What would they do back?" These 32 children either repeated their original answer or said nothing more would happen.

Approximate reciprocity Twenty-three children gave descriptions in which recipients performed some act approximating but not exactly duplicating the actor's original initiative. Examples are:

(M,7) His friend let him go first: *I let him sometimes use my ball.*

(M,8) His friend shared with him: *After school sometimes, maybe I invite him over.*

(M,8) His friend helped when he fell off his bike: *I let him ride my bike while I was inside. I told him something secret.*

(F,8) Someone invited her into a game: *Like at lunchtime, giving them something; sharing if you forgot your lunch.*

(M,11) Another peer gives him something: *When I give them a present, we play with it.*

(F,11) Someone let her in a game: *She was it and you were the one that got her to play. She wouldn't chase you as much as the other kids.*

(M,12) He shows a new kid around the neighborhood: *He goes home and the next day he returns to play with me and my brother. They're like a trio.*

(M,14) A peer helped him with homework: *Get closer to him and be better friends. (?) Call him; go out with him; let him know you'd help him.*

(F,13) Invite an acquaintance to your house: *They'd become your friend. She'd open up to you.*

(F,13) I helped my friend who got sick: *She'd go out with you to play.*

In each story of this type, reciprocity took the form of returning one kindness with a different kind act. In 10 of the 13 cases, the approximate reaction was play. This may mean that the recipient took the first act as a gesture and now returned it to become a closer friend of the actor. As several children said: *They would become friends; You'd get along better; They get to be freinds; He would get closer to him; They would be better friends;* or *She would try to be my friend.*

Direct reciprocity In stories of direct reciprocity, a storyteller had to say that the recipient would next perform the same act which the actor had just performed. This was the most frequently used category, accounting for 62 stories. Here are examples:

(M,6) My friend plays with me: *Thank him. (?) Next day I play with him.*

(M,7) His friend let him use his bike:*When I was using his bike, I let him use my bike.*

(M,8) His friend let him go to his house: *Say that sometime he can go to yours.*

(F,7) Her friend shared her jump rope with her: *I'll bring something like my Hula-Hoop tomorrow and let her go first.*

(F,7) Invite a friend to play: *Well the next day she played with me and invited me over to her house.*

(F,7) Give a toy to a friend in the hospital: *Say, 'Thank you,' then if they're ever in a hospital, maybe you bring them a toy.*

(F,8) She forgot her lunch and someone shared theirs with her: *Say "Thank you." (?) Maybe if they forgot their lunch sometime, you could share with them.*

(M,10) He visited a friend who was sick: *If the other friend gets sick, visit him.*

(M,10) A peer lets him play a 'good' position in a game: *Try to play my hardest. (?) I ask if they wanted to play instead.*

(M,11) A kid, who was beating up another said he was sorry: *He said he was sorry and so did the other guy.*

(F,10) She helped her sister: *She'd probably do me a favor. She'd say, "Well now I owe you one."*

(F,10) A friend helped when she fell down: *Say, "Thank you." If you ever fall down, I'll help you, too.*

(F,11) She was helped with homework: *By helping them with stuff they don't understand.*

(M,13) A friend helped him when he fell into a creek: *If something happened he would help me, like if I got injured.*

(M,13) His friend gave him a sandwich when he forgot his lunch: *Try to pay 'em back by one day bringing them something in your lunch.*

(M,14) A friend invited him over: *Thank him and invite him back.*

(F,13) When she was teased, her friend made her feel better: *Try to do for them the things they did for me.*

(F,14) Someone helped her with homework: *Explain to them what they don't understand in schoolwork.*

(F,14)   A friend helped with homework: *Help them sometimes on homework.*

(M,14)   A friend helped with homework: *Maybe do the same thing if the other person was absent.*

In all of these stories, children described a direct payback of act for act. The older children actually spoke as if they were aware of the act as a payback. Moreover, if the recipient had a need, the actor was often described as later having the same need—for instance, food or help with school subjects or assistance when hurt.

Results when
Children
Respond to
Adults'
Initiatives

Recall that only half of the children ($N=60$) in this study were to give a reaction to the story in which an adult does something kind for a child. The overall results are reported in table 11. The same three types of reciprocity that were found in child-child stories were found again. In this case, however, there were clear age differences in the responses. Fifteen of the 20 6 to 8 year olds said that children reciprocated to adults' acts of kindness with gratitude. Gratitude decreased by half in the two older groups. Approximate and direct reciprocity, in contrast, increased with age. Three of the youngest children used these two categories as opposed to 12 of the middle and 13 of the oldest age children.

In reviewing the actual stories below, the reader should keep in mind that the original initiatives were from adults to children. The stories then refer to ways children reacted to adult's initiatives.

Gratitude   The original stories were similar to those produced in study 1. Adults primarily gave material things or did favors, such as driving children to recreational events. Here is the way children expressed gratitude.

(M,6)   His mother drove him to soccer practice: *Play soccer.* (?) *Thank her.*

(M,7)   His mother gave him a surprise: *Say, "Thank you."* (?) *Give her a big hug.*

(M,8)   His parents helped with homework: *Say, "Thank you" and get better grades and mother would help him more and then he would thank her and she could help him a lot more and he would learn more things.*

(F,7)   Her father gave permission for her friend to sleep over: *Give him a big hug and kiss.*

(F,8)   Her parents gave her a present: *I gave them a kiss and a hug.*

(F,8)   Her parents helped with homework: *Say, "Thank you," and do the rest of my homework.*

(M,10)   His parents took him somewhere special: *Thank you.*

(M,10)   Parents helped with a school assignment: *Say, "Thank you."*

(M,11)   An adult helped a lost child find his way home: *My mother thanks them.*

(F,10)   A grown-up helped a child who was hurt: *Say, "Thank you."*

(F,10)   Her mother drove her to a ballgame: *Thanks her and promises her not to inconvenience her again.*

(F,11)   An adult drove children to a park: *They thank them.*

(M,12)   My parents helped organize a breakfast at school: *Thank them.*

(M,14)   His father did not punish him for getting in trouble: *I was grateful that he was kind to us and understood.*

(M,14)   His father drove him to his friend's house: *Thank him. I do what they tell me to do. (?) I do it or they won't let me go to a party.*

(F,13)   A lady counsels a girl with social problems: *Appreciate it. (?) Be happy and say, "Thank you."*

(F,14)   Her father helped her with math homework: *Thank him. (?) I give him a kiss.*

(F,14)   Her neighbors drove her to a party: *Say, "Thank you."*

Approximate reciprocity   In stories showing approximate reciprocity, children returned adult-initiated kindness generally by doing chores for adults. The following examples illustrate this type of reciprocity.

(M,7)   A grown-up helped a child who was hurt: *Like the mother has to go someplace and she has a baby; she could babysit.*

(M,8)   His father taught him how to play soccer: *By cleaning up the yard.*

(F,7)   Her mother took care of her when she was sick: *I was upstairs and she was downstairs and she asked me to get her slippers and I did.*

(M,10)   His dad bought him model planes: *I help him with things, like get tape and scissors for his work.*

(M,11)   His father drove him somewhere: *Tries to make his parents have a nice time.*

(M,11)   His neighbor took him fishing: *Talk and things like that.*

(F,10)   Her parents helped her with schoolwork: *Like if your mom's cleaning, instead of watching TV, you could help her.*

(F,11)   Her mother drove her everywhere: *Thank her. Help her and do whatever I can to pay her back.*

(F,11)   Her parents helped her with homework: *Thank them and help mother with dishes since she helped me.*

(M,13)   His parents helped him prepare a party: *I'd help around the house and do what they asked me to do.*

(M,13)   His parents let him build something: *Help them carry in groceries.*

(M,14)   His father drove him somewhere out of the way: *Do house-cleaning for my mother and live up to what I say to my father.*

(F,13)   Her mother listened to her problems: *Run errands, bake cookies, or do something nice to show you appreciate what they did for you.*

(F,14)   Her parents helped her with homework: *Help them in return around the house. Obey rules.*

(F,14)   Her parents let her go to camp: *Keep [babysit] the kids outside. Help around the house.*

Direct reciprocity   There were only 4 stories of direct reciprocity. They are:

(M,11)   Grown-ups give children presents: *Thank them or give something back.*

(F,10)   Her mother took care of her when she fell: *Say that I would do the same for her if she was hurt.*

(F,14)   An adult took time to talk with her and be friendly: *Talking to him. (?) Let him know he had a close relationship.*

(F,13)   Your parents help you with your house chores: *Do the dishes or what I could do around the house the next day.*

Results when Adults Respond to Children's Initiatives   Two of the three categories which applied to children's responses to peer and adult initiatives also applied to adults' responses to children's initiatives. These were "gratitude" and "direct reciprocity," with the latter including a new subtype of story, described below. The category of children's responses called "approximate reciprocity" was better defined as "reward" when applied to adults' responses, since adults either gave material things or granted privileges in return for children's kind initiatives. The overall results are shown in table 11. Children of all ages performed alike.

Gratitude   Most of the original stories dealt with children being kind by doing physical chores for adults. Adults reciprocated by acting with gratitude toward children. Examples are:

(M,8)   He babysat for someone: *She would say, "Thank you," and let you go over and babysit some more.*

(M,7)   I helped John's father who was carrying a lot of books: *Says, "Thank you. You're very nice."*

(F,8)   She helped her mother wash dishes: *She put dinner on the table with a smile on her face.*

(F,8)   She cleaned the kitchen without being asked: *They say, "Thank you," and kiss you.*

(M,11)   *He gave his father some candy: He thanks him.*

(M,11)   He helped his mother in the kitchen: *She thanked me.*

(F,11)   Gave her mother breakfast when she was sick: *She thanked me.*

(M,14)   He helped the teacher clean up the classroom: *She thanked me.*

(F,13)   She visited old people in an nursing home: *They smiled and said, "Thank you."*

(F,13)   She helped her mother prepare for a dinner party: *Making you feel real good by telling you they appreciated it.*

Reward   Fifty-four children said that after a child did something kind for an adult, the adult would reciprocate by rewarding the child. Although reward could be viewed as a type of approximate reciprocity, it has been renamed to reflect more accurately the meaning of the action for the child in the context of the child-adult relation. Here are examples of this category:

(M,6)   He swept the floor for his mother: *She gives you a big dinner.*

(M,8)   He helped his father with yardwork: *He gives me a reward.*

(M,8)   He babysat for his parents: *They give you money.*

(M,7)   He obeyed: *They reward you.*

(F,7)   She helped her mother, who was sick: *We went on a picnic.*

(F,8)   Her mother was busy; she helped her out: *Says, "Thank you," and give me something for doing it.* (?) *Maybe a piece of candy.*

(F,8)   She helped her mother with housework: *Gives me a little money; let's you eat outside with everybody.*

(M,10)   He got the newspaper for his parents: *Sometimes they pay me.*

(M,10)   He does chores for his mother: *She's nice, she gives me treats and stuff.*

(M,11)   He helps his mother, who has visitors: *Offer them a ride.*

(M,10)   He helped by washing dishes: *They say, "Thanks," and give us little candies. That's only if we work a lot. They give us pretty much, like M & Ms.*

(F,10)   She visited her grandmother: *Once she made a pillow for me.*

(F,10)   She did something for her mother: *[She let's you] go to your friend's house.*

(F,11)   She helped her mother: *She thanks us and lets us do a lot of things.*

(F,11)   I help her with something: *Ask me to go horseback riding with her.*

(M,12)   He did chores without complaining: *Slack off on him. Not as many chores and stuff.*

(M,14)   He took care of his neighbor's dog and yard: *Said, "Thank you," and gave me money.*

(M,14)   He was considerate of an older person: *He thinks of me as a grandson . . . praises me a lot.*

(F,13)   She helped with housework: *They'd let you go out.*

(F,13)   She helped her mother: *Do me a favor. Something in return. Like take us out to dinner.*

(F,14)   She looked after her neighbor's house while they were on vacation: *They gave me money for doing it.*

Direct reciprocity   There were only 10 cases of direct reciprocity, involving an exact trade of one action for the same action. Examples include:

(F,7)   She gave her mother a present: *She give me a pencil case.*

(F,7)   Obey: *The parent listens to the child.*

(M,7)   Give him a present: *Give you something back.*

(F,10)   Help with chores: *She can help you with homework.*

(M,11)   A boy helped his parents with work and chores: *Help them back, like if the child needs help with homework.*

(M,11)   A child visits a neighbor who has no children. He talks with him: *Talk and invite us over again.*

(F,13)   A girl respects a teacher whom the other children make fun of: *If you pay attention . . . and don't laugh, she'll answer your question when you get out of your seat and go up to her to ask.*

(F,14)   A girl listened and obeyed adults: *Be kind. It would alternate and go on and on.* (?) *You help them, they help you, you help them, and so on; etc.*

No reciprocity   There were 4 cases in which children said that adults would not have to reciprocate at all to children's kind initiatives. When asked whether adults reciprocated, children responded as follows:

(F,13)   She and her siblings gave their parents money to go out for an anniversary dinner: *Mom would cry. She'd probably say, "Keep it," or tell us to come, but we'd say, no.*

(M,14)   He helped an adult who was in a car accident: *No. But it didn't matter.*

(M,14)   He and his friends pushed a car which was stuck in the snow: *He drove away.* (?) *No.*

(F,14)   She called up her uncle when he was sick: *No. It would be nice to make him happier, make him higher in spirit.*

Interpretation of Results   Previous results led us to the conclusion that approximate and direct reciprocity were fundamental to peer relations. The present results substantiate this idea. Either type of reciprocity predominated in stories at all ages. They were used by children of the 6 to 8-year-old range, for whom the peer relation is at best a composite of practical rules for interaction. And they were used by children older than 9 years, for whom peers are understood as belonging to an abiding relation. The lack of differences based on age is important since it signifies that the method of interacting by reciprocity is known by younger children and may be the basis for a reconstituted principle later on in development. A similar conclusion holds for equality which is at first enacted literally and subsequently becomes a principle for the peer relation.

Prior results also suggested that child-adult relations function by way of complementariness. This was substantiated in two ways in the present findings. First, after adults did something kind for children, children reciprocated mainly by verbally expressing gratitude or by doing chores for adults. There were only a few stories of direct reciprocity for both child and adults in child-adult relations. Second, after children did something kind for adults, adults reciprocated mainly by rewarding children. They gave them things children wanted, payed them money, or granted them privileges. There were only 10 stories of direct reciprocity and 4 stories in which adults did not have to do anything in exchange for child-initiated kindness.

One might say that these results are obvious. Children are more likely to exchange similar actions because they have equal resources, capabilities, and interests. Likewise, children, practically speaking, cannot do for adults what adults are able to do for them. For instance, adults can drive children places, give them money, grant permission, and give privileges. However, independent of these rather concrete similarities among peers and differences among children and adults, it is important to realize that peers interact by treating one another in the same ways while children and adults do not. The practical facts, in themselves, may be the primary source first of methods for interacting and later for principles when the methods are reconstituted in relations. The present data show clearly that peers can exchange actions almost literally on a one-to-one basis. Peers share capabilities as well as interests, all of which promote direct reciprocity as the major method for their interactive functioning.

Children are not equals with respect to adults and, as the stories show, children and adults do not always share common interests. Children want to play, to be entertained, and to participate in peer activities with one another. Adults are interested in keeping the home well ordered, and, therefore they want children to work around the house. These diverse interests put exchanges on an unequal basis. In effect, each party gets what it wants in kindness, but both do not want the same thing. The high incidence of gratitude alone shows this same point with respect to children and adults. A verbal 'thank you' may be all a young child can offer at the moment when an adult extends a kindness. For children older than about 9 years, exchanges are more integrated. Doing chores is understood as obligatory in a unilateral relation. At the same time it serves as an appropriate exchange for adults' kindness. In turn, an adult's granting favors or privileges is considered fair exchange for a child's obedience or doing chores.

Study 7:
Reciprocity in
Unkindness

Sixty of the children from study 6 also served as storytellers in study 7 on reciprocity in unkindness. Each child was to describe two sequences of actions and reactions, one between peers who were friends and one between a child actor and a parent recipient. The child had to describe: (1) an unkind act, hereafter called an offense; (2) what the recipient would do next; (3) what the original actor would do the next day; and (4) what the recipient would do in reaction. In each relation, there were two action-reaction sequences between the same two persons which occurred one day apart.

Friend-Friend
Results

Most of the offenses described in step 1 fit into five categories. Three of these categories were used more by the younger children, while two were used more by the older ones. The three used more by younger children were *physical aggression, taking property*, and *refusing to play*. Offenses of these types were described by 13, 10, and 4 children respectively, from the youngest, middle, and oldest groups. Offenses referred to most by older children were *exclusion from groups* and *picking on* or *bossing*. They were described by 6, 10, and 15 children respectively, from the youngest, middle, and oldest groups.

Given these offenses, the second step was for the children to describe how the offended friends reacted or what the recipient of the unkindness did next. Most children described reactions which fit into three general categories. The most frequent reaction, described by 22 children, was *direct reciprocity*. In this category, the recipient was said to do back to the offender all or part of the same act that the offender had just done. Thirteen children described reactions of *indirect reciprocity*. This included acts which were negative and equivalent to but not identical to the original offenses. The last category is called *nonconfrontation*. It was used by 24 children. Reactions fitting nonconfrontation included the following subtypes: The recipient "walked away," "said nothing," "ignored," "backed off," avoided," "did not play with," or "asked for an explanation." The frequency of use of these categories was unrelated to age. This finding similarly characterized the study of kindness between peers reported in table 11. Apparently, the youngest children know as well as the oldest what peers or friends expect of them in negative as well as positive exchanges.

The third step in the sequence required children to describe the original offender's second action which was to be a reaction to the offended friend's reaction. Three types of second actions were observed. The first was a negative sort in which the original actor *repeated* the offense. A total of 12 children gave this type. The second was positive in nature and consisted of two subtypes. Sixteen children said that the offender would *undo* the original offense by substituting a new positive action for it. Twenty-one children said that the actor would *apologize* for the original offense. The third type was ambiguous. Eleven children said that the offender would *avoid* the recipient; this could have been a positive gesture or a negative withdrawal.

Finally, the fourth step, describing the offended friend's second reaction, cannot be analyzed on its own. It is best seen in terms of patterns which include the three preceding steps. Six patterns were obvious in the data. They are shown in table 12. Several results are apparent and are now discussed.

Patterns A and B describe sequences in which the friends did not resolve the original offense. In both patterns, the last reaction of the offended friend was negative. Thirteen nonresolved sequences emanated when step 2 was in the form of a direct or indirect reciprocation of the original offense, and 9 occurred in the form of a nonconfronting reaction to the original offense.

Patterns C and D describe resolved sequences in which step 2 was direct or indirect reciprocity to the original offense. In pattern C, step 3 on the part of the offending friend was an undoing of his or her offense. In pattern D, step 3 as an apology. Five children generated the former pattern and 16 described the latter sequence.

Patterns E and F depict resolutions for which step 2 had been a nonconfronting reaction. Nine children followed nonconfrontation with an undoing of the original offense. Six said nonconfrontation would be followed by an un-

Table 12   Patterns of Reactions Following Offenses of Unkindness

				Age	
			6–8	9–11	12–14
Patterns for Friends					
	Step 2	*Step 3*	*Step 4*		
A.	Reciprocate 1 (Direct/indirect)	Offense 2 (Avoid)	Reciprocate 2 (Avoid)	4	6	3
B.	Not confront	Offense 2 (Avoid)	Reciprocate 1 (Avoid)	3	3	3
C.	Reciprocate 1 (Direct/indirect)	Undo offense	Accept	4	0	1
D.	Reciprocate 1 (Direct/indirect)	Apologize	Apologize/accept	5	4	7
E.	Not confront	Undo Offense	Accept	3	0	6
F.	Not confront	Apologize	Apologize/accept	1	5	0
Patterns for Parents					
G.	Punish, etc.	Offense 2	Punish	2	3	4
H.	Punish, etc.	Undo	Accept/explain	10	6	6
I.	Punish, etc.	Apologize	Accept	4	7	1
J.	Punish, etc.	Apologize/forget	Apologize/forget	2	4	5

doing of the original offense. Six said nonconfrontation would be followed by an apology.

These patterns lead to several conclusions. First, in this sample of 60 children, there is no predominant sequence which follows from an unkind offense. Second, no particular reaction to an original offense predicts eventual resolution or nonresolution. That is, a total of 34 children said that the first reaction would be some type of retaliation. Of these, 62% said that the offense would be resolved while 38% said it would not be resolved. In comparison, 24 children gave a first reaction of nonconfrontation. Of these, 63% proposed eventual resolution and 37% described nonresolution.

Thirdly, patterns do not appear to be related to age in any obvious manner. There are minor but not substantive differences among the groups. For example, the 9 to 11-year-old group described the most instances of nonresolution; 11 said that the friends would end the sequence on a negative note, while 9 said the offense would be resolved. Further, all of the children in this group who proposed sequences of resolution did so by having the original offender offer an apology as step 3; none proposed resolution through a substitute act which would undo the original offense.

Examples of Patterns

Pattern A. Thirteen children described nonresolved sequences fitting the pattern: offend, reciprocate, offend again, reciprocate again. One example from each age group is now given.

(F,8) *Like if they were best friends and I asked if I could play ... and she says no./ Then I would say, "I hate you. I won't be your friend anymore."/ She wouldn't talk to me./ I wouldn't talk to her.*

(M,10) *Go up and punch him around. Hit him./ Punch him back. / He would call him names. Tease him./ Do the same thing back.*

(F,11) *She butts into line and pushes her around./ She'll probably push her back. Continue Fighting. / Fight back. It's a lifelong fight.*

Pattern B. A second pattern which did not end in resolution was: offend; not confront; offend again; reciprocate. Nine children described this pattern.

(F,7) *My friend Seth used to bug me. (?) Pour water on my head ... scare me./ I felt like kicking him but didn't. I ran away from him./ He'd tease me more./ I tried to tease him back.*

(M,10) *We would sometimes say we didn't want her to play because she was mean./ She was shy and wouldn't do anything./ Probably do the same thing because she's usually mean./ Just say, "shut up," and walk away.*

(M,12) *Most people didn't like what he did; he talked funny. Some of the guys wouldn't let him play./ He wasn't big and he was afraid. He'd walk away./ Tease him more./ He'd probably say something back.... Go tell the teacher.*

Pattern C. Five children, 4 from the youngest group, described the sequence: offend; reciprocate; undo offense; accept. Here are two examples:

(M,7) *You don't like the person. You don't want to play with them./ They tell on you. Say they don't like you./ You would play with them./ They play with you.*

(M,8) *Everyone wanted to play with him but he didn't want to play 'cause he was selfish./ He won't be kind either./ Ask the boy to play./ The other one asks, "Are you sure you won't quit?" He says he won't and they go and play.*

Pattern D. The most frequently used pattern (*N*=16) was: offend; reciprocate; apologize; apologize or accept. Examples include the following sequences:

(F,7) *By taking money from them./ He would take some from that person./ He would say he was sorry he had stealed his money./ He'd say he was sorry he had took his money.*

(M,10) *Fighting. They start hitting each other and get in a fight./ Start hitting him./ He'd make up. Say he was sorry./ They both say they're sorry and become friends again.*

(M,13) *Spread rumors or kick him out of game you're playing./ Try to retaliate. Take all the people out of the game./ He might say he was sorry. If he was nice, he would say, "Alright."*

Pattern E. Nine children produced the sequence: offend; not confront; undo offense; accept. The following are representative examples:

(F,7) *I wouldn't give her anything./ She wouldn't say anything./ I would be better to her. Play with her more./ She would play with me.*

(F,14) *Sometimes they make fun of others' mistakes./ Some people take it with a grin./ If the person had ignored it, the whole thing is forgotten./ If she had been treated normally, the whole thing would be forgotten by her too.*

Pattern F. Six children, none from the oldest group produced the sequence: offend; not confront; apologize apologize or accept apology. Examples are:

(F,7) *Someone fell down and my friend J. didn't help her./ She didn't do anything./ She said she was sorry./ They made up. They spent the whole day playing the same game, but they were more careful.*

(M,10) *Not letting him play with him. Let him play one day and the next day say, "Get out of here."/ If he's nice, he might just walk away . . ./ He might say he was sorry./ He would say, OK, and they would be friends again.*

Child–Parent
Results

Most offenses (acts of unkindness) in child-parent interactions were similar to those produced in study 4. Categories of offenses were: "disobey" (*N*=26); "answer back or sass" (N=18); "lie" (N=4); "steal" (N=4); and others (N=8).

There were two categories of parental reactions (step 2). Forty children described the parent as reacting to the child's offense with a *punishment*. Within this category, the youngest group tended to refer to physical punishment (N=11) while the oldest tended to describe punishment in terms of taking away privileges or restricting the child (N=7). Fourteen other children described the parent's reaction in terms of an *insistence that the offending child follow orders*. Of these 14, only 3 were from the youngest group of children.

Descriptions of step 3, the child's second action, fell into four categories. Twenty-two children said that the child would undo the original offense by substituting a positive act for the previous negative act. Fifteen children said that the offending child would offer an *apology*. Fourteen children said that the child would produce a *second offense*. This category implied that punishment or insistence did not have its intended effect. Instead, children reacted negatively to the parents' reactions. Finally, 6 children said that the child would *forget* the matter or just *act normally*.

To understand step 4 and to put the sequences in clear relief, the data were ordered according to four general patterns. These patterns are shown in table 12. Each is now described and illustrated.

Pattern G. Nine children produced sequences of the following sort: offend; punish/insist; offend again; punish again. The pattern thus was a case of nonresolution since it was concluded on a negative note. The examples below illustrate the pattern.

(M,6) *Disobey them./ They give you a spanking for disobeying./ He wouldn't talk to her because she gave him a spanking and he didn't like it./ She would get mad.*

(F,10) *Talk back to her; maybe not do as she's told./ She'd feel hurt, but she'd punish them./ Kind of be mad. . . . Maybe not talk to her mother. Wait until she asked a question, then sass back to her./ She'd still feel sad, if the child talks back. She'd give her another punishment.*

(M,12) *A boy who lives across the street, started a fire in our backyard./*

His parents were upset. They mostly restrict him./ He went out and did the same thing again. He doesn't listen./ Just restrict him. They can't really do much with him.

Pattern H. In the most frequently produced pattern, 22 children described the sequence: offend; punish/insist; undo offense; accept or explain. Acceptance refers to acknowledging the new positive act. Explain refers to the parent commenting on the new act in comparison with the previous offense. Examples are as follows.

(F,7)   *Not obey./ They spank you./ She obeys them./ They don's spank them.*

(M,8)   *When your mom wants you to set the table and you don't want to./ Paddle you./ Do what she says./ She'll let me do the things I want.*

(M,10) *The parent tells the child to clean up the yard and the child says no./ Tell him to come here and send him to his room./ He doesn't disobey them./ If he's good for a couple of days, they might let him go out and play again.*

(M,10) *He wouldn't listen to him./ Say, "Go to your room."/ Be kind and nice; say the breakfast was good and all that./ Say, "Thank you."*

(F,14) *When they don't do things they're supposed to be doing like clearing off dishes./ Remind them to do it./ He might do it to avoid trouble./ If the child does it, the parent may thank them, but not likely. It's something they're obliged to do.*

(M,14) *Steal some money from their purse or wallet to get something he wanted but wasn't allowed to have./ He punishes him./ Try to raise some money to pay them back./ Say he was forgiven.*

Pattern I. Twelve children, all but one from the younger two groups, described sequences which ended with the child apologizing and the parent accepting the apology. The pattern was: offend; punish/insist; apologize; accept apology. Examples are as follow:

(F,7)   *A child gave her mom a plant and then threw it on the floor./ She punished her. She couldn't go out for two weeks./ She might say she was sorry./ She might give her another chance.*

(F,10) *Talk back to them./ Punish them./ The child might say, "I'm sorry."/ She'd accept the apology. She'd probably still keep the punishment 'cause she still did it.*

(F,11) *If they ask you to do the dishes and you say no and go out and play./ Make you do it anyway or punish you./ She tells her parents she's sorry and does it now without being asked./ They might give her an extra allowance.*

Pattern J. Eleven children described sequences which ended with either a dual apology or a dual overlooking of the offense. The pattern was: offend; punish/insist; apologize/forget; apologize/forget. The pattern was produced mainly by children from the two older groups.

(M,10) *Getting bad grades deliberately./ Punish him./ Just act normal./ Sort of the same.*

(F,10) *Just go up and kick her. Not accidentally./ Probably send her to bed and tell her not to do it again./ She'd probably say she was sorry./ Probably say, "I'm sorry for yelling at you."*

(F,13) *Talk back to mother./ Send her to her room./ Usually forgets the whole thing./ Leaves her be.*

(F,13) *When you ask one parent and they say no and go ask the other parent and they say yes. Then the parents go into a discussion./ They probably punish the child for not going along with the first answer./ Just act normal./ Act normal.*

Friend-Friend and Child-Parent Results Compared

Several differences were observed in the results depicting unkindness between friends and between child and parent. First, children's descriptions of offenses correspond to differences between these relations as they were expressed in studies 1 through 6. For example, offenses between friends involve the idea of not acting as an equal; acts of physical aggression or exclusion from play, set one child over the other or set one child apart as less than another. Offenses to parents show the opposite idea. In not obeying or in talking back, child actors were failing to take the complementary part in relations. One may say that these offenses represent children's failure to conform to their expected subordinate roles toward adults.

Second, the descriptions of first reactions to offenses (step 2) indicate a further difference along the same lines. The most common reaction of friends was direct or indirect reciprocation of the offense ($N=35$). Only one child described a parent as reciprocating with the same action the child had initiated. Instead, punishment was the most frequent reaction ($N=24$). Moreover, 24 children said that friends might walk away from or otherwise not react to the actor's offense. This reaction did not occur at all on the part of parents. It is possible that parents' restrictions may be a rough equivalent to nonconfrontation, since they involved isolating offenders from their family or peers. Finally, the reaction of insisting that the child do some action occurred 14 times with parents but did not occur at all with friends.

These differences correspond to the now familiar distinction regarding equality in the two relations. Punishment, restriction, and insistence would emanate from a relation in which one person has the power to control another's activity. Punishment, a reaction which declined in use as the storytellers grew older, represents an exchange of disapproval for disobedience. Restriction implies that parents have the right to give and take away privilege. Insistence is a statement that parents can make children do particular things. In each case, the parent stands out as the controlling force while the child is being directed or led. Thus, inequality can take several particular forms, all expressed through unilateral authority.

Friends who are equals generally have two other paths available by which to express their displeasure. One is to return a like act for the offense in which case the offended friend asserts equality through direct enactment. This counters the offense of inequality with a definite enactment of equality. Nonconfrontation follows the same logic but from a different angle. By not returning the offense, the offended friend may be telling the offender that the original act of inequality is inappropriate. The message may be that if you act this way, I will not interact with you further. Or it may be, now that I have chosen not to harm you, you are obligated not to harm me.

Third, step 3, shows differences between the relations for each main type of reaction. Additional offenses occurred more often with friends ($N=23$) than with parents ($N=14$). This result could reflect the freedom of friendship in contrast to the limitations with authority relations. Undoing offenses by substituting positive for previous negative acts, occurred 22 times with parents versus 13 with friends. That is, parents can demand that offenses be undone by requiring new positive behaviors. Friends cannot make this demand with the power to enforce it; they can only ask for it.

Apology also differed in the two relations. Offending freinds apologized more often ($N=21$) than children who had offended parents ($N=15$). To see this difference more clearly, one may look to step 4, the reaction to apology. Friends who were given apologies by offenders actually apologized in return for having reacted to the original offense. Double apology occurred in 14 of 21 possible cases. Double apology occurred twice between child and parent.

Lastly, for step 4, 10 children said that parents would accept children's positive gestures but concluded their sequences by saying that parents would also give explanations of why the offense was wrong. Two possibly similar cases occurred with friends. In both instances friends asked whether the offender would be unkind again before they accepted the positive gesture as genuine. The difference is worth noting since ending patterns with explanation may stress the fact that parents have the right or duty to outline correct behavior even when the child has just tried to admit error and undo it.

Eight From Reciprocal Practice to Cooperation

The purpose of this chapter is to integrate the findings of studies 1 through 7 and to show how they serve to clarify the thesis. Two types of results are of interest. The first pertains to differences between relations as they were found to characterize different age levels. The second pertains to changes within each relation as they appeared across age levels. Emphasis is given to those findings which recurred from study to study. Consistency may be assumed to represent common conceptions derived from the general social reality which these various samples of children shared. Obviously, each child has an individual history of social experience with parents and peers. One child differs from another based on ways in which their own parents or peers characteristically interacted with them. The present interview techniques and classification of results were insensitive to these possible differences. On the other hand, the spontaneous grouping of results by similarity in accounts suggests that there must be a common base which underlies each child's particular exposure to reality.

A discussion of the connection between accounts and methods of reciprocity is presented first. This is followed by a consideration of concepts of two relations which were evident in children of the youngest age level. Next, changes in both relations are discussed insofar as they were manifested in accounts from older children. These

149

changes pertain to establishment of structure and to important functional products, in particular, concepts of self and other as persons. The next section attempts to reconstruct development as it appeared in both relations. Emphasis is given to transformations which occurred in child-adult relations at around early adolescence and to the continuous development of cooperation among peers which first appeared at around 9 to 11 years of age. The chapter ends with conclusions drawn from these studies first as they adequately summarize two course of development and second as they bear on and help to clarify the Sullivan-Piaget thesis.

Methods of Reciprocity   It is important that results of studies 6 and 7 concur with findings in studies 1 to 5. In the earlier studies, children produced accounts of single acts. In the thesis, acts from one person are said to be understood as parts of methods of interactions. Single acts are designed as reciprocations to previous acts from the recipient or as anticipations of the recipient's future reciprocations. Relations are ongoing and have a history. When two persons have occasion to interact, their mutual history structures the context of their new meeting. According to the thesis, single acts signify the structure since they represent a shared meaning which is known to the participants. Surely, when one child offers to share a possession, that child believes that the recipient understands the meaning of this gesture. This belief is not concocted on the spot, but stems from prior interactions between the peers.

Results of study 6 illustrate that acts described in studies 1, 2, and 3, can be interpreted as constitutive parts of reciprocal methods. Acts of sharing or assisting peers may be seen as reciprocations to prior initiatives or offers soliciting recipient's future reciprocations. Similarly, acts of obedience or doing chores may be understood as parts of the method of complementariness. They are either complements of adults' earlier signs of approval or requests for future signs of approval. It is proper to view single acts as elements within exchanges, when exchanges reflect understanding of methods of reciprocity. In this vein, the results of study 7 reveal the same methods as the single

acts obtained in studies 4 and 5. The question now remains to spell out the nature of each method and show
how each is developed during the movement from school
age to early adolescence.

Child–Adult
Relations: 6 to 8
year olds

For most 6 to 8-year-old children, kindness was expressed
through the theme of unilateral control. Children were
kind by obeying adults or acting in accord with standards
imposed by adults. The latter included statements about
being good, not lying, and acting politely. In return,
adults acted kindly toward children by giving them possessions they desired or granting them permission to participate in recreational activities. The same theme was also
represented in child-adult unkindness. Children were unkind when they were disobedient or failed to conform to
adults' standards of action. Adults, in turn, were unkind
by not giving children what they wanted, by placing ex-
cessive demands on them from their position of power, or
by punishing unfairly.

These results appear to represent the method of reciprocity by complement in unambiguous terms. Obedience already implies that children are to build their parts
in interactions in conformity to adults' wishes. In return
they receive adults' favor and approval. Seen from the reverse, disobedience meets with disapproval. The consistency of these findings was not entirely expected. Instructions directed children to kindness and unkindness.
They could easily have provoked stories about the exchange of pleasantries and unpleasant behaviors, respectively. Storytellers were, of course, free to supply
whichever content they thought fitting. The fact that they
spontaneously chose to bring out the theme of unilateral
authority is therefore important. It shows that kindness
may be represented by adherence to a method which is
understood as appropriate to a relationship. For example,
by obeying, children attest to their part in the method
which describes their relation with adults. When they disobey, children deviate from the method and step outside
the relation, thereby, being unkind.

This interpretation is solidified in studies 6 and 7. In
the former, accounts illustrate the fullness of exchanges.

Willingness to conform to the method of complement merits signs of approval through rewards and other pleasant expressions. In distinction, deviation is met with punishment as a first reaction. This sign of disapproval from adults is apparently perceived as a fair return since it is almost always followed by the child's undoing of the original act. The patterns observed in study 7 almost invariably took the course of eventual obedience which the parent accepted. That is, ultimately even untoward events ended with acknowledgment of unilateral authority.

There is in these data little evidence that children view this relation as unfair. Their accounts may indicate that adults are seen as deserving of respect for their superior knowledge and power. They may further indicate a sense of security which can be gained by remaining true to the method wherein adherence yields acceptance. From a pragmatic viewpoint, results may show that young children have learned to use their parts in the method to gain personal ends. Adults hold material resources as well as control over things children want. To get these things, children can work through adults. Conformity is therefore a tool for achieving self-satisfaction through interpersonal means wherein material rewards and maintenance of the relationship are nearly indistinguishable.

Peer Relations: 6 to 8 year olds   The focus of accounts of peer kindness was on giving, sharing, and playing together. Unkindness was manifested in physical or verbal aggression, in not sharing, or in not playing fairly. Two clear points were evident in these results. First, the symmetry of direct reciprocity dominated most accounts in studies 6 and 7. One child did exactly or approximately whatever the other child did. This method fits the single acts described in earlier studies. These acts were not heroic or outstandingly mean but could have been initiated easily by actors or recipients in most circumstances. In this sense, single acts could have been reciprocations to past or future initiatives as the results of studies 6 and 7 readily demonstrate. These results therefore highlight the method of direct reciprocity as the commonly understood form of exchange which applies to peers.

Second, in the accounts of kindness or unkindness there

was an obvious expression of equality between peers. One might call it an equality of enactment because the two peers were shown to have parts in interactions which are not distinguishable. Children seem to agree that when one shared, the other shared, and when one was nasty, the other would be nasty. This concrete demonstration of equality is not separable from the method of direct and symmetrical reciprocity itself. Seen from either angle, emphasis is given to each peer's freedom to act as the other has acted or is expected to act later. It is worth noting that the results of interactions also illustrate a concrete sense of equality. Typically, kind acts resulted in two peers having a material possession which prior to the act only one peer had. Playing had a similar result, since after the kind initiative both peers were enjoined in the same playful activity. Unkindness also yielded equal consequences insofar as the hurt resulting from the first initiative was transfered in symmetrical fashion to the original actor.

From Method to Principles of Relations

According to Sullivan and Piaget, methods are first understood through their practice, which constitutes the relation. Subsequently, the methods become reconstituted into principles which characterize the structure of relations. This developmental step should be evident in changes observed across the age span studied here. There appears to be support for this development in studies 1 through 7. The youngest children produced accounts in which unqualified acts were given as self-evident cases of kindness or unkindness. This result was corroborated by judgments from indepedent samples of children from the same age level (studies 3 and 5). In contrast, actions representing a method were not self-explanatory for the older groups. They generated stories in which actions were qualified and judged stories by imputing qualifications to actions. The major exception occurred at the 9 to 11-year-old level for child-adult relations. Interactions between children and adults followed the method of complementariness and were unaccompanied by qualifications. In this respect, 9 to 11-year-old groups were like the 6 to 8-year-old groups.

In which ways do the data imply a change toward relational principles? The answer is found in the nature of qualifications which older children brought to their stories and judgments. For interactions between peers, the most frequently cited condition was explicit need on the part of the recipient. For interactions with adults, recipient's need was one qualification and actor's attitude was another. These are now discussed separately.

Needs of peers, as recipients, were expressed variously, ranging from material lack to deficiencies in terms of emotional stability. Simultaneously, actors were generally depicted as not being in states of need. When these facts are brought together, a general qualification emerges, which is actor-recipient inequality. With inequality as context, interactions become immediately interpretable as following the principle of equality. Kindness ensues when one peer seeks to help another peer reach a state of equality. For instance, when one peer understands mathematics and the other peer does not (he is not smart; she missed class because of illness), the act of teaching serves as a means to put the two peers on a par.

Stories of unkindness reflect the same principle as for kindness seen in reverse. If kindness is represented by adherence to principle, then unkindness is expressed by failure to act according to the same principle. For many of the older children, unkindness was described as a failure to act predicated on recipient need. A careful look at the needs cited indicates what might have been at stake. Peers were typically presented as being in separate states, one peer deficient; the other not. Acts of omission were not negative in themselves. They were simply failures to take initiatives which would change states of inequality. It may be reasoned that when a peer finds another in a deficit position and leaves him or her there, the very terms of relation are denied. Denial in the face of knowledge of the principle makes a neutral act of doing nothing an omission and therefore constitutes unkindness.

This result contrasts sharply with the findings from 6 to 8 year olds. For them unkindness occurs in aggressive acts or other forms of administering hurt. Once such an act occurs, the recipient reciprocates. The action-reaction sequence: I hit you; you hit me, reflects the naïve and literal application of the method of direct reciprocity. For older children, however, direct reciprocity is a deeper matter. As a principle, peers are bound to use the method in a cooperative manner. Thus, kindness is represented when one peer shows a readiness to cooperate in benefitting another. Unkindness is shown when one peer fails to cooperate and leaves another in a deficit state. The children's judgments and reasons confirm this interpretation. For example, when given stories of not sharing food or a bicycle, older children declared that not sharing was neutral in itself. It became unkind when actor-recipient inequality was imputed.

A further source of evidence concerning this principle was obtained in study 7 in which several children said that one peer would walk away rather than retaliating for another's unkindness. Nineteen of the 24 such responses came from children in the middle and oldest groups. If relations were primarily a matter of method, then one unkind act deserved another and exact reciprocity would have been obtained. If, on the other hand, principle were the issue, then reactions should be designed to end rather than escalate unkindness. By walking away or refraining from tit for tat behavior, children may have been offering a signal that the original act had violated cooperation. At the same time, by breaking off contact, they may have been offering an opportunity for the offender to initiate a new act which could then be reciprocated.

Persons in Relations   Sullivan and Piaget suggest that a developmental change is made after about 8 years of age regarding the concept of persons in relations. They propose a complex of changes which include the following components. Recognition of individual personalities should occur chronologically earlier in perceptions of peers than of adults. And, individuals will come to be seen not as "objective" personalities, but according to the terms of the relation to which they belong. Specifically, peers will be described as persons with characteristics derived from concepts of peer relations, and adults will be seen as persons with characteristics derived from the terms of child-adult relations.

Peers as Persons   Only after about 9 years of age did storytellers regularly describe peers as individual persons. Younger children's stories and judgments consisted almost entirely of descriptions of methods alone. In these procedures, the two peers were not presented as distinct individuals; actors and recipients could have represented classes of children. But from 9 years onward, children described peers with particularization. In fact, the term, personality, might be used here in its most general sense to apply to any definitions of individuals that might distinguish them one from another or from a class of individuals. One type of distinction children made was based on persons' material possessions. For example, recipients were frequently described as not having, and thus needing, food, money, or an implement required for school. Lack of an object was due to simple nonpossession, having lost an item, or having it but forgetting to bring it. A second type of distinction pertained to physical health. Referents included getting hurt accidentally while playing as well as having been sick or being in the hospital.

A third type of distinction was made by children of this age, and this touches more directly on the personality in its usual sense. The main referent was the recipient's psychological makeup. In some cases it was characterized by talent to succeed in schoolwork. Peers were described as unable to do mathematics or as having trouble in a particular subject matter. In other cases it involved recipients' emotional conditions. Children provided a wide variety of descriptions, almost all of which were psychological in nature. They include loneliness, depression, homesicknesses, feelings of rejection, feelings of social isolation, hostility, sadness, jealousy, and general emotional upset.

It is important to note that descriptions of recipients were often accompanied by comparative descriptions of actors. For example, when the recipient was doing poorly in spelling, the actor was doing well and could help by sharing his or her knowledge. The same type of comparison applied to material possession—one peer had what the other did not have—and to physical health—one peer fell and was hurt while the other was well and able to offer assistance. A similar comparison was implied by stories predicated on emotional states. For instance, the recipient who was new and therefore had no friends was invited into a friendship group by one of its regular members. Or, when a recipient brought an emotional problem to an actor, the implication was that the actor was well enough to offer solace or understanding.

Three points stand out in these descriptions. One is that children from about age 9 onward define peers along scales which psychologists use to assess individual differences. Children seem to have a clear sense of what is normal or average and they recognize deviations from the norm in peers. When a peer is located on the negative side of average, identification of the state is an occasion which calls for action. The action is corrective since it helps to bring the peer into a more normal state, on a par with the actor.

Secondly, the content of these depictions tends to be restricted to the real-life interests of school-age children. Focus is on having food, health, and friends to play with. It also centers on success in school and being free of emotional ills. The concerns of storytellers for the persons in their interactions tended to hover around interests common to children. The same concerns were repeated from study to study. This point is significant when it is recalled that results came from independent samples and that storytellers were free to describe peers however they liked.

Thirdly, and most importantly, descriptions of peers are summarized by two main themes which characterize peer relations themselves. These are the themes of equality and cooperation. In depicting actors and recipients comparatively, storytellers emphasized factual inequalities. They did so by locating the peers at two disparate points along scales of individual differences. Kindness was then represented by initiatives which either removed the inequality or signified that the peer in the lesser position was entitled to be treated as an equal. Unkindness occurred in leaving the peer in the lesser position and letting the inequality persist. Cooperation was manifested by going out of one's way to assist another and by the expectation of reciprocity in return. There is here an interesting coupling of two conceptual advances. The principles become characteristic of the relation at about the same time that individuality is discovered. When storytellers put them together, their accounts take on a new cast. Kindness is no longer indicated by simple and naïve enactment of direct reciprocity. Instead, kindness involves acting on a principle of cooperative use of reciprocity for the end of equality. The action is called for because actual conditions of interpersonal existence do not conform to the principle. Children who follow this model show a developmental advance over those who do not. Younger children interact in acceptable procedural forms which attest to and result in literal equality. Older children interact to sustain a principle in the face of reality which contradicts that principle. These children do not have to achieve literal equality. For instance, in the case of emotional upset, listening or understanding will not always undo the source of the problem. Rather these children only need show one another that they accept the principle of treating one another as equals and are willing to cooperate to achieve it. In so doing, they testify to the terms of their relation while admitting the respective individuality of each.

Adults as Persons

According to the thesis, recognition of personhood evolves more slowly in child-adult than in peer relations. The results of our studies corroborated this. Children of 9 to 11 years were a pivotal group. They regularly described interactions between peers with qualifications about individuals. They typically described interactions between children and adults with emphasis on method but employed no qualifications. By 12 to 14 years, however, qualifications of persons was evident. Young adolescents either depicted adults as being in states of need or described adolescent actors as having attitudes which qualified complementariness. Needs of adults tended to be grouped around the single theme of enfeeblement. While younger children implied that adults were commanding and powerful, adolescents said that adults could be sick, old, overburdened, lonely, or otherwise needing someone's assistance. By describing adults in incapacitated states, young adolescents show that they have come to see adults as persons with needs of their own. Simultaneously, young adolescents have come to see themselves as capable of taking initiatives to help adults. Their actions are no longer complementary in the sense of emanating from adults' demands. Instead, they stem in part from adults' incapacities relative to children's strengths. Adults' deficiencies range from weaknesses due to status (old age), to momentary physical burdens (having too much work to do), and to emotional difficulties, which include loneliness, embarrassment, and depression.

A simultaneous change occurred in young adolescents' views toward themselves. Results of reasons for judgments given in studies 3 and 5 and from reciprocal sequences in studies 6 and 7 show a newfound stress on voluntary action and sacrifice. Kindness and unkindness were qualified by both factors. With this advance, obedience is no longer kind qua obedience. While the reality is that young adolescents must still obey adults' directives, they feel that they are obeying voluntarily or, at least, with sacrifice. The act of obedience still follows the form of complementariness, but it has new meaning. It is now more a free initiative than a necessary part of unilateral constraint, and stems from the adolescent rather than being simply a rule which must be followed.

A Transformation of the Child-Adult Relation   Present results show a modification in the child-adult relation beginning roughly at the time of adolescence, when the method of reciprocity by complement becomes qualified by the individuality of the adolescent and of the adult. There seems to be a movement toward a kind of equality between the persons in that both are free to take initiatives, both need help, and both can provide it. Recall that in study 6, younger children said that adults would reward child actors and that children would be grateful to adult actors. In distinction, over one-half of the older children said that child recipients could reciprocate directly or approximately to adult actors. This apparent reconceptualization of adolescents' relation to adults, shows a shift from the acceptance of unilateral authority to a bilateral sharing of power. Children interviewed emphasized weaknesses in adults and freedom in the adolescent. There appears to be a compromise between the principle of equality, as found with peers, and the reality of constraint exercised by adults. Adults still control and adolescents have to conform to their wishes. But adults sometimes need help and turn to children for it. This knowledge allows adolescents to sense themselves as free actors who at least glimpse the possibility of being the equals of adults and entering into cooperative relations with them.

The present discussion focuses on the viewpoint of the young adolescents who generated the data, hence, the stress on their reconceptualization of the relation. This is not to imply that adults do not also change their parts and begin to treat adolescents more as equals. This is probably a fact in these adolescents' lives, and the mesh of the two parties' changed conceptions may account for the transformation better than any suggestion that only one or the other is the cause. However, it is critical that in describing the change of relationship, young adolescents used terms that they first used in describing their relations with peers. While the impetus for change may be bilateral, the direction seems to come from adolescents' concepts of their own relations with peers or friends.

Further Consideration of Two Worlds   The remainder of this chapter looks more closely at the developmental transitions within peer and child-adult relations. The former relation appears to begin with enacted methods and moves in the direction of a principled bond between two individuals who deserve to be treated as equals. The latter relation also begins with a method, but one expressed through procedures of unilateral constraint. This relation moves slowly toward a recognition of personhood and then, still gradually, toward a belief in some sort of child-adult equality.

Child-Adult Relations   In study 3 (chap. 5) children were required to judge stories involving a child's obedience to a parent. It was found that younger children judged acts of obedience as self-evident signs of kindness, while for older children there was a tendency to qualify obedience either on the parent's need or the child's attitude. Upon giving their judgments and reasons, children were asked to perform an additional task, the results of which were not previously reported. Children were to modify the given story so that it would be *kinder*. These results help to clarify the nature of the developmental transition in children's conception of this relation and will now be reported as further illustrations.

The youngest group typically said that the act of obedience was kind. This result, in itself, suggested that the method of adherence to unilateral constraint is a sign of the child-adult relation. How could obedience be made kinder? Results show that the youngest group continued to focus on the method of complement but extended it quantitatively. That is, since obedience is kind, then more obedience was kinder. The typical responses from the youngest children were as follows:

(M,6) *If she helps her mother a lot.*

(F,6) *She does whatever her mother wants.*

(M,7) *To do everything his mother told him.*

(M,7) *He could do the whole thing.*

(F,7) *Helping her everyday.*

(F,7) *She did extra things.*

Recall that the 9 to 11-year-old group had given a mixed performance. Some children had focused on the method while others brought in voluntarism or sacrifice. When asked to produce modifications that would make the story kinder, children in this same age group again produced these conceptions. Examples which continued to emphasize complementariness by adding to it quantitatively were:

(M,9) *He helped her a little bit more.*

(F,9) *She did it as soon as she was asked.*

(M,10) *He helped both his mother and father.*

(M,10) *Do more of it.*

(F,10) *She did extra work.*

Examples which stressed the child's attitude were as follows:

(M,9) *If he'd do it when his mother didn't tell him.*

(F,9) *She helps without her mother having to ask her.*

(F,9) *If you were watching a TV show you really liked.*

(F,10) *If she did it when she wasn't asked.*

(F,10) *If she offered and [the mother] had a hard day.*

Only one of the 12 to 14 year olds gave a quantitative response for making acts kinder. The other children either imputed need to the mother or sacrifice/voluntarism to the child. Examples of need included:

(M,12) *If she was senile.*

(F,12) *The mother was sick.*

(F,12)   *The mother was probably sick.*

(M,14)   *If she's very old.*

Sacrifice was exemplified by the following answers:

(M,12)   *If it was something he didn't want to do.*

(F,12)   *If she gave up playing.*

(M,13)   *If he passes up something he wants to do.*

And voluntary action was expressed as follows:

(M,12)   *He could ask her if she needed help.*

(F,12)   *She does things her mother doesn't ask.*

(F,12)   *She offered to do something without being asked.*

(M,13)   *Doing it willfully.*

(M,13)   *If he offered to do it.*

(F,13)   *She did it without being told.*

These additional data help to sharpen the line of development for child-adult relations. At the beginning of school age, the relation is dominated by reciprocity of complement which expresses unilateral constraint. The method remains dominant for several years. But at around adolescence an innovative idea comes into existence. Young adolescents still see themselves bound to adult constraint but in a new way. They know the terms of the relation but accept them voluntarily. The implication is that young adolescents believe that they have become more the equals of adults. Nevertheless, this understanding of equality is realistically coupled with the fact that adults still expect children to act in complement to their wishes. Young adolescents resolve this mixture by acknowledging their inferior position yet seeing its enactment as a free choice. This shifts the meaning of obedience from naïve obligation to a voluntary selection on their part to abide by the old terms but with a newly found meaning.

Peer Relations.   Sullivan and Piaget propose that as children develop from early school age through young adolescence, the peer relation is reconceptualized along a single course. Equality and direct reciprocity are first enacted in procedures but continually give birth to a heightened interpersonal sensitivity and intimacy. It has already been seen that stories and judgments provide a substantial documentation of this proposal. It is worth inspecting the thesis in more specific terms so that the course of the peer relation can be shown in greater detail. For this purpose, Sullivan's ideas will be inspected for their correspondence with results.

A New Interest in Another Person

Sullivan suggests that between 8 and 10 years of age, children develop a novel interest—a concern for the other peer's well-being. This concern is not evident earlier for peers and does not manifest itself until later with regard to adults. The concern for other, in this age group, is as important as concern for oneself. The point is neatly shown in the following results. Children of about 6 to 8 years said that "sharing candy" or "riding bikes together" was kind and that "hitting" was unkind. A new type of story was presented by 9 to 11 year olds. Kindness took the following form: *When a new student comes in, don't make fun of him. Play with him.* Or, *If they don't have a lunch, share with them.* And unkindness took this form: *Some kids are playing kickball and someone makes an out. The other kids hit him and pick on him. (?) He couldn't help making an out.* One sees in these examples a constancy of the acts of sharing, playing, and hitting. What has changed from 6 to 9 years is the focus from acts as self-defining events to concern for the other peer's physical and emotional well-being.

Sensitivity to what matters to the other.

What matters to school-age children covers a range of human needs and interests. According to results, these multiple possibilities center around a few thematic interests. One is that a child should not be seen as different or as isolated. The other, which is its near complement, is that a child should be seen as similar to or connected to other peers. Sensitivity to these interests requires that they be identified and then acted on.

Being seen as different was a frequent occasion for accounts of peer kindness or unkindness. An example of kindness was, *A bunch of kids are out at the Hot Shoppes... and you don't have any money. They give you some so you can buy a coke or something.* And of unkindness, *My friend and I were going down the street and we saw the Good Humor man. I didn't have any money. She said,*

"Want some ice cream? That's your tough luck." She just got herself some. Kindness with peer isolation was exemplified equally clearly: *One is left out; you go over and talk with her.... Make her feel like somebody likes her.* And unkindness in this situation: *When you're choosing sides, sometimes the captain won't pick a person who's a lousy player.*

Perhaps the core concept is to feel a sense of relatedness with other peers. Apt illustrations are as follows: *Like a new girl ... other people poke fun. You make friends with her.* And in contrast: *Two boys, every recess one would have a lot of friends and they wouldn't let the other boy play.* Further illustrations dealt with emotional relatedness directly. For example, with kindness: *Someone messes up in diagramming. Instead of laughing, she helps out. Help him as an equal and don't look down at him.* And the converse: *If he's in trouble, you could help him get out of it. But you don't talk to him. Leave him there.*

Adjusting one's behavior to the needs of others
Children recognize needs in other peers and immediately accommodate their behavior to the other's needs and thereby acknowledge relationship. Some interesting further examples include the following: *Your best friend is in the back of the line ... you're in front. You give her fronts.* Or, *You're playing and one of them cheats. They argue. The other said,* OK *He let it go. They were friends again.* The countercase is exemplified by failure to adjust to the other's recognized need: *If they don't understand something in school and you understand it. You don't help him. Say you don't have time.* (?) *It's deliberately not helping them; turning them away.*

Intimacy.
As the peer relation develops and each peer discovers the other's personality, there is said to be a merging of the peers into a relational entity. The peers then share with one another their pleasures and their difficulties. There is, in Sullivan's scheme, no need to conceal oneself. Rather there is an openness to present one's most intimate self to another who will understand and show empathy rather than turn away in rejection. Recall that the settings of the studies involved the relatively neutral instructions to give accounts of kindness and unkindness. Niether would obviously induce storytellers to evoke thoughts of intimacy.

Nevertheless, several cases were forthcoming and they serve to illustrate the depth of intimacy which older children sense as essential to the peer relation.

Examples in kindness were: *Jane gets in trouble with her parents. Jill tries to comfort her . . . gives her advice.* Or, *He's a loner. . . . Help him to make friendships [and] learn to get along.* And, *I sort of got in trouble and sort of blamed it on my friend. He would let it stay.* With respect to unkindness, the following stories illustrate the point. *This person, a really good friend, knows her friend is really bad in school or has a problem in the house. This boy or girl would be unkind by not caring about the person . . . just ignoring her.* Or, *A girl is not liked by anyone in class. No one would play with her. You make no effort to let them know you want to be friends. Go along with everyone else. Make her feel awful.*

Conclusions   Sullivan and Piaget propose that children grow up simultaneously experiencing two social worlds of relations. In one, children look to adults who are thought to possess knowledge of the social order. Adults therefore have unilateral rights to tell children what to do and to evaluate children's behavior. Children, respecting adults' power and knowledge, try to understand the order in adults' minds and work to gain adults' approval. The present studies tap into this world as children begin school. Six to 8 year olds seem to substantiate Sullivan's and Piaget's description fully. Conformity to adults is the overriding theme found in results. But so is the risk which Sullivan and Piaget describe. The conformity-approval arrangement seems to keep the minds and interests of child and adult apart. It also separates them as persons by preventing them from recognizing that adults are individuals and not just authority figures. Only at about adolescence is this arrangement consciously understood. However, at this point, a change takes place. Adults come to be seen as persons with assets and shortcomings. And children come to see themselves as potentially in positions similar to adults. The relation then takes on a new form of bilaterality in which young adolescents see themselves as equals in some ways to adults.

The development just described is marked by a sharp transformation. The relation seems to be moving apace in the direction of stabilized unilaterality, but then takes a sharp turn near the adolescent area. The newfound reciprocity and equality between child and adult are in one sense a novel creation. On the other hand, they are not new at all. The very terms which are newly acquired are already well known to children. They have been developing within the second world, that of peer relations and may in fact come directly from this world.

The world of peer relations appears to have a straight developmental course. It starts with the method based on pragmatic practice of equality and direct reciprocity. These constitutive rules of interaction are then converted into principles of cooperation. Meanwhile the construction of persons as individuals is added. And eventually there is a consciousness of the relation and how interactions may serve to sustain it. Instead of keeping minds apart, practice of the peer relation brings children closer together. Children come to see one another's individuality. They also see the need to cooperate in attending to one another's strengths and weaknesses. Needs, interests, concerns, and even emotional states become occasions for expressions of mutual understanding. Instead of concealing themselves, peers present themselves openly with the assurance that the other person in the relation will be accepting in a sensitive and sympathetic manner. This assurance no doubt comes from the fact that peers together have constructed the principles of their relation. Thus, as persons who abide by the relation itself, both peers can be secure in their own worthwhileness while respecting and being respected by the other.

In summary, it may be concluded the results of studies 1 to 7 have helped to clarify major points of the Sullivan-Piaget thesis. The technique of having children generate or judge accounts of interactions yielded clear evidence for two reciprocal methods. Children's parts in interactions were complementary to adults' parts. Children's parts in interactions with peers were directly reciprocal and symmetrical to the parts taken by peers. These two methods help to illustrate the structure of relations. Complementariness gives way to unilateral constraint and authority in relations with adults. This form of relation is established by the beginning of school age and is maintained until about entry into adolescence. Functional products of this structure are seen in the absence of qualifications regarding persons and the immediate correction of deviations from the method, tolerance of punishment, and readiness to conform. "Figures" give way to individual personhood once this structure is transformed into a more symmetrical relation. Thereafter, adults are recognized as having deficiencies, and children are seen as having a choice in their dealings with adults.

While the relation of unilateral authority is being lived out, children are simultaneously experiencing interactions with their peers. Near the start of school age, peer relations are tentative because they are constituted by the practice of direct reciprocity which yields uncertain results. Children know that, when one shares, the other is free to share, and they also know that, when one is unkind, the other is free to return the unkindness. A definite structure is established at around 9 to 11 years of age when direct reciprocity is reconstituted into the principle of cooperation and used to serve the principle of equality. Functional products follow with a clear recognition of individual personhood and the several components of mutuality which include criteria of worth and intimacy with all that they imply.

Results in no way provide proof for the thesis. There are alternative ways of viewing the findings and giving them theoretical organization. Nevertheless, the consistency of the data from study to study may be taken as illustrating Sullivan's and Piaget's insights in more than a passing fashion. Methods of reciprocity and themes of relations were not guided by the open-ended interviews. They were freely generated by children and agreed upon by each independent sample. The congruence within age levels which held up across studies was matched by the sturdiness of differences among the levels. It is evident that the thesis is pertinent to interpersonal existence as children understand it and helps to uncover the nature of development in two basic relations. What remains to be seen is whether the thesis can be further clarified when children's concepts of friendship are inspected as a means of documenting more carefully the development of cooperative relations. For this question, additional results are presented in the next three chapters.

Nine   Children's Definitions of Friendship

Results of studies 1 through 7 help to bring the Sullivan-Piaget thesis to life. The 500 children who were interviewed seem to divide social reality into two forms of existence. Adult-child interactions imply a relation of authority while peer relations imply mutuality of interest and concern between persons who think and feel alike. In this and the next three chapters, studies are reported which were designed to look more closely at the development of children's understanding of peer relations. Specifically, focus was on *friendship* as that special case where peers are presumed to achieve the highest sense of mutual, interpersonal understanding. Before study 8 is presented, relevant parts of the thesis are summarized in order to provide a context for the empirical findings.

Sullivan on Friendship   Sullivan proposes that friendship contributes to the child's social development in two important ways. First, it broadens the child's understanding of social reality by providing new possibilities for social exchange. Secondly, it expands the child's self-understanding by providing a sense of mutuality with others. According to Sullivan, before entering school children have learned to get along in the restricted milieu of family and neighborhood. They have mastered the dos and don'ts which apply to the few people they know. Although this is a significant achievement, it leaves children with a parochial view of reality, since they do not realize that their viewpoint is but a lim-

168

ited slice of society at large. In addition, children tend to think of themselves as special individuals. They are aware of their achievement in mastering procedures which allow them to function well with others, and they see themselves as the focus of adults' concern. Thus, upon entering school, children feel confident that they understand social reality, and that they are special individuals in the minds of others.

For Sullivan, peer experiences and, in particular, friendship experiences provide essential correctives to these illusions. In the first place, the child's view of reality is expanded as a necessary consequence of participation in free, reciprocal exchanges with friends. Neither friend has absolute 'say.' One child's version of reality can be and often is countered by another's version. Through dispute, discussion, and compromise, children discover the value of collaboration, and with this come new ideas which neither child alone previously saw. Simultaneously, friendship provides the means for the child to transcend his or her sense of uniqueness. In the 'two-group' which friends experience, children come to recognize their commonality with one another. This realization was not possible with adults, who children viewed as all-knowing and all-powerful figures. Sullivan summarizes the point concisely:

> I would hope that preadolescent relationships were intense enough for each of the two chums to get to know practically everything about the other one that could possibly be exposed in an intimate relationship, because that remedies a good deal of the often illusory, usually morbid, feeling of being different, which is such a striking part of rationalizations of insecurity in later life. [P. 256]

Sullivan was aware that this proposal ran counter to the mainstream of thinking, which holds that parent-child rather than child-child relations provide the child with a fundamental understanding of self and others. He said, "It is self-evident . . . that I am conspicuously taking exception to the all-too-prevalent idea that things are pretty well fixed in the Jesuitical first seven years" (p. 248). He pointed out, however, that his perspective was not a matter of personal taste so much as a conclusion forced by the experiences his clients brought to him. Hence, he argued that friendship should be seen for its positive place in social development and that, given the nature of the child-adult bond, friendship is truly a socially curative and healing relation. It provides children with a new perspective which is necessary for further progress in social development.

It has already been seen in chapter 1 that Sullivan assigns numerous positive functions to friendship, particularly during that period spanning the beginning of school up through early adolescence. It is "the actual time for becoming social" (p. 227) and is "marked by the appearance of a new interest in another person" (p. 245). It is when the other person "becomes of practically equal importance in all fields of value" (p. 245) and the self "begins to develop a real sensitivity to what matters to another person" (p. 245). The self starts to ask, what should I do "to contribute to the happiness [and] to support the prestige and worth-whileness of my chum" (p. 245). The *we*—the sense of commonality and empathy with others—develops from the collaborating self and other who discover in the process the necessity for consensual validation (p. 246). In practice, peers learn how to adjust their own behavior to each other's expressed needs, (p. 246) and as the relation continues to develop, friends find themselves involved "in the pursuit of increasingly identical and, more and more mutual, satisfactions and in the maintenance of increasingly similar security operations" (p. 246).

The Self in Friendship If Sullivan were approached without a clear reminder of his relational outlook, his developmental prospectus might seem misdirected. In many theories, the focus is on children's discovery of 'self', that unique composite of individual characteristics which separates one person from another. Sullivan definitely is arguing the opposite, with an emphasis on the need to find sameness between self and other and on the merging of identities. However, the two approaches can be reconciled if Sullivan is understood to be saying that children discover themselves through relations with other persons. The relational self is not an objective entity. Its definition does not begin with a pre-existing individual but starts with knowledge of a relation. Working with adults and friends, children create characteristics which give the self definition and construct values for evaluating themselves and others. The process is individual, insofar as each child must participate in construction, and it is social, because the work is done jointly.

The product of friendship is a self clearly located within a jointly constructed system of meaning. The consensus on which the system is built does not diminish any child's individuality. Each child remains a person with distinction. But simultaneously for each child there exist others who are similar as well as different along those dimensions by which the self is defined. A relation such as friendship provides a necessary frame of reference without which individuals would scatter in diverse directions and be able only to glimpse any other individual. Friendship provides the social glue which makes societal functioning for mutual benefit possible.

Sullivan offers two examples which help to show how the self-concept is sustained, rather than erased, through relations. The first example involves competition, which in traditional theory epitomizes the self as an independent entity. Competition involves, among other things, individual expression of one's talents in order to assert the self over someone else. Sullivan sees the friendship 'two-group' as teaching one how to use one's talents in socially productive ways. Any friend is liable to be related to a more talented friend as children acquire more friendships and participate in more areas of social life. Through intimate relations children "discover that if they are lucky enough to have gifts, these gifts carry responsibilities; and that insofar as gifts are used for the discharge of social responsibilities, one is to a certain extent spared the great evil of envy" (p. 255). It is necessary to remember only that friendship operates by reciprocity in order to see that self-interest and the interest of another are relationally compatible and not necessarily competitive.

The second example involves loneliness. To feel apart is neither positive nor negative in itself. But once the possibility of relatedness is seen, to feel cutoff or excluded can cause anxiety. Thus, Sullivan reserves loneliness for preadolescence, after children have discovered friendship. It then becomes a feeling of being apart from others, which induces tension and compels the child to seek companionship with another. To be recognized, to be needed by another is a relief which, if not experienced, denies the child a sense of personhood (pp. 261–62).

Piaget on Friendship   Piaget suggests that young children's experiences with adults lead to a belief that all situations will be dominated by rules. This is true even when children enter games with other children. Young children state that there are rules and that the rules have always existed, being passed from adult to adult, and from adult to child. This belief is carried into peer relations, but undergoes transformation when peers interact with one another. Piaget emphasizes that peers operate on equal footing so that the weight of one's opinion does not overwhelm the opinion of another. Through reciprocal presentation of opinions, peers soon learn that rules do not simply preexist but can be constructed through discussion and compromise.

Piaget's focus is not on the content of rules that children make, but on the procedures which they adopt as their modus operandi. From the naïve practice of reciprocity as equals, peers arrive at what Piaget believes to be universal, social-psychological results: the norms of equality and cooperative reciprocity. He sees these norms as the means by which children move out of the subjective realm of thought, which child-adult relations have placed them in, toward rational, objective thought (p. 104).

This conclusion and the line of reasoning leading to it are similar to those put forth by Sullivan. It is in taking their ideas of social reality to peers that children come out of their narrow-minded world view into the realm of possible other worlds. Going to new authorities cannot have the same effect since it carries the risk for the child of being left with only a subjective understanding of ideas. In contrast, the exchange of ideas through discussion and continuing compromise allows peers to construct new ideas which are mutually validated and, therefore, nonsubjective (pp. 93–95).

Piaget uses the term *cooperative relation* for friendship. His discussion of friendship considers both the relation and the self within it. The relation is described as one of increasing solidarity which Piaget attributes to the collaborative construction process. As peers practice and become conscious of the procedures on which they agree, they advance in a sense of solidarity of "we-ness." In turn, "a rule becomes the necessary condition for agreement [and] the fairest rule . . . is that which unites the opinions of the [peers]" (p. 71). The practice leads to the relation, which reinforces the practice, which unites its members.

As to the self, Piaget contrasts the "ego" with the "personality" (p. 96). The personality is established through the norms which peers construct and is sustained by respect for the self and other who adhere to these norms. These cannot be just any norms which two persons agree to, but are specifically the norms of cooperative reciprocity and equality, which can be applied to any relation. While mutual control may derive from a few instances of friendship, as a principle it extends to other peers and persons in general. It insures justice or fairness on a societal scale because ultimately it entitles all persons to equal treatment.

Mutuality is the theme which permeates friendship. It comes from the very process by which friends interact and construct rules and ideas. Friends can, of course, disagree, because they are individuals. But even with differences friends can reach mutual understanding. They can follow each other's reasoning and respect divergent opinions. This allows them to maintain their sense of solidarity and still appreciate one another's individual personalities.

Piaget introduces the notion of *equity* in accounting for the self in a friendship relation. At the point of entrance to adolescence, children understand equality as a principle. They apply it, however, not in an absolute way but by taking account of the individual person and the situation at hand (p. 317). Young adolescents take "into account extenuating circumstances . . . and personal circumstances" (p. 317). Instead of a legalistic attitude, young adolescents have learned to balance norms of friendship with the individuals in it.

In summary, Piaget sees friendship as beginning in the naïve practice of reciprocity and equality. Children treat methods and procedures as rules. Subsequently, the rules are reconstituted into conceptions of relation and become norms or principles. A system of meaning develops which allows children to define and identify individuals as personalities who adhere to this system. The system is a mutual construction, and functioning within it engenders respect and solidarity. At the same time, the individual personality is recognized and reconciled through the concept of equity. This personality is not a free-floating ego, but a member of a relation belonging to this system. "With children . . . there exist two psychological types of social equilibrium—a type based on constraint . . . which excludes both equality and 'organic' solidarity . . . and a type based on cooperation and resting on equality and solidarity" (p. 320).

With the foregoing as a framework, it is now possible to approach empirical findings on children's conceptions of friendship seeking clarification for Sullivan's and Piaget's perspectives.

Study 8: Children's Definitions of Friends   One hundred twenty-seven children were interviewed, 41 between 6 and 8 of years age, 45 between 9 and 11 years, and 41 between 12 and 14 years. About half of the children from each age level had also participated in studies 1 and 4. The other half constituted a new sample of a similar socioeconomic makeup and also came from a parochial school. All children were asked to define friendship. They were asked several questions: "What is a friend?" or "What is the difference between a friend and not a friend?" or "What is a best friend?" These various instructions were necessary, since not all children reacted in articulate ways to the first question. As in previous studies, the four interviewers asked children to elaborate on their answers posing such questions as: "Can you tell more more?" or "What do you mean by [e.g.] loyalty?"

Children's definitions are now presented as representations of major points in Sullivan's and Piaget's analysis. Most definitions fit one or another of these points and some fit several of them. Since various children emphasized one or another aspect of their ideas on friendship, the data were not placed into strict categories according to age. In general, younger children gave definitions in terms of methods and procedures, equivalent to the unqualified stories observed earlier. After age 9, definitions took a new turn. Children brought in explicit statements of equality, equity, solidarity, reciprocity, or mutual respect and understanding. At the end of the chapter, general age trends will be summarized in quantitative terms.

Playing and Sharing   Children in the 6 to 8-year-old range concentrated on two procedures to describe peer interactions. These are now familiar through the same-age children's accounts of kindness. Children said that friends are peers who play together and share things. Those children who defined "best" friends did so mainly by saying that best friends play together *all of the time* and share *everything*. These definitions thus distinguished "just" a friend from "best" friend in quantitative terms reflecting the frequency with which certain procedures were practiced.

The rule "to play" was expressed in the following examples:

(M,6)   *They play with you.*

(M,6)   *Somebody that likes you. (?) You play with him.*

(F,6)   *He lets me play soccer with him.*

(F,6)   *It means they like to play with you.*

(M,7)   *A next-door neighbor you play with.*

(M,7)   *He likes me and he comes to my house all the time. We go swimming in his pool.*

(F,7)   *Someone who likes you. (?) Play with them.*

(F,7)   *Play with them. (?) Invite you to a party.*

(M,8)   *When they play a lot together.*

(F,8)   *A friend is a person who I play with.*

The rule "to share" was expressed by the following children:

(M,6)   *They always say yes when I want to borrow their eraser.*

(F,7)   *Play with them and give them stuff.*

(M,7)   *He gave them a lot of stuff and likes you.*

(F,7)   *Like them. Give them something they really like.*

Adjustment to Need   In Sullivan's proposal, one function of friendship is to teach children to be sensitive to the needs of other persons. Children learn to subjugate their own personal interests of the moment to the needs of another. An adjustment is made so that another's need is met and the person is relieved of trouble. Piaget makes a similar proposal with the idea of equity. Friends see themselves and each other as equals. But circumstances often cause an imbalance which places one of the friends in an inferior position. At that moment, the less fortunate friend cannot interact as an equal. If the principle of equality is to be sustained, the better-off friend must make an adjustment of personal interest and initiate some action toward the friend in need.

Were the principle of equality an absolute, the better-off friend could ignore a friend in need and simply move on to interact with other peers who are capable of acting as his or her equal. At the moment the other friend is in need, he or she is incapable of reciprocating and there can be no immediate payoff to the actor. But if the relation is ongoing as a conception, stopping what one is doing or giving up what one has cannot be considered losses. They become instead investments in the relation and serve to sustain it.

Results for kindness and unkindness have already shown that, after about 9 years of age, children become sensitive to needs of peers. They are especially attuned to inequalities which differentiate peers into better and less well-off states. Need and inequality were conditions spontaneously introduced by most children as qualifying conditions for actions. This no doubt indicates an awareness of the individuality of persons. One friend may be in need now or one friend may be inferior in a particular domain. Later, however, the friend may be in a position to assist and the actor may be in a state of need. Or, another domain may become relevant, in which case the present recipient might be more talented and better off than the actor.

Needs and inequalities abound in children's societies, and the question immediately arises as to whom are peers responsible. This is when friendship takes on significance. Practically speaking, a child cannot be expected to attend to everyone's needs. Equal treatment may be a general principle, but the facts of social life demand its selective application. It is possible then that friendship solves the child's problem. One is responsible to peers but expected to act overtly with regard to friends. The two-group, in Sullivan's terms, is the sphere to which friends are committed. Need or inequality within it demand attention and action. This would explain why acts of omission were considered unkind in studies 4, 5, and 7. If need or inequality were ignored, the very principle which makes for the relation would be undermined. Continual ignoring would then eventually lead to the dissolution of the relation.

The definitions culled from the present study appear to represent the above-mentioned aspects of friendship. In each instance, the child offering a version of friendship chose to focus on one friend's sensitivity to the other friend's need as a way of emphasizing that inequality is a condition which must be attended to in a friendship. Examples are reported below.

Physical or material welfare   Four definitions focused on the recipient's welfare.

(M,7)   *He's a person who helps you. Like if I fall down, he helps me.*

(M,10)   *Someone you play with. If you need heep, like you're hurt, he'll help you or get you help.*

(F,10)   *If you're hurt, they come over and visit.*

(F,11)   *Someone who is nice to me. Like when I was sick, she brought me flowers.*

The last two samples begin with a physical need, but describe help which indicates response to a psychological need. The visit and the gift do not repair the physical deficiency but are obvious signs of concern.

School   Four children stressed that friends helped one another with schoolwork when one of them needed assistance.

(M,7)   *A friend means that they like you and want to help you. Sometimes when you have homework and don't know what the instructions are, they tell you the instructions.*

(F,9)   *Help someone out. If the person is stuck, show them the answer but tell them why it's the answer.*

(M,11)   *[Someone] who'll do things for you; help you when you can't understand something.*

(F,12)   *Caring about them. (?) If somebody falls, helping them. If they don't know certain problems with homework, you help them.*

These definitions are reminiscent of other children's stories about peer kindness in the specification of the need to do well in school which can be attended to by a peer who is more academically capable.

General help   Six children gave definitions which referred to a type of general assistance friends provided.

(M,8)   *A person who you like the best and who reminds you and helps you . . . . He reminds me of what we're suppoesd to do when we get back from gym.*

(F,9)   *Being nice to each other. If something happened to you, they's run over to help you.*

(M,11)   *Somebody you like. (?) Someone you can depend on. Like if you wanted him to do something for you that you couldn't do, he would do it.*

(F,11)   *Someone who really cares about you and doesn't want to betray you . . . a person who would want to help me out if I was in trouble; just to help out when you need his help.*

(M,13)   *If he has a problem, he helps him out.*

(F,13)   *Help you with your problems. Very loyal to you. (?) They're not turning to somebody else.*

Loneliness and exclusion   Five children focused on the problem of loneliness as a state of need which friends attended to and remedied by offering to be with you when you are down are alone.

(F,7)   *Someone who comes to you to help them. (?) If you see someone doesn't have people to play with, then you go try to be friends with her. You may like someone else more but she may have friends to play with so the girl who is alone needs it.*

(F,9)   *Somebody that plays with you when you don't have anybody else to play with.*

(F,9)   *When you're lonely she plays with you. You go places and do things with them.*

(M,9)   *You're lonely and your friend on a bike joins you. You feel a lot better because he joined you.*

(M,13)   *Somebody who could help you and stay with you when you're in trouble. Plays with you when there's nobody else around.*

Shared feelings   Seven children described friendship with situations in which one friend needed to share an emotional state with someone else. Stress seems to be placed on reliance; the friend will not ignore your state but stays with you because you need companionship and support in times of doubt or trouble.

(M,9) *We mess around. He agrees with you. If you get in trouble, he won't say you did it but stays with you.*

(M,10) *Someone who sticks up for you. Someone you can trust.*

(M,12) *A person who will help you, like if you have problems. Depend on you and won't leave you if you get in trouble . . . tries to console you if you have problems. Tries to relieve you of some of your problems.*

(M,13) *They help you. Like if you're sad, they'll help you feel better.*

(M,13) *He's there when you're down to get you up. Have happy times together.*

(M,13) *When you need help, he helps you. . . . Never turns you down. If another person picks on you, he comes and helps you, if the other one is bigger or smaller. Never runs away and leaves you.*

(F,14) *A person that would always be around whenever you needed them and you always could talk to them.*

Establishment of
Principles of
Friendship

The stories so far reported correspond to accounts of kindness observed in earlier studies about peers. Younger children describe friendship with unqualified procedures of playing and sharing. After about 9 years, two changes occur. Accounts become qualified by need, and the content of interest expands across several dimensions of importance, from physical well-being to emotional troubles. The remaining stories to be reported are not so simple in that they go beyond descriptions of attending to another's state of need. These stories or definitions bring out the mutual nature of friendship with emphasis on the symmetrical character of the relation. The categories are: cooperative reciprocity, equality, trust, and mutual understanding. The last category is composed of at least three subclasses: self-revealment, working out problems, and being understood. These categories are not totally independent of one another. Individual definitions show emphasis on a major characteristic but also include reference to other characteristics, and therefore, there is overlap between and among categories.

Cooperative reciprocity   The following definitions provide clear reference to the symmetry which children understand as a principle of friendship. Whatever one does for the other, the other friend is said to do also for the one.

(M,7)   *They're nice. If I forgot my lunch, they share with me. And I like someone and he forgets, I share with them.*

(M,9)   *A person who helps you do things. When you need something, they get it. You do the same for them.*

(F,9)   *She lets you have things she doesn't want and I give her things I have.*

(M,9)   *When I had problems, he helped me. And when he had problems, I helped him.*

(M,10)   *You exchange kindness for a long time, not just for a day.*

(F,10)   *Somebody you can keep your secrets together. Two people who are really good to each other.*

(M,11)   *They like each other very much. (?) If you're playing a game and you hit on the ball and they say you didn't, and they all agree on it . . . even if they did or didn't. There won't be a big argument.*

(F,12)   *Someone you like. Someone you can depend on. (?) Well, if you're in trouble or if you need help, they can help you out . . . . They tell you their secrets and you tell them yours and you talk about things you wouldn't tell other people.*

(M,14)   *He's always interested in what you're interested in and vice versa . . . his interests are like mine. I'll give in to him and he'll give in to me.*

One can note a change in tone with increasing age. Younger children tended to deal with more concrete problems while older children put stress on interests and emotions. The latter represent clearer cases of mutual adjustment whereby each friend takes on the other's concern, holding their own in abeyance in the process.

Equality   These definitions illustrate the belief that friends are persons who share a common outlook, even to the degree of having a similar personality. This category was not used by younger children at all.

(M,11)   *They would have the same personalities and like the same things. Someone you can talk to and they won't always make fun of you.*

(F,12)   *Both agree on the same things. You like their personality. Because you have the same ideas, you can talk more freely.*

(M,13)   *Someone who knows you and wants to be equal to you. Helps you when you're in trouble and wants to come and talk about your problems.*

(F,13)   *They'll understand your problems. They won't always be the boss. Sometimes they'll let you decide; they'll take turns. If you did something wrong, they'll share the responsibility.*

(F,13)   *Somebody you look up to (?) They think the same feelings I do. About equal to me in gym and other things.*

(M,13)   *These guys are friends because they have the same personalities. Someone who will give in but you can do what he wants. He'll do what you want. He'll give in for you and you'll give in for him.*

(M,13)   *They would believe in the same things and they would value the same things.*

(M,14)   *They have something in common. You hang around with him. (?) We're more or less the same; the same personalities.*

Again the theme of adjustment comes out in these definitions. Stress is put on the process of "giving in" or checking one's own interest for the sake of the other. And giving in is obviously seen to work in both directions; it is symmetrical.

Trust   The following definitions highlight the characteristic of trust or dependability. In most of the instances, trust contained the additional meaning of being seen as entailing risk. The risk followed from the fact that a friend made a self-revealing statement. Additionally, there was the hope that the recipient would hold the information as privileged.

(M,11)   *He's dependable. (?) He keeps a promise. He does what he says.*

(F,11)   *Someone you know and like and trust. (?) A true friend is someone you can tell everything. They're not going to tell.*

(F,12)   *Someone you can trust. (?) If you tell them a secret, they wouldn't tell.*

(F,13)   *Somebody you can trust. Know what they're like and can help you with their problems.*

(F,13)   *Somebody you can trust. You can tell them things and won't expect them to tell everybody else.*

(F,14)   *They are open and care for people. (?) You can trust them more and they are more your type.*

(F,13)   *A person you always trust and who will help you when you need it. You can tell her everything. You know she won't tell anybody anything. You just do everything with her.*

Mutual understanding   The foregoing statements of trust imply mutual understanding in the sense that one friend tells another something that is meant to be understood by that friend and no one else. Mutual understanding is further evident in the following definitions in which the two-group is given special status as the means within which one can be understood clearly and can understand another uniquely.

Self-revealment. A subset of children described friendship in terms of providing opportunities to reveal your true self to another person and for that person to make reciprocal self-revelations.

(M,11)   *A person you can talk to—you know, show your feelings. You can talk to him and he'll—you can trust him—he'll talk to you. Like I can trust him.*

(F,11)   *Someone you can talk to and tell your problems and she can tell you her problems—and they can trust you that you won't tell anybody.*

(F,11)   *A person you can really tell your feelings to. When you're lonely, you'll always have a friend to tell your problems. (?) I know her so much that I can do anything with her.*

(M,12)   *A person you can trust and confide in. Tell them what you feel and you can be yourself with them.*

(F,12)   *Someone you like. Someone you can depend on. (?) Well, if you're in trouble or if you need help, they can help you out . . . . They tell you their secrets and you tell them yours and you talk about things you wouldn't tell other people.*

Working out problems. A special version of mutual understanding was manifested in definitions where children said that friends would be able to face problems together and find solutions through discussion. These definitions perforce include statements also about self-revealment.

(M,12)   *Sharing interests with them. A friend helps you out in time of need and talks problems out with you.*

(F,12)   *Someone who can help you in time of need. (?) You know*
          each other good and talk things out.

(M,13)   *Hangs around with you. (?) He would just listen to you and*
          you would listen to him. If he had a problem, maybe the two
          of you could come to a conclusion on what you could do.

(F,14)   *A person you can lean on when you need help . . . she'll help*
          you understand how you feel and give advice.

(F,14)   *Someone you can talk to. They're even closer to you than*
          a brother or sister. . . . They can tell you what's wrong and
          what's right in a way. You sort of think things out with them.

Understanding and being understood. Definitions which
stressed that friends understand each other follow:

(M,12)   *A friend is someone you can trust. (?) If you kind of had a*
          problem, you'd tell them. (?) You got to know them and they'd
          have to know you.

(F,12)   *Always listen when you have problems. Stick up for you. A*
          friend always understands your problems because they go
          through the same experiences. Even if they can't help, they
          sympathize.

(F,13)   *Someone you can share things with and who shares things with*
          you. Not material things. Feelings. When you feel sad, she feels
          sad. They understand you.

(F,14)   *Someone you can depend on; share your feelings. She under-*
          stands you and knows how you feel.

(F,14)   *Just like a person who you can talk to all the time who will listen*
          and tell you their problems.

(F,14)   *Friendship . . . being able to understand somebody. Helping*
          them when they need it and not brushing them off. (?) If you
          tell someone something, they won't use it to get revenge on you
          when you get in a fight.

A further subset of definitions extend the theme of
mutual understanding further. They address the issue of
being understood by contrasting friendship with other
relations in which, presumably, there is less likelihood of
mutual understanding between the child and other
persons.

(F,13)   *Friends try not to hurt you or embarrass you. They understand*
          you more than other people do.

(F,13)   *A person I trust, have faith in. If I have a problem, I can go to them. I would probably go to my friend more than I could go to my parents because they might understand it more than my parents.*

(M,14)   *When you have a problem, you can tell that friend and talk it over with him and he'll understand. Sometimes . . . you can't tell your parents, then you can go to your friend and he would know what to say.*

(M,14)   *Somebody you can talk to and share your problems with. Like you can't talk to your parents because they have a one-track mind.*

Quantitative Summary of Study 8

There were 47 definitions which stressed sharing and playing in unqualified descriptions. Of these, 34 were given by children in the 6 to 8-year-old group. There were 30 definitions in which assistance was predicated on need. Only 5 of these were produced by children in the youngest group. The remainder of the definitions, almost all coming from children older than 9 years, emphasized principles of cooperation and equality or described functional outcomes of friendship in terms of trust and mutual understanding.

Conclusions

At the 6 to 8-year-level definitions of friendship were indistinguishable from descriptions of kindness between peers. Friends share, play together, and help one another. Apparently, friendship, like kindness, represents the positive side of direct reciprocity by which peers are nice rather than mean or hostile. The relation of friendship is nearly the same as that in interactions in which peers are "friendly." These definitions give no indication of lasting relation nor any sign that the persons who enact these procedures are individuals with enduring personalities. From age 9 onward, friendship takes on new meaning. Personhood is now evident. As before, individuals are shown to differ by talent as well as momentary states. In addition, differences between individuals are coupled with recognition that friends share like interests and share characteristics which children call "personality." These two points are put together as friends are seen to be interested in each other's welfare. They attend to one another's problems and emotional welfare and are prepared to help because they understand needs through their shared personality.

The change with age appears to reflect a continuity with a qualitative advance. Whereas, younger children focus on the enactment of reciprocal procedures and equality, older children are able to address the same points as principles. Direct reciprocity can now be "depended on", having helped a friend, the actor can count on the friend to help him should circumstances warrant. Equality no longer refers to symmetry of action; friends "want to be" equals. Dependability is further articulated by "trust" and equality by the fact that one is "really" oneself in the presence of a friend who thinks and feels "practically like I do." There is a building of mutuality so that one is assured of the other's understanding even to the extent of sharing blame and responsibility. It is clear just how far the naïve practice of reciprocity has gone during the period from 6 years to early adolescence when the *we* of the adolescents' definitions is taken in its full sense. Adolescents describe friends as almost wholly dependent on one another in time of trouble as well as in moments when the self is most truly itself.

The curative potential of friendship as Sullivan views it can readily be seen from children's viewpoints. As adolescents, children have progressed out of the enclosed society they knew when they first left family and entered school. Through friendship, children have learned how to admit their weaknesses, present their ideas and feelings openly, and "talk things out" together. Adolescents are aware that exposure carries risks such as being "brushed off" and "laughed at." Yet they believe that friendship insures against these negative consequences. This would be an empty belief save for for the gains it might bring. Thus, adolescents say that friends will help them understand "how they feel" and give advice and validation so that the self can be relieved of doubt and uncertainty. If children enter the school age with false senses of self and society, they enter adolescence with a radically new posture. Adolescents can more realistically see their own weak and strong points and realize that others have assets and shortcomings too. Focus is not on taking advantage of one's strengths or competing to promote the self at the expense of another's weakness. Friends work together to enhance one another through interactions which preserve their relation.

From Piaget's perspective, friendship should function to create a sense of solidarity and mutual understanding. Results illustrate that both appear as products of the earlier naïve practice of direct reciprocity. Solidarity was represented by several of the definitions especially those emphasizing trust, taking blame, and giving in. The focus seems to put increasing burden on the stability of the two-group as more privileged information is put in and both friends become relied on to protect one another and themselves. Mutual understanding at its core means that another person understands the self in the same terms that self understands self. This idea was most frequently articulated in adolescents' statements. They were sure that they could take problems to a friend who would "know what to do" and grasp the self's feelings fully. No doubt this level of mutual understanding is derived from a continuing process of revealment and a going back and forth. With continued exposure of this sort, friends come to know each other at a depth that even "brothers, sisters, mothers, and fathers" may not achieve in the minds of adolescents.

It is apparent that the years 9 to 14 are by no means a time of psychological dormancy. Rather, it is a time when the method of direct reciprocity is seen as problematical and is converted into the principled practice of cooperation. The child identifies individual personhood and perceives similarities between personalities. These new perceptions are then reconciled within the principle of equal treatment. It is this principle and its accompanying abilities that appear to provide the structure of friendship that, in turn, enables the relation proper to take effect. The relation's functional products then appear in rapid succession. By adjusting to another's needs, friends experience the other's adjustment to them. Friends then find the value of seeking order together. In the process they learn how to expose themselves, to remain open to the other's ideas, and to figure out reality together. Gradually friends build a common viewpoint which is the framework for mutual understanding. The "I and You" of earlier eras has by early adolescence become definitely articulated into a *we* at which point one's individual motives, interests, feelings, and the like are meshed with the other's and the two become symmetrical parts of the unifying relation. That is why adolescents can say that they are most like themselves when they are feeling at one with their friends. The following elaborate definition was provided by a 14-year-old female: *Friendship is being able to do what you want, feel comfortable about what you're doing, and having fun doing it, with someone else . . . . It's being able to tell someone your problems and not get laughed at. Instead they try and solve their problems with you . . . . Friendship is never putting on a show or false personality, but knowing you're accepted as you are.*

Ten   The Natural Histories of Friendships

The results of studies, described thus far, point to an interesting possibility. Up to about age 9, younger children seem to identify friendship with momentary interactions. When peers are practicing direct reciprocity through positive interactions, they are friends. When, in contrast, reciprocity is practiced negatively, they are not friends. For older children, and especially young adolescents, friendship is a more enduring relation. For example, in study 7 it was seen that untoward exchanges did not end a friendship but could be overcome through appropriate remedies. In study 8, it was found that with increasing age friendship becomes more than an enactment of particular procedures. Friends have personalities which endure, and in their relations with one another, friends accumulate knowledge of each other and develop attachments which are as deep as the sensing of self through other. This suggests that at some time during the span under study, children develop a clear conception of the structure of friendship and come to know the relation as a continuing form of interpersonal existence.

The present chapter examines concepts of friendship from this perspective. In a typical child's life, there are probably numerous friendships whose natural histories contribute to children's knowledge of the relationship. For example, the definitions obtained in the previous chapter probably reflect experiences with one or more friends. If the foregoing results are representative, then one might expect that older children who understand the structure of the relation will be articulate about the dynamic process which friendship entails. They should be able to differentiate important moments within a friendship—how a friendship is started or how it comes to a natural end. Further, older children should be able to describe how these aspects of friendship are coordinated in terms of the themes observed in the preceding chapter.

Study 9 is an attempt to capitalize on children's life experiences and therefore to bring definitions of friendship, which tend toward the ideal, more in line with reality. In practical functioning, friendship is not so much a stable entity as a goal which is being pursued. Children have to work to get a friendship started. Once it is established, they have to work to keep it going. Effort is needed if only because circumstances of events and other peers continually intrude on and tend to change the relation. To move on to a best or close friendship, the friends have to attend to one another and keep in mind the direction in which they want to go. And despite these efforts, we know that in most instances a friendship will not last. Eventually, the friends will move apart and their relation will change so that they become less attentive to one another and hardly have contact.

Sullivan gives only general attention to the internal dynamics of friendship. He emphasizes the unidirectional and cumulative effects which accrue from continuing within a two-group. Friends, who stay together long enough, grow in their sense of mutual understanding and progress in their concern for intimacy. This view, however, represents friendship only partially. Children who partake of everyday social life must learn that friendships break up as well as grow. And they must learn that termination occurs even in the face of effort not to lose the friendship.

Piaget touches more on the dynamic process of friendship. In several sections of his 1932 study (1965), he points out how children come to understand interpersonal interactions as a means to an end, the end being maintenance of relations. He offers a general model of the following sort. In any relation, circumstances bring moments of difficulty. For instance, an adult or a group of peers might pressure one friend to take sides against another friend. What the friend then does at the moment can be seen in two lights. His or her action might interrupt the relation; for example, the one friend might side against the other. This act not only harms the friend, who is left on his or her own, but it may harm the relation. If the children are to remain friends, further interactions will have to be performed to undo the previous act and to reestablish the broken bond.

The results now reported do in fact add to the definitions already obtained. They show that children have a practical sense about the relation and that this sense changes developmentally. The particular findings support quite well the general trends observed previously. The younger the child, the more likely friendship will be equated with procedures of playing and sharing. When these procedures are not enacted, the relation will go out of existence. In contrast, the older the child, the more likely single interactions will be subjugated to the recognition that friendship is based on interpersonal similarities which are coupled with individual differences through the principle of equality. In sum, it will be shown that younger and older children propose quite different accounts of how a friendship might start, be fostered, and then ended, because they operate from disparate concepts about the structure of the relation.

Study 9: Aspects of Friendship as a Process   Eighty-four new children, who did not participate in the previous studies, were interviewed by two adult females. There were 28 children from grades 1, 4, and 7, of a parochial elementary school. Half were boys and half were girls. The children comprised three age groups of 28 each: 6 to 7 years, 9 to 10 years, and 12 to 13 years.

The interviewer began with a story in which two children (e.g., Mary and Sue) were described as newcomers to a school whom the teacher had placed in adjoining seats. The storytellers were told first to assign a number from 1 (least likely) to 5 (most likely) indicating whether they thought these two children would become friends. Then they were asked to give accounts representing four phases of the possible natural history of a friendship. (1)

What might Mary and Sue do or what might happen so that they become friends? (2) What might they do or might happen so that they would *not* become friends? (3) What might they do or might happen so that they become best or close friends? And (4) What might they do or might happen so that they were not friends anymore?

Results   Accounts are contingent on children's belief that two new-comers to a school could in fact become friends. Scores of the 28 children in each age group were summed and averages were obtained. The mean scores, based on the numbers assigned by the children were, for the youngest, middle, and oldest groups: 4.5, 4.1, and 3.9, respectively. They indicate a general belief that the peers in the story could become friends. Of the total 84 children, only 14 assigned a score of 3 (the middle rank) or less. Thus, most children were fairly confident that the two peers had a strong chance of becoming friends.

To Start a   Accounts of how the peers might become friends readily
Friendship   fell into three general categories. Forty children said that a friendship would begin if peers *played, shared,* or *talked* together. These accounts usually appeared as unqualified descriptions of interactions. They are similar to stories of peer kindness and to definitions reported in the previous chapter. Over half of these 40 accounts came from the 6 to 7 year group. Frequencies of these accounts decreased across the three age groups.

A total of 23 children said that friendship would begin if one peer would *help* the other or if the peers would help one another. Most children either specified need on the part of one peer or reciprocity in helping between both peers. Over half of these accounts were given by children in the 9 to 10 year group.

The remaining category contained 20 accounts, all of which followed the reasoning that friendship might begin if the peers *got to know* each other. These accounts implied that friendship was based on the personalities involved. Thus, finding out about common interests, abilities, and the like, was a prerequisite to establishment of the relation. Frequencies for this type of account increased from near zero in the youngest group to 13, or almost 50%, of the oldest group. Frequencies for each category are reported in table 13.

Examples are now presented for the three categories as well as subcategories within each.

Table 13   Four Aspects of Friendship

Interactions	Age					
	6–7		9–10		12–13	
	Male	Female	Male	Female	Male	Female
To Start a Friendship						
Play; talk; share	12	11	8	2	4	3
Help	2	2	3	9	4	3
Get to know	0	1	3	3	6	7
Not to Start a Friendship						
Not play; not talk; not share	6	9	1	4	2	1
Fight; argue	7	3	12	8	3	4
Third-person enters	1	1	1	2	3	4
Persons differ	0	1	0	0	6	5
To Become Best Friends						
Play; share; help	12	10	10	10	3	6
Like each other	1	4	1	2	1	0
Know each other	0	0	1	2	10	8
To End a Friendship						
Not play; not share; not help	4	2	1	4	0	0
Fight; argue	7	8	8	6	4	2
Third-person enters	2	3	4	3	7	8
Persons differ	0	0	0	0	3	4

NOTE: Some columns add up to only 12 or 13, because one or two children gave accounts which did not fit into the categories.

Playing   There were 21 accounts in which children said that peers would become friends by playing together. The probable implications were either that because the newcomers played they were friends or that playing was a first step toward friendship. The majority of these accounts came from 6 to 7-year-old children. Examples are:

(M,6)   *They play with each other.*

(M,7)   *At recess they might play around and have fun.*

(F,6)   *They would play with each other and they would be friends.*

(F,7)   *They would play out on recess together.*

(M,9)   *They could play with each other and come over to each other's house.*

(F,9)   *If they play games at recess.*

(M,13)   *They'll play around on the playground and talk to each other.*

(F,12)   *First they'll talk and might play together and then they'll invite each other over to each other's house.*

Talking   Twelve children said that the peers would become friends by talking to one another. Characteristic examples are:

(M,7)   *Tell jokes to each other.*

(F,6)   *They'll talk to each other and just become friends.*

(M,9)   *Just say, "Do you want to be my friend?"*

(M,13)   *Talk to him. Ask him if he wants to play a game or something.*

(F,12)   *They didn't know people so they'll start talking and become friends.*

Sharing   There were 7 children who described sharing as the interaction which would lead to friendship. All 7 gave accounts resembling the following:

(M,6)   *They would share and play with each other on the playground.*

(F,7)   *They have to share and be good.*

(M,9)   *If someone brought a toy to school and the other one asked if he could play with it. They'd be having fun together and they'll be friends.*

(F,9)   *They'd share stuff.*

Helping   The 23 accounts of helping covered the content areas other children had described in previous studies. These areas were: general help ($N=5$), material need ($N=5$), physical welfare ($N=3$), and schoolwork ($N=10$). The implication was that by helping one another, the newcomers would form a special two-group of friendship.

General help:

(F,6)   *By helping each other.*

(F,9)   *Mary could help Sue do everything.*

(F,10)   *Play with each other and help each other and they will be friends.*

Material help:

(M,7)   *Probably one forgot their lunch and asked the other one and he shared with him.*

(M,10)   *If one breaks his pencil, he could let him use one or an eraser.*

(M,13)   *If David forgets his lunch, Bill would buy him his lunch and he'll think he's a good guy.*

Physical help:

(F,9)   *Like one person might fall and the other might try to help . . . . They'll start liking each other.*

(F,13)   *Probably on the playground someone got hurt and they wanted to help.*

Schoolwork:

(M,6)   *Sometimes I help Ed and we become friends that easy. I helped him when he was absent. When he came back, everyone was ahead of him. So I saved my work [for him].*

(M,9)   *Bill calls David to ask him to help him with is homework and David does.*

(M,13)   *One person might have problems with his work and the other helps him. They work together on projects.*

(F,12)   *Ask questions to each other. Talk over assignments. Help each other.*

Getting to know each other   This category of accounts was used predominantly by children 9 years or older. Statements indicated that two peers who were new to a school, would probably become friends by getting to know one another. Of the 20 such accounts, 14 contained the phrase "get to know each other" and 6 emphasized that the peers would discover their mutual similarities. Here are examples of these accounts.

(F,7)   *They're in the same classroom, so they'll get to know each other.*

(F,9)   *They didn't know each other in the beginning and they know each other and would become better friends.*

(M,9)   *Because they would get to know each other.*

(M,13)   *They'll talk at first and get to know each other.*

(F,13)   *They may have to work together on a project and play together.*
         Then they know each other better than the other people.

         Discovery of similarity:

(F,9)   *They would like each other's personalities.*

(F,12)   *If they have something in common, they will talk and get to be*
         friends.

(M,13)   *Start talking to each other and find out they like the same*
         things.

(M,13)   *Find out they like each other and they just build up a friendship.*

(M,13)   *They might be on a winning baseball team and be proud of each*
         other.

(M,13)   *They might find out they like the same things. Both are good*
         students or both are good in sports.

Summary of | Accounts of how two newcomers might start a friendship
Starting a | agree with the developmental findings for definitions in
Friendship | the previous chapter. Younger children tend to equate the
existence of the relation with the enactment of particular
interactions. These are the pleasurable and positive activities of playing, talking, and sharing. Older children see
the relation differently as involving the joining of two
similar persons. For them, the prerequisite step toward
friendship is that children learn about one another as persons. Once peers discover who the persons are, they can
find what the persons have in common. If there are com-
monalities and the peers like one another, friendship becomes possible.

The transitional point between simple procedures and
joining of persons is represented by the 9 to 10 year group.
About half these children emphasized reciprocity in assistance as a means for becoming friends. The idea seems
to be that the two peers pay attention to another's need
for help. In helping, the peers show one another that they
have each singled the other out for attention and concern.
They recognized their individual needs and see their
common problems, for example, the importance of doing
well in school.

Not to Start | Accounts of why the two newcomers might not be friends
a Friendship | fell into four categories. The first set, which included *not*
playing, not talking, and *not sharing,* was the opposite of

the simple procedures younger children had said would lead to friendship. Over half of the youngest group used this type of account. Frequencies then declined sharply with increasing age.

Fighting or *arguing* made up the next category. Thirty-seven children gave this type of account with the predominant number coming from the 9 to 10 year group (see table 13). The typical account described an unconditioned, negative exchange between the peers. Apparently these children were saying that fighting was either equivalent to not being friends or that it was incompatible with friendship.

Twelve children, all but 2 from the older groups, said that friendship would not begin because a *third person* would enter and form a relation with one of the two newcomers. This intervention would then prevent the two new peers from establishing a relation.

The last category was used only by 12 and 13 year olds, save for 1 other child. These accounts focused on the possibility that the peers would find out that they were dissimilar persons. This discovery would therefore show that there is no basis for starting a friendship.

Not playing, not talking, not sharing   These accounts were simple negations of interactions, which were previously said to lead to friendship. They were also similar to accounts observed in study 4 describing unkindness between peers. Almost all such accounts were unqualified in the sense that neither the persons nor the circumstances appeared to provoke the interactions. These accounts add nothing new to the picture already formed. Apparently, young children equate the absence of particular procedures with the nonexistence of the relation. Statements like,

(F,7) *They wouldn't play together.*
(F,9) *If they didn't share.*
(M,13) *They might not talk to each other.*

represent the belief that, to be friends, peers have to be performing the activities of playing, sharing, or talking. Peers who do not are not friends.

Fighting, arguing   The 37 accounts in this category are also not new and conform to other children's stories of unkindness. Accounts were mainly unqualified, negative acts with stress on physical aggression. The following are typical examples:

(M,6) *They might get in a fight.*

(F,6) *Get in a fight.*

(M,9) *Probably got in a real bad fight. They beat each other up.*

(F,9) *They might play and one cheats and they start having an argument.*

(M,13) *Bill might show off and punch him and they'd get in a fight.*

(F,12) *Fighting. Kicking. Stealing. Playing rough. Talking mean.*

Third-party intervention
This category is composed of two subtypes of accounts. One refers to the possibility that one of the potential friends starts up a relation with someone else rather than the other newcomer. This relation then deters the establishment of a bond between the two newcomers. The second subtype includes all of the above details but adds a factor. It is that the excluded peer sees in the others' relation a difference between him or herself and them as persons. Examples of simple exclusion are as follows:

(M,6) *They will play with someone else.*

(F,6) *One of them might play with someone else.*

(F,10) *She would get another friend and the other girl would be jealous.*

(M,13) *If someone else got in the friendship, that might ruin it. Like Bill might play with someone that he liked better.*

(M,13) *If one of them picks up a lot friends all of a sudden and leaves the other cold.*

(F,13) *One might become popular with the other girls in class and the other one would be left out.*

Examples of discovery of interpersonal dissimilarities through the others' friendship are as follows:

(M,9) *One might want to be friends with someone else who was really tough and he started acting really cool and just followed him around.*

(F,12) *One of them became friends with a group that the other didn't like.*

(M,13) *Maybe David might get another friend that Bill didn't like and that would break it up.*

(F,13) *If Mary goes along with some other people that Sue doesn't like. Then Sue won't want to be friends because of the people*

*she hangs around with. Or, they have personal differences. Sue
may be shy and Mary is bossy and outgoing.*

Persons Differ   The 12 accounts in this category resemble the last set in that
they focus on the lack of similarity between the peers.
Children said that the two newcomers would not become
friends because they were dissimilar persons who therefore lacked common interests or ways of thinking. Finding
that they were different, the two peers had no basis for
starting a relation. The 12 accounts are:

(F,7)   *If Mary didn't like Sue.*

(F,12)   *They may have different opinions; attitudes. Like religion or
something . . . and just not get along.*

(F,12)   *If they didn't have anything in common.*

(F,12)   *They may not like the way the other person dressed or acted or
looked. They just wouldn't get along.*

(M,12)   *One might not like what the other does. They might come from
different areas. . . . One's poor and the other is rich.*

(M,13)   *Sometimes your personalities have to meet. Be similar. And if
they weren't then you won't become friends.*

(M,13)   *One doesn't like the way the other acts. They might disagree.*

(M,13)   *Maybe David is sort of slow and Bill is stronger than him and
he won't want to play games with him.*

(M,13)   *One could make a serious mistake, like flunk a test. The other
would look down on him.*

(M,13)   *They'd like different things.*

(F,13)   *They may not be each other's style. Like to do different things.
Have different interests.*

(F,13)   *They may have different ideas. Different personalities.*

*Summary of Not
Starting a
Friendship*   Results support findings for the process of starting a friendship. The youngest children focused mainly on procedures
which if enacted, would start, and if not enacted, would
not start a relation. The oldest group described both processes in terms of the peers' mutual recognition of one
another as persons. To start a friendship, peers have to
learn about each other, their psychological makeup, their
interests. Friendship cannot be built when peers discover
that they have little in common.

    The 9 to 10-year-old group was less articulate than their
older counterparts. These children said that a friendship

would not begin when the two newcomers had a fight, an argument, or a disagreement. These accounts may be seen as focusing on the peers' incompatability. This would square with the same children's view that reciprocal helping, expressing compatibility, would lead to friendship. Nevertheless, these children did not bring out the specific importance of similarity of personhood so clearly as the young adolescent group.

To Become Children described three ways in which friends could
Best Friends become best or close friends. The first was to repeat those interactive procedures which were said to lead originally to friendship. These were playing, sharing, and helping. Eighteen children reiterated these procedures almost verbatim. Thirty-three children repeated them with an interesting addition. They extended the procedures quantitatively in amount or in time. Best friends were said to play *all the time* or *every day* and to share *always, really,* or a *lot*. Children describing playing, sharing, and helping included 22 of the 28 youngest children and 20 of the 28 middle group. Only 9 of the oldest children described this type of procedure (see table 13). This result corresponds to answers to the question of how kind acts could be made more kind (chap. 8).

The second way to become best friends was used by a total of 9 children, all of whom said that the friends *liked each other*. These accounts go beyond simple procedures but do not quite reach the level of saying that best friends know each other well as persons.

Interpersonal knowledge makes up the third category and describes the majority (18 of 28) of the oldest children. In this type of account, children speak of trust, equality, common interest, and mutual understanding of one other as persons.

Playing, sharing, Accounts fitting this category were indistinguishable from
helping simple procedures used to describe how a relation might begin save for quantitative extensions. The following examples characterize the category as a whole.

(M,7) *Always play with each other. Always talk to each other. And never hit.*

(F,6) *Play with each other every day.*

(M,6)   *Bill wanted him to and he would give him his lunch every time.*
(F,10)   *One could help the other all the time.*
(M,9)   *Always work together.*

Liking Each Other   Emphasis in these accounts is on the friends coming to like each other. They contain two implications. One is that the friends not only partake of friendly interactions, but they learn to like each other in doing so. The second is that liking is mutual or reciprocal. Here are the 9 cases of this type.

(F,6)   *They like each other.*
(F,7)   *If they like each other very much.*
(F,6)   *If they really, really like each other.*
(F,7)   *If they like each other a lot.*
(M,6)   *Being really happy . . . 'cause they like each other.*
(F,9)   *By liking each other a lot.*
(F,10)   *They get along with each other.*
(M,9)   *They think each other are nice.*
(M,13)   *They find out they really like each other.*

Know Each Other   Examples are now given for each of the subcategories of this type. All seem to represent the core concept that best friends understand each other because they know and trust each other as persons. These accounts appear to be the logical extension of how peers came initially to be friends. First they have to learn about one another and find a common ground. Having done this, they can move even closer in the relation by prizing each other as special persons.

Trust:

(F,9)   *They keep each other's secrets.*
(F,12)   *Keeping things to themselves.*
(M,13)   *They trust each other.*

Equality:

(F,10)   *They play together all the time and find out they're equally good.*
(F,13)   *One girl is teased and the other sticks up for her.*

(M,13) *Do everything together. Both are really good at everything.*

(M,13) *They could be about even . . . get to know each other better.*

Common Interests:

(M,9)   *Read the same books. Get the same report cards. They're almost identical.*

(F,12) *Get along. Have things in common.*

(F,12) *If they both like the same things; get along really well together.*

(F,13) *If Mary liked her personality and they had something in common.*

(F,12) *They found out they had something in common and they liked each other.*

(F,12) *Having the same interests. Liking the same things.*

(M,13) *If they found out they had the same interests, like a hobby or something.*

(M,13) *Spend a lot of time together and like to do the same things.*

(M,13) *They have something in common.*

(F,12) *Get along. Have things in common.*

Understand one another:

(F,12) *They could be exactly the same and get to know each other really well.*

(M,12) *Get to know each other better.*

(M,13) *Get to know each other.*

(M,13) *Really get to know each other.*

(M,13) *They know each other really well and they like each other.*

Summary of Becoming a Best Friend   Accounts of how peers become best friends were found to be quantitative or logical extensions of the processes by which peers become friends in the first place. The developmental pattern was again clearly shown to be a progression from procedure to person with the latter being a new step toward interpersonal understanding within the two-group.

To end a Friendship   The same categories found for the question of why peers might not become friends applied for accounts of how a friendship, already started, might end. Eleven children, all from the youngest and middle groups, reiterated that not playing, not sharing or not helping would lead to the end of a friendship. Thirty-five children said the friendship would end through fighting or arguing. Again, accounts were similar to those given previously for why the friendship might not begin. As before, this category was used frequently by the youngest and middle groups then dropped off in the oldest group.

The last two categories were used with increased frequency as children grew older. The first of these was made up of accounts in which a third person entered to break up the existing relation. The second involved recognition that the friends, who were previously thought to be alike, were now seen as different.

Not playing, not sharing, not helping

The following accounts exemplify the 11 making up this category.

(M,6) *By not playing with him anymore.*

(F,6) *They won't share anymore.*

(M,7) *He might not like him anymore . . . not playing.*

(M,9) *Like one could not share. Lie or cheat.*

(F,10) *They wouldn't share anymore and start to tell stories about each other.*

(F,10) *They wouldn't help each other anymore. Like if Sue doesn't know a math problem, and asks Mary and Mary says no.*

(F,9) *If they've been playing or helping for about three months and then for a week one of them doesn't want to.*

The point of these accounts seems to be that the friends had built up expectations about interactions. For unexplained reasons, one or both peers stopped meeting the terms of playing, sharing, or helping. Use of the adverb, "anymore," makes the point clearly. Since the relation is equated with these interactions, failure to perform them terminates the relation.

Fighting, arguing

These accounts are similar to the above examples but focus on the content of aggressive and disputive behavior.

(M,6) *Someone hit one of them. He thinks his friend did it and he starts a big fight.*

(F,6) *If they had a fight and didn't talk to each other.*

(M,9)   *He pushes him off the swing and he gets mad.*

(F,9)   *If they got in a big fight and said, "I'll never speak to you
again."*

(M,13)   *They could have a disagreement.*

(F,13)   *They get jealous, like over a better grade, and get in an argument and never make up.*

*Third-party
intervention*   Twenty-seven children said that the friendship would
end when one of the friends began a new relation with
another peer. Examples include the following:

(M,6)   *One would get a new friend.*

(M,6)   *They found another friend.*

(F,6)   *One of them would play with someone else, and they wouldn't
be friends.*

(F,6)   *Play with other people.*

(M,9)   *A new guy makes friends with one of them.*

(M,9)   *Someone might say bad things about one of them. He believes
them.*

(F,9)   *Like one of Mary's other friends could want to play and they
would leave Sue out of it.*

(F,10)   *Somebody else could tell something about one of them to the
other.*

(M,12)   *They meet people they like better and just drift apart.*

(M,13)   *If one of them picks up a lot of friends all of a sudden and leaves
the other cold.*

(M,13)   *A new kid likes one, and the other guy gets jealous and starts
putting him down.*

(M,13)   *If someone else gets in the friendship and ruins it. Then Bill likes
him better.*

(F,12)   *One could meet someone else and be their friend instead.*

(F,12)   *One of them met someone else and became better friends with
them.*

(F,13)   *Someone says something about Mary to Sue. Sue believes them
instead of Mary.*

(F,12)   *Mary might get another friend that she'd like better than Sue
and would leave Sue out in the cold.*

Two underlying reasons for ending a friendship can be
seen in these accounts. The younger children seem to be
saying that the act of taking on another friend automati-

cally replaces the old friend. Older children appear to be saying something more than that. They are acknowledging that persons change. For example, it is possible to discover someone you like *better* than someone else you knew previously. The movement to the new relation is then a matter of the principle that friends are similar and have things in common. When one friend finds a new person who is more similar to him or her than an old friend, the former basis of the friendship has changed. It is time to switch friends and establish a relation with the new person.

Discovering Older children understand friendship as a bond between
dissimilarity like persons. When circumstances reveal that friends are no longer similar, the reason for their relation is removed. As was just shown, one means for this discovery is to see that one's former friend has affiliated with a third party who is different from oneself. Statements reflecting this discovery of dissimilarity are now inspected more closely.

(M,13) *Bill might get another friend that David doesn't like and that would break them up.*

(M,13) *One could get jealous of the other because he was better. He would look for friends of his own ability.*

(M,13) *One is smart. The other is athletic. They bug each other by saying, "What I do is better."*

(F,12) *Find out something about the other one that makes them not like her. Like, she was mean to someone.*

(F,12) *One became friends with a group that another one didn't like and she was left alone.*

(F,12) *One might become friends with someone else and they think they are better.*

(F,12) *Another friend comes along who likes one but not the other.*

Conclusions Accounts of processes in the natural history of a friendship reveal developmental changes similar to those found with definitions in the previous chapter. Young school-age children identify friendship with the here-and-now enactment of interactive procedures. With the advance toward adolescence, these same procedures become means for establishing a relation. Older children look on these procedures as ways of coming to know persons and

discovering whether there are sufficient similarities between them to continue within the friendship.

The here-and-now perspective shown by 6 to 7-year-old
children highlights two features of their conceptual understanding. The first is the precedence of procedure over
person. Young children say that whomever they play or
share with is their friend, and whomever they do not play
with or fight with is not their friend. The implication is
that procedures are constant, but the persons in them and
the relation are not. Any peers who partake of these procedures are de facto friends or not. And any time these
procedures are enacted, the relation is operative.

The second feature pertains to the interchangability of
peers. One peer is substitutable for another in this concept. A peer who plays today is a friend. If this peer does
not play tomorrow, he or she is not a friend. That peer is
replaced by another who does play. In equating the relation with procedures, young children maintain a sense of
orderliness in social activities without building upon their
own or other peers' individuality as persons.

These features fit commonsense observations of young
children. Parents and teachers sometimes express surprise
at the number and frequency of changes among young
friends. It is not uncommon for children to announce that
someone they just met and only talked with briefly is their
friend. It is equally common that young children drop
friends of long standing unabashedly when they have had
a fight.

The temporariness of young children's friendships
results not so much from fickleness as from a lack of
appreciation for the persons behind the procedures. This
is true even where best friends are involved. Young children do designate selected peers as their best friends. The
designation seems to apply, however, to peers who practice the proper procedures repeatedly together. Frequency
of interaction may give the appearance of a close meshing
between the friends, but it is apparent that it covers over
the fact that the children have not developed an appreciation of each other as persons.

This level of understanding gives way to a different
conception as children practice, reflect on, and reconceptualize procedures into the relation proper. Procedures

become means to an end, the end being the relation. And secondly, the persons have to form a bond of understanding in which the procedures are given a common meaning.

The first point is seen clearly in the integration of accounts across the phases of friendship. Two newcomers play, talk, and work together. These interactions do not make a friendship but allow the peers to get to know each other as persons. As the friends continue to practice these procedures, they can come to an even closer mutual understanding. This involves the discovery of their common interests, equal abilities, and like personalities. And when the friends have been joined on the mutual basis, their relation cannot be so easily ended. Termination will follow only if the persons are no longer similar. One of them, therefore, has to change. Change is recognized either by observing a former friend in a new relation with someone else or by noticing behavior which contrasts with one's own. In either case, the grounds for the relation are undermined and the friends move apart.

In our studies, the young adolescents' descriptions of the dynamics of the relation agreed with other young adolescents' definitions of friendship. Those definitions emphasized mutual concern and understanding accompanied by a feeling of closeness and openness. Present results show why friendship can evolve in the direction of intimacy. From the beginning the peers focus on one another's personhood. The peers look for psychological qualities which make them similar. Being essential parts of the persons, these qualities endure. Thus there is a constant factor around which the relation can be built.

The two-group of the pre- and early adolescents' friendships appears, as Sullivan suggests, as an innovation in social development. Within its confines, self and other see themselves as special persons who share a mutual outlook on the world. The friends work to achieve it, attain a sense of closeness in it, and benefit by fostering it. Interestingly, the relation terminates when a third party enters almost as if the bond requires exclusivity. When one of the peers starts a relation with someone else, the new friendship takes away from the old. One reason it does is that it induces the old friend to see differences which now make the previous friend a changed person. The reason for the bond is destroyed and the two-group is broken.

Eleven   Offenses and Their Repair

Results of studies 8 and 9 indicate that friendship becomes
a relation proper sometime in the middle of the school-
age period. But these same studies show a potential source
of difficulty children must face in conceptualizing the relation. Definitions illustrate what friendship may ideally
mean, but results of study 9 demonstrate that friends do
not always live up to these ideals. The results are similar
when studies 1 and 2 are compared with study 4, or study
6 with study 7. In each comparison, the former show
friends interacting as they should to enhance relationships, while the latter show that friends can be cruel,
harmful, and insensitive. If a fair appraisal of children's
concepts of friendship and their development is to be
made, a further study of the untoward side of peer life
is necessary. Practically speaking, friends cannot consistently act in accord with norms of equality and cooperation. Friends are individual persons with interests and
separate emotional lives to protect. Yet friendship can be a
lasting relation. Therefore, it must be the case that
friendships can tolerate conflict and violations of norms
and persist in spite of them. Put differently, children's
conceptions of friendship must include awareness of violations and knowledge of how to handle them when they
come up.

   This conclusion raises the questions, What constitutes an
offense to friendship? and How do children deal with of-
208   fenses? These questions, in turn, raise others: What role

does the offended person play in mending a breach in relation? How, specifically, does the offender make an adequate apology if this is the chosen remedy? Does repair of a breach occur all of a sudden or must both persons gradually work toward reinstituting their relation?

Study 10 attempts to answer some of these questions. The data for this study were already reported in study 7. They are now reinspected with the aim of understanding the patterns leading to repair from the perspective that older children are working toward maintenance of their relation. Study 11 is a new study, deemed necessary for several reasons. In study 10, children were told to generate accounts of "unkindness" and then asked to describe what would happen. In study 11, children were to generate acts which would be "harmful to a friendship" and to describe exchanges which would repair the breach and make the persons friends again. These latter instructions are more explicit with regard to maintaining relationship and necessary to the purposes of answering the original questions.

It may be helpful to reiterate a point made earlier. Studies 10 and 11 can be seen as instructive complements to studies 8 and 9 which emphasized positive norms, rather than the starting or ending of a relation. The present studies are designed to uncover the realistic parts of children's conceptions through analysis of negative interactions which occur but do not terminate a relation. These data are necessary adjuncts to earlier findings, since they are intended to reveal how children reconcile the understanding of positive norms with the practical facts of everyday deviations from these norms. At the same time, descriptions and choices of offenses themselves should help to elaborate concepts of friendship by identifying norms of the relation from their reverse side. This follows from the same rationale by which unkind acts helped to explicate the positive nature of relations.

Study 10: Special Cases of Friendship: Violation and Repair   In this study special instances of offenses which occurred within friendship will be focused on. Attempts are made to draw conclusions from patterns by which these offenses were repaired. The data come from the sample of children reported in study 7. Recall that 60 children described

unkind acts between friends, then gave accounts of reactions which might have occurred immediately or one
day later. Results were summarized in general patterns
(see table 12) which contrasted friendship with child-
parent relations. Particular accounts will be cited to illuminate more fully the variety of friendship concepts children
hold.

Results   As previously reported, there were two model sequences
for offenses and subsequent reactions. The first can be
called a *negative chaining* in which the initial offense was
followed by a reciprocated negative action. This reaction
led to a further offense and another negative reciprocation.
The second pattern may be called *arbitrary breaking of the
chain*. In this pattern, children began with an offense and
immediate reciprocation, as above. However, they then
broke the chain by having the offender initiate some positive action (undoing the offense or apology) and having
the offended child accept it.

Both of these general patterns reflect the characteristics
of equality and reciprocity in the sense of practical, constitutive rules. Children who proposed these sequences
may have been saying that one friend has the right to do
whatever the other does. When one initiates an unkindness, the other may return it. If one initiates a positive
action, the other may do the same. The point is made in a
particularly sharp manner in sequences which ended with
double apology. First the offender performed an unkindness. Then the other friend initiated an unkindness in
reciprocity. Next the offender offered an apology for the
initial unkindness. And then the offended child offered an
apology for his or her reciprocation to the original offense.
In other words, the child who was originally offended saw
him- or herself also as an offender for having reciprocated
the unkind act.

While these patterns reflect equality and reciprocity,
they do little to help explain dynamics. Both patterns
begin in the same way: offend, then reciprocate. It is not
evident why in some cases the negative beginning led to a
negative conclusion while in other cases the chain was
broken and friends concluded on a positive note. There

was little in most of these accounts to differentiate negative progression from sequences which resulted in resolution. However, there were two exceptions in the cases where resolution occurred. Both appeared in accounts given by the oldest children, and in both, the offender's apology was stimulated by conscious consideration of the nature of the offense. The accounts follow: (M,14) *If he really thought about it, he might apologize.* (Then) *The offended friend would forgive him.* The second example was: (F,12) *Later that night, it would probably bother me. I would apologize. I would say, "You can't do things I can do and I can't do things you can do. I'm sorry. Next time, you can be on my team, because games are just for fun."* (Then) *She would probably say, "Don't worry about it. We're still friends."*

Not reciprocate   Twenty-four children, or 40% of the sample, said that the offended friend would not reciprocate upon being offended. A reaction of nonreciprocation is important, since it may indicate that the child understands reciprocity as a higher principle. That is, if a negative act is returned, then the pragmatic rule of reciprocity would logically lead to continued negative exchanges. If, on the other hand, the negative act is not returned, a different consequence should follow. A burden is put on the offender to initiate some other type of action. Presumably, it would be a positive act which the offended friend could reciprocate. It would follow that the friends could then resume positive exchanges on a reciprocal basis.

It was indeed observed in 15 of the 24 cases that nonreciprocity of unkindness led immediately to positive action on the offender's part which the offended friend accepted. As would be expected from previous results, such higher level understanding of reciprocity as a principle was more evident in older than younger children. Four, 3, and 8 children, respectively, in the youngest, middle, and oldest groups gave accounts with nonreciprocity followed by resolution.

Examples from the youngest group were:

(F,6)   *If he says, "I won't let you play with me."/ Go home. Tell him he's mean./ He would tell me I could play./ I would say, "Thank you."*

(F,7)   *I wouldn't give her anything.| She wouldn't say anything.| I would be better to her. I would play with her more and be better to her.| She would play with me.*

(F,7)   *One time my friend, J., didn't help someone who fell down.| He didn't do anything.| J. said he was sorry.| They made up.*

(M,9)   *They interrupt somebody who's talking.| Go home.| Ask if he could play.| He would say he would play.*

Examples from the middle group were similar.

(M,10) *Not letting him play with him. Let him play one day. The next day say, "Get out of here."| If he's nice, he might just walk away. If he's nasty, he might pick a fight with him.| He might say he was sorry.| He would say OK and they would be friends again.*

(M,9)   *Like if a guy asks you to play frisbee and you say, "No-o"; Something mean.| He should walk away . . . . Drop him for a while.| If they were friends, he'd say he was sorry for what he had said.| He would play with him again.*

(M,10) *He steals their things.| Don't play with the person who stole it.| He'd give it back and say he was sorry.| He'd play with them again.*

Examples from the oldest group include the following:

(M,13) *Tease them about something they can't do.| Say he would fight him.| Maybe apologize.| Say he was sorry for saying he was going to fight.*

(M,12) *The friend doesn't do anything to help the other guy. He picks on him all the time.| Just not like him very much. Tell everyone to keep away from him 'cause he's really a brat.| He wouldn't pick on you. He'd say, "Hi"; be nicer.| Be nice to him too. Tell everybody he's OK now and he's nicer than he was.*

(F,13) *Like when you get into an argument.| Instead of fighting back with words, I would walk away.| She'd apologize.| Apologize back and the thing would probably be all over.*

(F,13) *I had a friend and when there were three of us, she'd say, "T. come here"; and they would go off and talk. I'd be left standing there. I felt just awful.| Sometimes I get in arguments. Sometimes I'd talk to my mom. Finally, I just stopped being friends with her.| It depended on my reaction. If I was still mad she'd ignore me. Mostly, we forgot about it; she would act friendly.| If she was friendly, so would I be.*

(F,14) *Sometimes they make fun of others' mistakes.| Some people take it with a grin. Others get mad and retaliate in some way.|*

*If the person had retaliated it, sometimes they'd continue
teasing. If the person had ignored it, sometimes the whole thing
is forgotten.| If the teasing continued, they'd probably try to
get back again. If it had been treated normally, the whole thing
would be forgotten by him too.*

These accounts give a new perspective to concepts of
friendship. In each example, the offended party refrained
from retaliation. A direct confrontation was avoided. As a
consequence, the next act in the sequence was a positive
gesture—a direct undoing of the original offense or an
apology. In all cases, the gesture was accepted and the
relationship could be resumed in its normal vein.

Some of the children in the middle and oldest groups
spontaneously articulated the difference between retaliation and nonconfrontation. They saw the former as leading to
continued negative exchange and contrasted it with the
latter, which they saw as potentially resolving the problem. This distinction exemplifies an advanced understanding of reciprocity and shows how a pragmatic rule
may differ from a conceptualized principle. In the latter
vein, it is precisely by not retaliating that the offended
friend induces the offender to acknowledge reciprocity.
Once negative action is stopped and positive action substituted, the offended friend reciprocates and presumably
the relational bond, which was breached, becomes
repaired.

Inequalities   Of the 24 cases of nonreciprocity to offenses, 15, as were
just seen, resulted in apology or resolution. The remaining
9 cases did not. These accounts were discovered to have a
common element. The sequences began with clearly stated
inequalities between the friends. Before discussing the
possible significance, these accounts should be looked at
in detail.

(F,7)   *I used to have a friend, S. [a boy] and he used to pour water
on my head. On Halloween he had a ghost costume and he
scared me. I felt like kicking him. I didn't 'cause he would tell his
mom. I started running away from him.| He'd tease me more.| I
tried to tease him back.*

(F,10)   *K. used to make sure a certain girl wouldn't play soccer with us.
She was mean to everyone smaller than her.| She was shy; she*

wouldn't do anything./She'd probably do the same thing. She's usually mean./ Just say "shut up" and walk away.

(F,10)   *If somebody has glasses and somebody teases them./ They'd probably walk away./ He might tease him again./ Yell at him to stop doing that.*

(M,10)   *Like in a football game, a pass is wrong. Or a wrong call. You might get into a fight./ He'd probably back off./ He'd stay away from him./ He'd just ignore him.*

(M,12)   *This year we had a new student. Most people didn't like what he did. He talked funny. We liked to play 'keep away'./ He wasn't big and he was afraid of the people. He would walk away. He got upset./ Tease the new boy. Crack jokes about him./ He'd probably say something back. They might hurt him. He would go tell the teacher.*

(M,14)   *Sometimes big kids pick on little kids. Once they took a little boy and put him on a hanger./ He started laughing, but he must have been embarrassed./ They'd probably tease him some more./ He takes it as a joke.*

In these 6 cases, one sees the offense originating in the context of an inequality between the friends. In 4 instances, the offender was bigger than the offended friend. In 1 instance, the offended friend had glasses, and in another he had made an error in a game. The smaller or lesser peer's failure to retaliate can be seen as a matter of being in a *one-down* position. The friend having the upper hand was then described as adding to the original offense, in 5 of the 6 cases, by repeating the offense and taking further advantage of the "lesser" peer.

These stories make a telling contrast with those reviewed in the previous section. There it was shown that nonretaliation led to apology. Now it is seen that this reaction can have other consequences. When one friend has a stated advantage over the other, failure to retaliate may be a matter of inability to react in kind, especially if the lesser is afraid of the *one-up* offender. The reaction is then ineffective for stopping further offenses since the one-up friend is free to offend again. The difference between these and the former stories can thus be seen to hinge on inequality.

As was found in study 4 (Stories of Unkindness), older children said that it is unkind for peers to recognize an inequality and then not act to undo it. For instance, you are unkind by not helping a friend with schoolwork when you know, and he or she does not know, an assignment. It is now clear that children are fully aware that peers do not consistently act for the sake of establishing equality. Some peers take advantage of it to harass others repeatedly. There is apparently little the friends in the one-down position can do to retaliate. They may call the offender a name or threaten to tell an adult. In either case, they still must suffer the consequences of being treated unkindly by the stronger peer.

The remaining three stories represent the same point but in slightly different ways. All these stories were begun with the contextual setting of one friend being excluded from a group by another friend. Insofar as the latter did the excluding, this peer acted with unilateral authority over the former. Thus, inequality was factually enacted. All 3 stories resulted in failure to resolve the offense. One was similar to the above cases of inequality and 2 were different.

The one story similar to those in which inequalities were predicated follows:

(F,7)   *Like when you're playing and they won't let you play./ You say you won't be their friend./ They run away from the child they wouldn't let play so she won't know where they were; so they can play./ Go find someone else. Pretend the other kids aren't even there.*

This story expresses inequality in a different form. The offense is done in the context of a group wherein several children will not let one child play. The offended child can do little to retaliate and therefore moves away. Exclusion is then carried one step further, and again the excluded child can only feel isolated.

The other two instances of exclusion were the following:

(M,10)   *When they meet someone new, they just say, "I don't want to play with you."/ He feels sad and he might start calling them names./ He might want to play with the person./ He might not want to play because the other person was mean to him the day before. He's still kind of mad.*

(F,10)   *A girl in my class has favorites. If someone tries to talk, she tells them to shut up and acts like she's the head of everybody./ I just try to ignore her./ Then she tries to come back and make friends*

and goes away from her other friends./ I don't want to be
friends with her because when she's a friend, she's not that
much of a friend.

In these 2 stories, the offended friend's nonconfronting
reaction induced the offender to offer a positive gesture.
But the gesture was rejected. In both cases, the offended
child was wary of being hurt again and therefore chose not
to reenter the relation.

Interpretation   The foregoing examples show the complexity of children's
concepts of friendship. There was considerable variation
among the actions children considered detrimental to the
relation. These ranged from direct physical aggression to
one friend acting superior to the other. Then there were
variations in the reactions to these offenses children proposed. Some children (about 60%) chose reactions in the
form of reciprocations, while others (about 40%) proposed
reactions of nonconfrontation.

Reactions of retaliation will be considered first here. For
some children, retaliation led to a second offense and this,
in turn, to a second reciprocation. For others, the first
retaliation was unexplainably followed by a positive initiative from the offender, and this gesture was accepted or
reciprocated. There were only 2 children who clarified this
pattern by saying that the offender would think about the
consequences of his or her actions and then decide to
undo the offense in order to resume positive relations. For
the remainder of these children, however, the transition
from the second to third step in the sequence was either
reciprocate/offend again or reciprocate/stop offending.

These latter two sequences illustrate pragmatic rules of
equality and reciprocity. One friend can do whatever the
other does. This is exemplified within steps one and two
and within steps three and four.It is also represented in
negative chains where step two is reciprocating to step one,
step three to two, and step four to three. It is represented
differently across steps when an *arbitrary break* occurs
between steps two and three. When this happens one can
only conclude that children know that offenses need not
be taken too seriously. Friends who hurt each other one
day can interact positively the next. The positive overrides
the negative in a type of matter-of-fact way.

Sequences with first reactions of nonconfrontation appear to show a higher level understanding of equality and reciprocity. In slightly more than half the cases, nonconfrontation in response to an offense led to positive gestures which were then accepted. This pattern may exemplify comprehension of reciprocity as a principle. That is, if friendship operates by reciprocity, then returning an offense logically leads to an endless series of negative exchanges. But friendship cannot be maintained with purely negative actions. Therefore, the logical means for returning to a positive mode is for the recipient to walk away from the offender, calling attention to the offense without extending it. Nonconfrontation serves to mark the event and call the offender's attention to the risk of losing the relation. When a positive gesture is then offered, the recipient can accept it and the relation can move out of its negative state into its more normal mode of positive reciprocation.

Failure to reciprocate an offense is not, however, a simple act. For some children, nonconfrontation appeared to be based on a lack of equality. These children described recipients who were in one-down positions relative to offenders. There was little these recipients could do when offended except to accept the insult. The superiority of offenders was reinforced in that the original offense was repeated. Again, all the lesser recipient could do was accept it also or give a verbal response which, in itself, could not stop the attack. This pattern seems to reflect a realistic understanding of friendship insofar as children often meet the disadvantages of inequality in real-life events over which they have little control. It is interesting to note here that children identified the offenders who misused advantage, and thereby violated equality, as "mean," "nasty," and "having no good in them." These appear to be children's adjectives for persons who should but do not enact the principle of equality with their supposed friends.

Study 11: Patterns for Resolving Violations   In this study 36 new children, 12 each from the same three general age levels, were interviewed. This interview was directed toward offenses within friendship and the subsequent process of repair. Children were told to describe an event which would harm a friendship and then to describe how the actor and recipient would become friends again. Thus, unlike the previous study, children were required to describe actions and reactions leading explicitly to the repair of the relation.

The interview format was more elaborate than in the previous study. First, children were instructed to tell a story in which a friend does something that another friend doesn't like; something that might be harmful to their friendship. The children were then told to say how the offended and offending friends would react in sequence; for example, "What would happen next time they were together?" Finally, they were asked to describe what would happen to make things better again, to patch things up. Depending on individual responses, children were asked additional questions like: "Is that all that has to be done?"; "Does the other one have to do something?"; "Is it really serious?"; "What if it were more serious?"

Results   About two-thirds of the stories conformed to patterns of resolution just reported in study 10. For present purposes, focus will be limited to 12 children, whose stories dealt specifically with offenses committed in the context of inequality. As was just shown, inequality between friends frequently led to nonresolution. In the present study, children were instructed to have the friends reach a resolution. The question of interest is therefore to see how children dealt with the facts of inequality in the process of repairing breaches in relations.

The Better-off   In the 6 stories now presented, children described friends
Friend Offends   as being unequal in some regard. One friend was better off and the other was worse off. The friend in the better position committed the offense. The process of repair then proceeded from this starting point.

(F,7)   *My friend, D. [a boy], calls me names a lot when they play hockey because I can't play hockey so good.* (What do you do when that happens?) *I go inside and just ignore them.* (You don't say anything?) *No, I just mind my own business and do other things.* (What happens next time you see him?) *Sometimes he makes friends with me. Different times, whenever I come along they have to leave, or he would make friends.* (How would you become friends again?) *He says, "If you go get it, I'll be your friend." He's silly. He makes deals with me.* (Do you ever get really mad at him? What do you say?) *"I can do things with my dad, you're not the only one."* (How do you become friends again?) *The next morning he's playing and he wants me to be face-off lady. And I do a couple of favors for him that he wasn't expecting.*

Throughout this account, the girl remained in the lesser position. She identified the boy's act of exclusion as the offense, yet it is she who had made up to the boy. When she abided by his "deals" or did him favors, they became friends again. Thus, there is a reversal from the common-sense view that the one who commits an offense is responsible for the work of repair. In this case, the superior boy never lost his advantageous position.

(F,8)   *My friend, J., went to my other friend, L., and said: "L., you're dumb and stupid and I'm in a higher math group and higher reading group than you." And then she hit her. And I saw them getting into a fight and L. was crying and I went over and tried to stop the fight.* (Did you say anything to J.?) *"J., if you didn't start anything, you guys wouldn't have gotten into a fight."* (What did J. say?) *She didn't say anything.* (What happened the next time you and J. met?) *We played together and had fun.* (You weren't mad at J.?) *Right.* (What do you think might have happened the next time J. and L. met?) *They would be nice since we talked about it.* (What did they say?) *J. said she was really sorry and she didn't want to do it and L. said she was really sorry and she didn't want to start hitting. They both said they were sorry to each other.* (Do you think one of them had to say they were sorry first?) *J.* (Why?) *Because J. started the fight.* (What would happen if it happened again?) *Probably fight and get really hurt.* (Do you think they could be friends again?) *If somebody helped them. If I went down and said, "Why don't you guys try to be friends instead of fighting and fighting?"*

If the premise is that J. was doing better in school than L., L. can be seen to be in the lesser position. The storyteller recognized this by not having L. direct the remediation process. Instead, the storyteller intervened by talking to the offender. When J. apologized, however, so did L. The storyteller had to intervene again when a second offense occurred, as if J. would not stop offending and L. could not stop her on her own.

(F,11)   *B. is friends with A.; and H. [The storyteller] likes A. too. B wants to take her away from H. like she does most other people*

'cause she likes to have friends all to herself and not share them
with other people. (How does she do that?) *If you're playing a*
game, she won't let you in . . . . She'll tell A. how icky I am. (B. is
your friend?) *Sometimes, yeah.* (What might H. do?) *I don't*
do anything but A. is still friends with me because it doesn't
work. (After B. tells A. how icky H. is, what does H. do?)
Nothing at all. (Nothing?) *No, because she'll still be friends*
with me. She still likes B. but she doesn't like B. She can be
friends with whoever she wants. (What do you think happens
to the friendship of B. and H.?) *We'll still like each other, I*
suppose, but sometimes we hate each other and don't get
along very well. (What could happen so that they become
friends again?) *For her mother not to work at school anymore*
because B. thinks she's big and shows off.

B. was obviously the more popular girl. She committed
the offense, but at no place in the story was she required to
undo the offense. She and H. became friends again, but
the relation remained a mixture of liking and hating. H.
said that if B's mother were not in the school, B. would not
have acted so assertively and her relation with H. might
have been better. In the interim, however, H. seems willing to stay in the relation and suffer the disadvantages of
being in the lesser position.

(F,13)   *There's this one girl—she has lots of friends, and one of her*
old best friends doesn't have too many friends. So the girl with
a lot of friends–we were going on a trip and it was a long ride.
She told the other girl she would sit with her and she also
promised another girl she would sit with her and she also
promised another girl she would sit with her. About a week from
the trip, she told her that she couldn't sit with her. (What
happened?) *She got really upset because there was no one else*
you could sit with. Everyone else had seats. (What happened?)
She got really mad and said the least she could have done was
told her and she could have found someone else . . . . She cries a
whole lot and said she just didn't like her anymore. (How did
they become friends again?) *They got back together after a*
while. (How?) *She didn't really hate her. She was just mad at*
her. She doesn't have too many other friends and she really likes
her a lot. (Did anyone have to apologize?) *No, no one apolo-*
gized . . . . She'd just talk to her and they got back together
because they have lots of classes together.

This is another example of a popular and an unpopular
friend where the latter was in no position to control the
relation. She could get mad and ask why, but ultimately to

stay in the relation meant she had to live with her one-down position. The storyteller noted that she had few friends to turn to as alternatives. Thus, to remain a friend with the popular girl, she had to suffer periodic insults.

(F,13)   *J. is trying out for the basketball team and so is T. T is much better, and they want the same position. J. talks to T. and says, "Why don't you try out for that other position since we're friends?" (What does T. say?) "Why should I? Why don't you?" (What does J. say?) "You're good at the other position too. This is the only one I can do fairly well." (What happens next?) At the tryouts, T. tries out for the same position as J. J. thinks he did it just to make him mad. They're not good friends after that. (What brings them together again?) It's not too smart to ruin a friendship. They talk. (And what if they were not good friends to begin with?) There would be more competition.*

In this case the inequality pertained to talent in a sport. The offense was committed by the better player. At no point in the story did he apologize or make up in some other way to the lesser player. The lesser got upset but did not want the friendship to end because "that wouldn't be smart." Consequently, the two remained friends even though they have competed, and the better friend made no concession to the lesser's lack of ability.

(F,13)   *D. is really popular. She thinks she's hot stuff. A. has a crush on the same guy. He likes D. She went with him and makes A. mad. (What would happen?) If they're best friends, it wouldn't affect their relation. But A. is upset. She's mad for a while. (What would D. say?) D. would be mad but she couldn't do anything.*

As above, the more popular girl committed the offense. She competed for a boyfriend and won out over her less popular friend. The latter was upset. But, in the storyteller's mind, she could do nothing about it, and the more popular girl simply offered the excuse that she could not help being popular. Thus, the relation continued presumably with both friends recognizing their inequality and operating around it.

The Lesser Friend Offends   There were 6 stories in which offenses occurred in the context of inequality and were committed by the lesser of the two friends.

(M,8) *My friends tease me. Well, like I'm the smallest one in class.* (Do you get mad?) *Yes. I used to get mad, but now I just go over and tell the teacher.* (What does the teacher do?) *She punishes them. Puts them in the hall and stuff.* (Do you ever do things your friends don't like?) *Yeah. When they start teasing me, I used to go and say something to them or hit them.* (Why did you stop doing that?) *Because that wasn't right.* (After they tease you, are you still friends with them?) *Not always. But we make up sometimes.* (How do you make up?) *I say I'm sorry or something.*

This story could be classified either according to the offense of teasing or the smaller boy's telling the teacher. The inequality was based on size. The only remedial action was given by the smaller boy who apologized. This apology refers either to having reacted to the teasing with aggression or to having told the teacher. The bigger boys who did the teasing did not offer an apology.

(F,8) *This girl had lots of Nancy Drew books and she had a friend who didn't have many at all. One time they were playing hide-and-go-seek [at the friend's] and she found a lot of Nancy Drew books. She took some and hid them and she brought them home.* (Did she say anything to the friend who took the books?) *She didn't like it at all. They costed almost all her money. She said, "Did you steal any books of mine?" and she said, "No, I didn't steal any of your books."* (What do you think happened the next time they saw each other?) *They would get into a fight.* (About what?) *About you took my book.* (Were they still friends?) *Yes, they really were friends, but they didn't want to admit it. But they really felt sorry.* (What do you mean, they really felt sorry?) *Well, they were hurting each other's feelings—you know, they were really friends.* (Is there anything that could have happened to make them friends again?) *Yes. The girl who took the books could have given them back.... Then they'd talk about it and be friends again.*

The disparity in this story was based on material wealth. The poorer girl stole the richer girl's books. The burden of repair fell to the lesser girl who had to admit the theft and return the property.

(F,11) *A boy and girl were best friends. The boy was really super at sports and the girl was awful. But she was a good actor and the boy was dismal, not very good.... The teacher said the boy could have the part of directing the play. Everyone wanted to be in it . . . . He picked someone else [not his friend].* (What did the little girl do?) *She got angry because she was the best actor.* (What could happen later to make things better?) *The one who played the part was awful. The teacher said you did a bad job picking. He said he was sorry and they were both happy.* (Who was happy?) *He said he was sorry to the teacher and the girl. Both.*

The inequality was acting talent and the offense was not picking the better actor. The offender, the poorer actor, resolved the breach by apologizing to his friend as well as to the teacher.

(F,11)   *S. said she wouldn't tell what M. had said but S. told another girl M's secrets.* (What do you think M. would do?) *M. would get mad. Nobody would believe S. M. has so many friends. She's one of the most popular girls. Nobody listens to S.* (How does S. patch things up?) *By trying to do things. S. is going to have a party for her. She tries to be real nice and give her things . . . . S. will have to stop lying and promise not to tell everybody's secrets.*

This is a straightforward account in which the less popular girl offended her more popular friend. The friendship was upset until the offender went out of her way to appease the popular girl and then promised not to tell her secrets again.

(M,11)   *B. gets straight A's every single day and his best friend didn't seem to like it. That presented a problem because his best friend was bigger than he was. He always got mad and beat him up. B. solved that problem by telling the teacher about the bigger kid and the bigger kid got in trouble.* (What happened to their friendship?) *He was still mad at him for telling the teacher.* (What could happen that would get them to be friends?) *One thing was if the bigger kid was smarter in the first place, he might not have to be mad at him if he studied or if he just laid off B.* (What could get them back together? Go back to the first part of the story.) *It would be pretty hard. Only if B. saves the bigger kid from getting smashed by a truck or something like that. I don't know. So then the bigger kid would be indebted to him. That's about the only way it could work . . . . It's basically jealously.*

As with the first story in this set, the offense could be attributed either to the smarter, smaller boy, for telling the teacher, or the less smart but bigger boy for physical aggression. In either case, the burden of remediation fell to the smaller, less aggressive boy who had to get the bigger boy in his debt in order to resolve the dispute. The larger boy's jealousy was not easily handled, especially because the smaller boy had used the teacher's intervention against him.

(M,10) *They were having a gambling game and I told the principal. I threatened to tell the principal and they didn't like that and they were going to hold me back. So what I did was break out.* (What will happen?) *Probably, they're going to try to mess me up. They'll try to neglect me.* (What will have to happen for you to be friends again the same as before?) *Tell the principal I made a mistake, that I lied. Lie to the principal so they can get off.*

The inequality was between the group and an individual. The offense was committed by the individual in telling on the group. The burden for repair, therefore, fell to the individual who had to try to undo the offense to get back into the group's good favor.

Conclusions: Studies 10 and 11   The results of studies 10 and 11 are instructive in showing the varieties of friendship concepts which children hold. Insofar as children described several forms of resolution and nonresolution, one has to conclude that there is no single conception of what friendship is or how friends should operate. The process of repair is obviously variable. When it begins with an offense and retaliation, either a second offense or an apology may follow. The same problematic situation follows from offense and nonconfrontation.

If a general construct which fits all results is sought, equality is the most logical candidate. It is seen in study 10 in patterns of negative chaining as well as arbitrary break. The latter pattern was replicated in about half the stories obtained in study 11. Children proposing these patterns appeared to be asserting that friends have the right to reciprocate either positive or negative acts. When one friend initiates a negative act, the other can return it as an equal. If one friend then offers a positive gesture, the equal friend can do the same in return.

This concept was phrased differently in study 10. Using

equality as a principle, older children proposed that non-retaliation would be an effective means for stopping negative action. They seemed to be following a special line of reasoning. If friends are equals who can reciprocate, then not reciprocating a negative act obliges the offender to offer a positive gesture. If the offender accepts the invitation, the friends can return to their normal mode of functioning, which is to exchange positive acts reciprocally. The alternative would be to retaliate and then allow the rule of reciprocity to carry the friends along an unending path of negative exchanges.

It was also seen in study 10, and even more clearly in study 11, that nonretaliation serves other purposes. It may in fact be a response to *inequality* between friends. Several stories indicated that friends in lesser or one-down positions may have been unable to retaliate. They had to accept offenses as insults. Further, when repair occurred, they were responsible for carrying the burden. Or as some children put it, the better off, or one-up friend who committed the offense, was not responsible for undoing it or for offering an apology.

These data indicate that children come to understand inequalities and their consequences in realistic ways. Friends compete as well as cooperate. Because of differences in talent or circumstance, some friends possess more power in relations than do others. In some of the stories seen in study 11, the lesser friends appeared to be enduring the one-down position. They rarely reciprocated an offense. Although they got angry, they could do little to retaliate. They sometimes called on adult authorities for assistance. But ultimately they suffered the disadvantage of inequality and waited for the stronger friend to invite them back into the relationship.

These results are probably best understood in the context of a broader picture. Inequality within friendship is a valuable experience. One can learn to see oneself in realistic perspective with others. For any asset a person might have, someone else may have it more abundantly, just as another may have it to a lesser degree. Similarly, some friends abide by the norms of equality, while others do not. The latter are exemplified by friends who exploit their better positions to the disadvantage of others. Recognition of these facts no doubt helps children gain a sense of self and uses of the self in interpersonal relations. In ordinary circumstances, children need not remain fixed within relations of inequality with friends. Knowing the potentially negative consequences, children can seek other friends with whom they can work out more equitable and mutually comfortable relations. This would follow from the voluntary nature of the relation.

The definitions obtained in study 8 indicate that most children simultaneously recognize the ideals achievable within friendship. These include shared identities, deep mutuality, mutual concern, shared intimacy, and openness. Were study 8 seen by itself, one might guess that the friendship concept develops along a single positive line, perhaps even in counterpoint to child-adult relations. But parts of study 9, and more clearly studies 10 and 11, call for a different assessment. Friendship is not a singularly pure, positive relation. In reality, it partakes of cooperation as well as competition, unilateral constraint, insult, embarrassment, jealousy, and private suffering. These facts contribute to a sense of self and understanding of relationship. Still, from these facts as well as positive experiences, children are able conceptually to articulate ideals and norms which, by all accounts, center on equality.

It is important to note that the theme of inequality has been brought out and shown to recur in those studies in which children were asked to address the negative side of friendship (studies 4, 5, 7, 9, 10, and 11). This suggests that children are most likely sensitive to inequality because they understand equality to be the basis of friendship. Knowing the norm, they are keenly aware of real-life deviations from it. What these results show then is that friendship is not solely a positive experience but one through which children can see the ideal, which is a relation in which two persons voluntarily agree to treat each other as equals in all respects.

Twelve Reciprocity: Ideal Principle and Real Practice

The aim of the concluding section of this book is to present an integrative description of interpersonal development for the age period of 6 to 14 years. The focus so far has been on two relations, the goal being to document children's understanding of these relations as it developed during the period. The present chapter is concerned primarily with peer and friendship relations, which is the chief interest of Sullivan's and Piaget's thinking and perhaps the most innovative part of their thesis. In general, other theorists have tended to neglect these relations in favor of children's relations with adults. Theoretical treatment of peers and friends has either made these relations into adjuncts to socialization paced by adults or stressed the deviancy which peers encourage. In either case, the contributions which peer and friendship relations make to healthy social development have been minimized or simply ignored.

The key to the Sullivan-Piaget thesis is the construct of reciprocity. It leads first of all to the proposition that development must be studied through interpersonal relationships. Conventional appraisal of "behavior" or the cognizant child's reasons for action do not adequately take account of the two sides of social life. The child who acts, or thinks and then acts, continually receives reciprocal actions and thoughts from other persons. These are not simply additions to the child but become essential parts of the child. Interaction, which includes initiatives and

227

reciprocations, is the unit of analysis that replaces the child's acting or thinking alone.

Reciprocity also serves as the basis for differentiating two relations, and is the means by which children can analyze interactions and find their parts in interactions with respect to other persons. It explains the structures of relations and accounts for the logical origin of the functions which follow from putting relations into everyday practice. From the major findings about the naïve practice, the structuring, and the functional products of direct reciprocity, symmetrical reciprocity will be discussed. Two conclusions can be drawn. One is that the thesis gives valuable insight into the developmental course within peer and friendship relations. The second is that the thesis can be used to account for development from pragmatic peer relations to the structuring of friendship as a dialectical process. This change, which occurs between 6 and 14 years of age, seems to emerge from the discovery that direct reciprocity is a problematic method which has ambiguous outcomes for the participants. One solution is found in the reconceptualization of direct reciprocity into principles of cooperation and equal treatment. At the same time, these principles have to be adapted to the fact that persons differ, have conflicts of interest, and do not always act in ideal ways.

Before reviewing the findings which bear on these points, it is important to recall the goals of our studies. The Sullivan-Piaget thesis was offered as an innovative perspective on social development and the place of two relations in that development. At the same time, it was noted that the thesis was composed of broad constructs in need of sharpening and deficient in suggesting definite behavioral measures. The empirical data generated by our studies thus serve two purposes. One is to suggest ways by which major constructs, like the principle of reciprocity, may be converted into more testable form, and to find ways to submit constructs, such as mutual understanding, to plausible measures. The second is see to how well the thesis would fare in the face of children's thinking. Children's accounts of interpersonal interactions are descriptive data and have the weaknesses of all such data. They are not amenable to conventional hypothesis testing and are not properly ready for standard statistical analyses. However, if approached cautiously, these data can be used to evaluate the thesis, clarify its constructs, and serve as springboards for future studies in which more rigorous methods may be applied. For the present, the descriptive accounts will have served well if they sus- tain the thesis sufficiently to engage others in its pursuit.

The Major Findings   A review of results indicates that Sullivan's and Piaget's out- line of the chronology of peer relations corresponds fairly closely to children's accounts. At the same time, each step in the continuous progression was found to be accom- panied by an understanding of the ambivalence of the method, its structual basis, and the functions which follow from it. These results show that direct reciprocity can lead to relational development which forms the composition of social understanding appropriate for relations to be established in later life. They also show, however, that the ideal form of existence which direct reciprocity engenders is attained with struggle and carries risks and liabilities which children's concepts must realistically include. The chief results are as follows:

1. Children of the 6 to 8 year level have already ordered interactions between peers according to the general method of direct reciprocity. In almost every study, the majority of children at this age level gave spontaneous accounts in which one child's contribution to an interac- tion could have been or was actually matched to another child's contribution. It is evident that children understand their parts in peer interactions and feel free to make like contributions. This result contrasts with children's parts in interactions with adults, where the method of rec- iprocity by complement dominates and children make their contributions conform to the anticipated wishes of adults.

2. To be appreciated in full, direct reciprocity has to be seen from a double perspective. Children of this age level applied the method to unkindness as well as to kindness and to the process of establishing friendship as well as to offending a friend or ending a relation. In summary, chil- dren said that "When I share, you will share back." They also said, "When you hurt me, I will hurt you back." This

stable finding has two implications. The first is that children of this level practice direct reciprocity concretely and naïvely. They use it for positive as well as negative social purposes either to bring two peers closer together or to drive them apart. The second is that direct reciprocity used in this manner discourages formation of a stable interpersonal relation. It leads to closeness or separation depending upon circumstance.

3. At round 9 years of age children appear to have made a major advance in their understanding of this method. They showed in their accounts an understanding of cooperation in its usage and treated cooperation as a norm or principle. They also appear to begin to define friendship as a relation which is sustained by cooperation in the method. Friends were described as ready to make adjustments of personal interests for the sake of someone else's needs. Moreover, they described the process of adjustment as mutual. The person who offers help to someone can count on being helped in the future when personal circumstances are reversed.

At the same time, understanding of the principle does not preclude peers or friends from failing to cooperate. Storytellers had no difficulty generating instances of unkindness or offenses to friendship. This finding may be taken to mean that children are aware of and familiar with breakdowns in cooperation. Results also show, however, that these children view breakdowns as violations of a norm. Several specific results point to this conclusion. They include descriptions of acts of omission as cases of unkindness, accounts of patterns of undoing offenses in which retaliation was avoided, and explicit mention that offenses were deviations from a norm.

4. Two simultaneous changes seem to accompany the above finding: Cooperation appears as a principle, and children begin to articulate the importance of personhood. Peers were described in accounts as being in separate psychological states and as making adjustments to these states. Actions subsequently taken appeared to be directed toward achieving equality or equity between the states. These results point to establishment of a second norm, which may be called the principle of equality or of equal treatment. Children recognize that leaving a peer in

a state of need, when one has the capacity to help, is a violation of relationship. It is not simply unkind but will prevent a friendship from starting, and, within a friendship, it is grounds for remedial actions which are necessary to reestablish the relation. Other grounds for repair include dominance, exclusion, and taking of advantage of one's superior position, all of which constitute exceptions to the principle.

As with the basic method and the norm of reciprocity, children admit that peers and friends do not always treat one another as equals. Their accounts show they understand that violations occur, and they were able to offer specific proposals for correcting them. They also recognize that not all friendships are founded on equality and clearly see these relations as entailing risks. In particular, friends in lesser positions may have to live with the burden of being treated with less than sensitivity and respect. This identification of the fragileness of such relations emphasizes, by implication, knowledge of the norm coupled with a realistic coming to grips with everyday facts of peer society.

5. Further changes were noticed in the advance from middle-school age through early adolescence. The norm of equality was expanded into a sense that friends had similar personalities and nearly shared identity. Cooperation was elaborated as friends not only adjusted to needs but openly came to one another revealing problems and admitting to difficulties. A fuller grasp of the relation as an enduring entity was evident in adolescents' descriptions of mutual understanding, intimacy, and exclusivity. All of these changes may be seen as logical outcomes of the structure of cooperation, and all show how far approximately eight years of extensive experience with peers have carried development from the naïve starting point of literal use of the method.

As with other advances, these changes were accompanied by knowledge of the actual impediments to realizing friendship in any ideal way. While a shared identity binds friends, either friend may alter his or her personality and consequently undermine the grounds for relation. While friends feel free to reveal their problems and shortcomings, opening of oneself involves the risk of

being laughed at or brushed off. Mutuality, intimacy, and
exclusivity can also be liabilities. Friends know so much
about each other that each has to trust the other not to let
this privileged view become public.

**The Nature
of Friendship**

The foregoing summary of results shows support for the
thesis and adds an important aspect to it. The path from
peer interactions to knowledge of friendship appears to
follow a continuous progression in use and understanding
of the method of direct reciprocity. The two critical
changes are seen in the step from naïve practice to the
decision to use the method cooperatively and, once the
latter step is taken, to derive the functional fruits of the
structure which allow a near merging of friends into a unit
where "I and You" become a *we*. What results add that the
thesis does not make clear is the struggle involved in
movement toward the *we*. At any moment in the process,
the persons who make up the relation remain individuals,
and this gives each the freedom to step outside the relation
to act for personal rather than mutual ends. To stay within
the relation and sustain it, children have to coordinate
self-interests and act in accord with the principles which
they know will serve the relation in the long run. Results
indicate that, while children come to understand this fact
as they advance toward adolescence, the struggle does not
necessarily become easier.

At the 6 to 8 year level, the ambivalence of direct reciprocity is clearly manifest in children's descriptions of
its dual uses. Sharing material possessions and playing
obviously bring peers closer together. For instance, when
one offers to share, it is highly likely that the other will
then offer to share. But the same method applies in negative instances, so that when one hurts the other, the other
is likely to retaliate. In such cases, one peer is pitted
against the other, and the result of the method is to drive
them apart, even to the point of instigating an endless
series of negative tit for tat. The discovery of cooperation
and its establishment as a norm does not end the ambivalence. This was brought out most clearly by the young
adolescents who cited the real possibility of disap-
pointments in close friendships. The very interactions
which serve to enhance closeness, like self-revealment,

carry the inherent risks of not being accepted or of being exposed to other persons outside the relation by the friend whom one has trusted.

Despite the duality, the overriding conclusion has to be that friendship is a relation much as Sullivan and Piaget say. It is founded on direct reciprocity and becomes structured when peers discover how to convert the method to cooperative usage. In the process, the persons who participate in the method become articulated individuals. Friends then discover characteristics they share in common. Meanwhile, by continuing to practice friendship, children formulate norms which, in turn, insure that their relation will endure. Subsequently, friends learn how to admit to their inner feelings, doubts, and weaknesses. They bring these to one another for validation, advice, clarification, and for "figuring out problems together." Such honest presentations of self are protected by the norms of the relation and eventuate in interpersonal trust. They also give rise to mutual understanding which is described by adolescents as knowing that one will be understood by the other as one truly is.

While this picture of development stops short with the observations of 14-year-old adolescents, Sullivan's and Piaget's projection of friendship to the adult personality now can be seen more clearly. Their argument is that friendship is the originating source of adult intimate relations. They mean to say that friendship gives rise to those components which make intimate relations possible. They explicitly identify the elements of interpersonal sensitivity, willingness to adjust to the other person, and mutual respect. It would be incautious simply to draw a straight line from the manifestation of these components in the findings to an imaginary moment in adulthood. It is, however, plausible to speculate that young adolescents' conceptions of friendship are the first signs of these elements and may very well be the seeds to be nurtured in later development.

A subsidiary conclusion is appropriate at this point. Upon first reading, the Sullivan-Piaget thesis may appear to be overly idealistic. This perception may be enhanced by the general skepticism which many theorists have about development which is not guided by adults who are society's agents. The present findings provide an alternative to both views. The thesis is not built upon a hypothesized inherent goodness in children. On the contrary, the positive sociality of friendship and its powerful cohesive force are grounded in a method of interacting which is dualistic in nature and ambivalent in its results. Norms of cooperation and equal treatment are not obvious but have to be discovered. This entails a struggle wherein self-interest has to be woven into a perspective and made compatible with mutual benefit. As to the need for adult guidance, the present findings suggest that the norms which make intimacy possible may be logically seen to arise from peers conjoint efforts. By working together to establish and maintain relationship, peers can on their own evolve those principles which supply the logical material of what one would ordinarily call the backbone of mature morality. They are cooperation and equality. This is not to deny that child-adult relations may be a necessary background or context for development within the world of peers. It is, however, to suggest that they are causally secondary during the span in question and that peer relations provide the primary arena where interpersonal understanding is developed during this era.

The Nature of Reciprocity   Sullivan and Piaget propose that children discover early in life that their actions cannot be understood as isolated events. Actions can have reliable meaning only when they are understood as reciprocal to the actions of other persons. In the present research, the earliest observations were of children who just entered school. Children of this age have already accumulated a wealth of social experience with family members, neighbors, relatives, playmates, and strangers such as clerks in stores and workmen. Children ought to have drawn from these experiences a pervasive wariness of what can be accomplished by exclusive focus on their own actions. They should be clearly experienced in the fact of reciprocity in interactions and the invariant characteristics which Sullivan and Piaget treat as methods of exchange.

Studies 1 through 7 supplied supporting evidence. Direct or symmetrical reciprocity was seen to apply widely to accounts of interactions between peers. In study 6, the majority of children said that peers would exchange kindness with identical or equivalent acts. For example: *In a game my friend let me go first.* (Then) *I let him sometimes use my ball.* Study 7 displayed the same method with acts of unkindness, for instance: One kid says, *"I will not walk to school with you."* (Then) *the other said, "I won't walk to school with you."* As was shown in chapter 8, the data from these two studies confirm earlier results pertaining to accounts of single acts. These acts may be seen as essential parts of an ongoing system of exchange. While only single acts were described, they may be logically understood as being reciprocations to previous acts or invitations for subsequent reciprocations.

Accounts of interactions between adults and children were also consistent in revealing knowledge of a system of reciprocal exchange. Instead of direct reciprocity, this system took the form of reciprocity by complement. It was illustrated in study 6 when children initiated kind acts and adults reacted. For example: *I do what they say,* (then) *they reward you.* Or, *When my mother asked, I swept the floor.* (Then) *she gives you a big dinner.* Complementariness was evident also when adults initiated kind acts and children reacted, for instance: *My father helped me learn to play soccer.* (Then) *I was nice by cleaning the yard.* Unkind exchanges of study 7 were equally illustrative of the same method. Instances were as follows: *Disobey them.* (Then) *They give you a spanking for disobeying.* Or, *Maybe not do as she's told.* (Then) *The mother will feel hurt, but she'd punish them.*

These results clarify the thesis on two major points. First, they show that children of 6 to 8 years have already grasped the methods of reciprocity and sorted them out respectively for interactions with peers and adults. It should be remembered that instructions given the children did not obviously suggest use of these methods or their differentiation by actor-recipient designations. Second, children's choice to express kindness and unkindness in these methodological terms indicates that they have come to order themselves in somewhat definite relations to others. It is plausible to suggest that children believe that adherence to methods is a positive sign of relationship. They said, in effect, that interacting within an established method was a way of showing that one person liked another. The congruent result was that deviation from established methods was considered unkind or a sign of not liking.

It is worth pointing out an interesting perspective which Sullivan and Piaget bring to the concept of kindness. In conventional thinking, kindness is said to be a function of a person's attitude or motivation. Generally, this attitude is understood as a suppression of one's self-interest for the sake of another person and is sometimes called altruism. A main interest of developmental researchers has been in finding when children become altruistic by initiating acts which help another even though there will be no payoff to themselves. The conventional viewpoint may be seen as founded on a model in which the actor and recipient are considered separated individuals who act to the benefit of one or the other. The perspective offered by Sullivan and Piaget, which may be seen in the present results, differs. Instead of being individuals apart, actor and recipient are seen as persons belonging to a more fundamental unit, which is their relation. Children appear to believe that preservation of the unit represents a positive social statement. When actors initiate kind acts by showing adherence to a mutually understood method of exchange, they affirm their own and the recipients' relational existence.

There is no doubt that particular kind acts have immediate benefits for recipients. In this respect, it may reasonable to say that actors suppress their own interests for those of recipients. But from the present perspective such an analysis would overemphasize individuality and overlook the interpersonal factor. As a member of an exchange system, a person's actions cannot be assessed meaningfully unless they are seen either as reciprocations to previous acts by another person or as expectations of future reciprocations by that other person. For example, when a child shares a possession, the momentary loss of something has to be weighed against what that child has previously gained or will gain later through the method of exchange. This is to put single acts into a broader context which is the conservation of the method and the relation. Within this context, it becomes difficult to sever interests and place them into separate personal compartments. It is more plausible to conclude that acts which preserve methods of exchange benefit both persons because they serve to affirm and therefore enhance the relational existence of the persons.

It is important to recognize that differentiation of the two methods occurred within children's own examples of interpersonal accounts. There was nothing obvious in the given instructions to lead children toward one or another selection. One might argue, of course, that children thought the interviewers wanted to hear that they shared, played, obeyed, and did not misbehave. As in all interview studies of the present sort, social desirability is a potential factor. It may also be argued, however, that this factor is a weak candidate for explaining why children generated the particular interactions which were obtained. There was no obvious reason why children did not describe child actors being kind by doing the bidding of other peers or by sharing or playing with adults. A few children did in fact. But, in the main, the methods of direct and complementary reciprocity were kept separate for peers and adults, respectively. And in a telling manner, the same differentiation by method was applied by independent samples of children when they described unkindness as a failure to reciprocate directly to peers, and as not conforming or behaving in a noncomplementary manner to adults.

The Development of Reciprocity	In a system of reciprocity by complement, one person has the power to take charge of interactions. If the other wants acceptance or approval, he or she must act according to the demands of the person in charge. Once the system is established, the exchange of one's obedience for the other's approval allows interactions to proceed smoothly. This is true even when the two persons might have different opinions about some event. The person in charge may insist that his or her opinion be followed and enforce this belief by withholding approval until the other person follows it. If the other person maintains a separate view, disapproval or punishment is risked.

As Sullivan points out, nonapproval provokes anxiety, especially when the complementary system is predicated on the belief that the person in charge has a privileged view of reality. If children believe adults to possess such knowledge, then failure to gain acceptance has the additional risk of isolating one's opinion from society at large. As Sullivan also notes, while the balance obviously tilts toward avoidance of such risk, children may still occasionally want to maintain their own opinions. One way for them to do this is to act in a manner which will lead to acceptance but, simultaneously, keep their opinions private. Sullivan refers to this as a potentially unhealthy secretiveness which may deter communication generally within the complementary system.

Direct reciprocity involves a different interpersonal arrangement in which one person's actions can be identical or equivalent to the other person's actions. Neither person alone can take charge and direct the other, except insofar as the other person allows it. Were one to atempt unilaterally to control the interaction, the method itself would permit the other person to do the same. Therefore, when one presents an opinion, saying, "I believe this," the other is free to accept it or say, "But I believe something else."

This method immediately fosters the image of two persons, each going in a separate direction. Each is entitled to an opinion, a feeling, or a thought, and is free to express it independently of the other person's expression. If left to its own devices, the method would logically lead to a *stalemate,* with each person free to express opinions and neither unilaterally powerful enough to enforce an opinion. This method does not seem to fit Sullivan's and Piaget's assumption of the interdependency of action. Rather it seems to promote the opposite, which is total independence of two persons' actions. How do Sullivan and Piaget conclude that this method of interrelating is the source of mutual understanding and intimacy in peer relations? If two persons start interacting with different opinions, the method does not in itself contain any element which would bring the persons together; at best, one could imagine them leaving the interaction as they started, which is with different opinions.

If the above analysis is accurate, it follows that the method of direct reciprocity can work only when *two per-*

sons agree to cooperate in its usage. Since the method allows for disagreement, consent must be *voluntary.* Indeed, voluntariness, consent, and cooperation hold the key to this method's social workability and explain the social outcomes which may be derived from it developmentally. When all these components are present, the potential exists for mutual understanding and intimacy. Friendship is an obvious candidate for this constructive state of affairs since the relation involves free selection between peers who agree to work for their mutual benefit. At the same time, however, each friend remains free to back out of the agreement or to stop cooperating in it. There is no mechanism within direct reciprocity comparable to that within complementariness by which one person could force the other to continue to abide by the method.

With this clarification in mind, the reader should be able to approach the results with a fresh perspective. There is an ambivalence in friendship which is clearly expressed in children's conceptions of it. These conceptions show that children think of friendship in all of the positive aspects which Sullivan and Piaget propose. Children simultaneously show, however, that friendship builds upon an inherently fragile process. Adolescents know that friendships may end, that friends who reveal themselves can be harmed, or that investments of concern in another might not be paid back. The very method which makes for friendship's uniqueness in children's interpersonal existence contains the seeds for friendship's own destruction. The nature of direct reciprocity makes children's conceptions of these relations ideal and at the same time realistic. Children appear to find in these relations possibilities for positive interpersonal feelings, bordering on unity, which could not come from participation in other types of relations. But the procedures by which friends interact are available for other uses. One friend can at any time freely drop out of the relation. One friend may stop cooperating in reciprocity and turn it around to negative ends. If either happens, the other friend can do little except invite renewal of the relation. The offer will be effective, however, only if both friends consent to their previous agreement.

The foregoing discussion adds a final point of clarity to

the theoretical differentiation between peer or friendship relations and child-adult relations. Many instances of the latter, in particular those between parent or teacher and child, are not voluntary nor do they persist by agreement. They are more like fixed arrangements which require collaborative effort to be sustained. For the age period of present interest, these relations are given to children and remain in effect aside from any consent on the part of the child. As with peer relations, those interactions children have with adults require adaptations on the child's part as well the adult's. But collaboration in the method in child-adult relations cannot be freely dropped by children, and it is doubtful that they see their participation in it as voluntary. This conception may change in adolescence, as was shown in our studies when 12 to 14 year olds began to speak of *voluntary obedience* or *conforming by free will*, and described *talking back* as an offense toward adults. The possibility will be considered later that such descriptions imply a changing conception of the child-adult relation, a change which may have its impetus in the understanding that friendship relations exist through two persons' voluntary consent.

How Direct Reciprocity Is Advanced   It has already been demonstrated that the method of direct reciprocity has no inherent developmental directionality. At the same time, the evidence is that children come to understand that the method can be used cooperatively to establish and sustain friendships. According to Piaget, the reconstitution of the method into a principle marks a change from simply acting, to controlling one's part in interactions by a conceptual norm. But this step only opens children to a new problem, which is to discover ways of converting the principle into practice. The requirements are complex because they demand a balance between presenting and suppressing oneself, speaking out and listening, holding on to one's views and letting them be modified by another's viewpoint. Requirements apply equally to self and other, and adaptation of the norm to reality must involve constructions based on equal effort from both persons.

For Sullivan and Piaget, this adaptation is described generally as the evolution of *procedures* which are particular extensions of the normative method. They refer to such procedures as compromise, debate, and discussion. Their argument is that, if such procedures are not constructed, cooperation will fail. Reversion to concrete practice of the method will result in dominance by one or the other person or lead to stalemate as each's person holds on to views and refuses to give in to the other. The object here, then, is to see whether our results contain clear evidence that procedures have been constructed and, if so, what they look like in practice.

Developing procedures   The cooperative use of direct reciprocity is a method for preventing a stalemate situation, possible when two peers of equal power assert their respective individuality. For example, in study 7, some children said that one unkindness would set off a chain reaction; first one peer would assert superiority, then the other, then the first again, and so on, with no resolution. As one child put it: "They would have a lifelong fight." In Sullivan's and Piaget's reasoning, the need for cooperation can be learned from just such instances. Instead of allowing individual viewpoints to collide, with personal interests pitted against one another, procedures of cooperation permit children to discover the benefits of working together and the value of adapting their respective selves to the *we* of a relation.

It has already been shown that older children believe that acts of omission are unkind (study 4) and offensive to friendship (studies 10 and 11). These results may indicate that older children recognize the importance of acting cooperatively. A child's failure to assist another can be seen to be a matter of not living up to an obligation. If friends are to take turns in helping each other, then one friend's failure to act on a particular occasion is a violation of principle. The general point is illustrated in the following account given by a 13-year-old boy.

There was these two boys [who] help each other build go-carts.... One of them breaks. [The boy whose cart broke asked] "Should we build another one?" The boy who still has his said, "No we can just race in mine.... One of us can run, and since it is mine, I guess I'll have to drive it.... You can run alongside." The kid's really sad his friend won't

help him build a new cart because he already has his. (The
storyteller indicates here the recognition of a violation.) *The
boy builds his own cart and this one's really sharp. I mean
this one's all out good. [They race and] the boy who had the
old go-cart lost by really a lot. The boy with the new go-cart
thinks, "Maybe his will break. Maybe I would help him or
maybe I won't." He thinks he should tell him that he should
have helped. So he tells him, "Maybe you should have
helped me when mine broke, because then we could have shared
the pleasure of having a good go-cart."* (This is the boy's
articulation of the principle.) *So the boy with the old one
said, "You know, I think you're right. Should we build another
one out of my parts?"* (Now we see the other boy's agreement to the principle.) *He says OK, so they end up building
another one that's just as good as his.* (The resolution.)

At its core, the agreement to cooperate in direct reciprocal exchange requires mutual coordination of self-
interest. The method allows each child to assert a viewpoint, hold to an opinion, and defend a stand, but, at the
same time, it necessitates that each will also attend to the
other's position. In the process, there is a check on the self
matched by a check on the other. Clearly, the method will
not work unless both parties cooperate in the same manner. Were just one of them always to give in, the method
would be distorted and border on becoming another version of unilateral constraint. As seen in the example just
cited, both boys recognize the principle, one by stating
what should have been done and the other by admitting
he was in error. Further, both make an appeal to the
mutual benefit cooperation would have produced, in this
case, a better cart that both boys could enjoy.

As in the complementary method, cooperation should
yield payoffs to both parties in the exchange. For example,
the 11 year old's conformity in doing chores benefits the
parent, and, in turn, the parent's granting permission to
go to a movie benefits the 11 year old. Direct reciprocity is
also an exchange system in which two peers benefit. What
the findings show is that children come to recognize
the difference between immediate payoff to the self and
the longer term gain of cooperation. They seem to understand that, at any moment, one child may be called upon
to give up something for the other. Were this act isolated

from the principle, the crucial motivating source would have been missed. In conceding to another at the moment, a child realizes that a turn will come up when the other will concede to his or her interest. Therefore, suppression of self is not so much a case of a competition between "self or other," but more a matter of sustaining a system which in the long run benefits both self and other.

Although the interviews were not designed to uncover details of particular procedures, they yielded accounts which may exemplify a variety of these procedures. The following list provides a tentative summary where each procedure represents a different attempt to adapt the principle to particular cases.

1. Taking Turns: *The one who has a bike will take turns [with the boy who doesn't have a bike]; You let them take turns on a swing; They won't always be the boss. Sometimes they'll let you decide, they'll take turns [deciding]; She lets me have things she doesn't want and I give her things I have.*

2. Conceding: *Like if I wanted to play baseball and they wanted to play tennis.... Go along with them; You're playing and one of them cheats.* (They argue.) *The other one says, "OK" He let it go; He's always interested in what you are interested in and vice versa.... I'll give in for you and you'll give in for him; If... you hit on the ball and they say you didn't, there won't be a big argument.*

3. Supporting the other: *Take up for him if someone's picking on him; I sort of got in trouble and sort of blamed my friend. He would let it stay; If you did something wrong, they'll share the responsibility; If you get in trouble, he won't say you did it but stays with you; Someone who sticks up for you; [A friend] won't leave you if you get in trouble.*

4. Explaining: *If the person is stuck [with schoolwork], show them the answer but tell them why it's the answer; if someone's being mean to that person... you can tell them not to and ask why; Talk over assignments. Help each other; She gets in trouble with her parents. Jill... gives her advice; [When she quit a game] go to her house and ask her why.*

5. Discussion: *You know each other good and talk things out; [Friends] talk problems out with you; You can talk to*

> *him and . . .He'll talk to you; [Friends] asks questions to
> each other; Talk over assignments; [A friend] wants
> to come and talk about your problems; He would just listen
> to you and you would listen to him; A person you can talk
> to who will listen and tell you their problems.*

6. Reflecting Views: *When you have a problem, you can tell
   that friend and talk it over with him and he'll understand; She'll help you understand how you feel and give
   advice; Someone you can talk to . . . . They can tell you
   what's wrong and what's right in a way . . . . Then you can
   go to your friend and he would know what to say.*

Each procedure gives a slightly different look at processes by which peers or friends coordinate their possession of material goods, their thoughts, their feelings, and
their problems. In each case, there is an opportunity for
one of the persons to act unilaterally. For instance, the
child who has a possession might keep it rather than
give it up. The child who is in trouble could be left to take
blame without the other getting involved. Or, the child
who comes with a problem need not be listened to. But
these procedures indicate that children have developed a
sense of cooperation which counteracts the tendency for
the self to act independent of the interest of the other.
There is reason for giving up one's own interest and taking on the burden of another's problem if in so doing, the
other is committed to do the same for the self. Note that
children also describe procedures in which peers or
friends practice reciprocity only with difficulty. The
clearest instances of this were shown in studies 10 and 11
when friends were depicted as arguing. For example, two
friends had different opinions about some event in a game
or disagreed about someone's social behavior. For the
majority of children, the argument went back and forth
with each child presenting a different viewpoint. However, in the majority of accounts, one of the children
stopped the argument by offering an apology which, in
general, was usually accepted. For other children, the argument was stopped by one of the children who simply
walked away from the dispute.

These procedures are essential to a realistic concept of
friendship. Friends cannot always give in to one another;
circumstances sometimes force them to disagree, espe-

cially when one of them feels hurt by the other. If friendship is to be workable, children have to develop procedures which can be used to handle such situations. Some children say, *I'm sorry;* others avoid the dispute by *walking away;* and still others simply initiate new positive behavior, e.g., *go to their house and ask them if they want to play.* The typical response to these procedures was acceptance so that the friends could return to their normal mode of functioning. They were recognized as attempts to correct earlier violations and seen as signs that offenders wanted to reestablish relationship.

Interestingly, the process of arguing rarely occurred between child and parent. It may be important to note that adolescents, but rarely younger children, described *talking back* as unkind (see studies 4 and 10). Talking back is precisely what friends can do in following the method of direct reciprocity. They talk back when exchanging opinions or in argument. But the very act of expressing a view contrary to the parent's was identified by storytellers as unkind. This characterization, however, was stated almost exclusively by adolescent storytellers, which may indicate that, at this age level, procedures of direct reciprocal exchange have become well-developed and have been tried out in child-adult relations, but were found not yet to have been accepted by adults who generally disapproved of their use.

Almost invariably, in our accounts, when children talked back to adults and said they would not do what adults asked, adults either punished them or insisted that children act as requested. With few exceptions, children accepted the punishment and did what they were told. Adults' right to control was acknowledged and children's differences in interests were discounted. In effect, children's opinions were not listened to and the possibility for dialogue was suppressed when children apologized for speaking out and reformed their behavior to conform with adults' expectations. This is a case of self-suppression which is unilateral on the child's part. With friends, the speaking of one's mind became more and more taken for granted with increasing age. As children said, friends will listen in the same way they expect to be heard. Dialogue in the form of argument was the norm. When one child came to another with a different personal viewpoint, the expressed expectation was: *He won't brush you off; They won't laugh at you; A friend never puts you down; . . . or, turns you down.*

The conclusion to be drawn from this set of results is twofold. First, factually speaking, children show an increasing awareness that direct reciprocity is a method which binds their particular relationship. They also show that the method requires mutual adaptation of one friend's interests with respect to another's interest. To adapt this principle to real-life circumstances, children work together to develop procedures which allow speaking out and listening. Procedures range from elemental taking turns to sophisticated reflection of one's feelings in front of another person for the sake of validation. The second aspect of this conclusion pertains to the outcome of these procedures. Sullivan and Piaget propose a series of developmental achievements which include conceptualization of equality, discovery of one's personhood in common with another, mutuality in understanding between friends, and intimacy in relationships involving caring and respect. These achievements are logical outcomes of a relation based on the method of direct reciprocity and grounded in cooperation. Once peers choose to use this method voluntarily, they must agree to develop procedures to make it workable. Thereafter, the positive outcomes which are proposed become possible. Thus, in demonstrating that children do recognize both sides of reciprocity, and that they do develop adaptive procedures to this end, the groundwork is laid for interpersonal development of relations in which friends can coordinate their respective interests and gain respect in the process. This implies a conceptual framework within which self and other subordinate themselves to the relationship and enhance each other through it. This achievement will be discussed in greater detail in the next chapter.

Thirteen   Transitions to Adolescence in Two Relations

The present chapter elaborates the conclusions presented in the previous chapter. It will focus on the structural basis of friendship and will consider in detail the functional products which should follow from it. It is evident that several new insights into interpersonal understanding become possible once children make a compact to cooperate. The period roughly corresponding to 9 to 14 years of age witnesses numerous conceptual breakthroughs. Almost suddenly, friendship takes on characteristics which earlier relations with peers did not have and relations with adults did not provide. Four of these characteristics will be considered: equality, sharing personhood, mutual understanding, and intimacy. I admit this division is not the only possible method of sorting; however, it helps to illuminate the thesis and pulls together several of the findings.

While, as just noted, friendship takes on new characteristics for children in the 9 to 14 year range, results also suggest that, during the latter part of this period, changes also occur in their relations with adults. This chapter will also focus on these changes. The possibility was raised earlier that the chief change involves a transformation from complementariness to a system more in keeping with direct reciprocity. The transformation includes definition of adults as individual personalities, which enhances the change from unilateral authority to equality. These possibilities fit with the hypothesis that the impetus for change comes from children's knowledge of friendship. Having seen the possibilities in this relation for consent, voluntary participation, and intimacy, children may begin to view relations with adults in similar terms. Data will therefore be reviewed to see how well this part of the thesis is sustained by children's accounts.

Equality and Personhood   In Sullivan's and Piaget's reasoning, the practice of direct reciprocity engenders further conceptual change in middle childhood. Most notably, children come to see one another as like persons who share characteristics and power. At first this appears to contain contradictory elements. Personhood implies individuality, and individuality entails the recognition of differences between persons. Equality, on the other hand, involves likeness in the sense that persons who are equals share qualities to the same extent.

Before describing the resolution of equality with individuality as it can be found in the data, one should consider the construct of equality from an analytic viewpoint. There are two general treatments of it in the social science literature (see Coleman 1976). In one, people are said to be equals by right because of some philosophical orientation. For example, Rawls (1971) holds to the position that, were persons blindly to choose a general condition for man, they would opt for equality out of a sense of justice. Not knowing how resources would be distributed, people would select as fair a distribution in which each would receive the same amount as the other. Resources refer to goods, talents, and abilities. An alternative is described by Nozick (1974) who suggests that, given a blind choice, people would not have to see equality as Rawls proposes. Instead they might hold that all persons were entitled to fair treatment. For example, persons would agree on fair ways for making distributions. But the fact of individual differences would dictate that even fair distribution would probably result in inequalities.

Coleman distinguishes these two viewpoints in the following way. He sees Rawls's point of view as based on a model in which persons would form society from a naïve position. Not knowing what their own talents were, persons would safeguard their chances by asking for equal distribution. This would insure that they would get a fair share, equal to everyone else's. If confronted at some historical moment with actual inequality, the principle would require redistribution. This is a safe choice since, even were a person to possess more than an equal share, circumstances could change and the person would need the principle as a personal guarantee. In contrast, Nozick's society would not be based on blind self-protection but rather, on the realization that persons are different, as are their needs. Instead of asking for equal distribution, which might at any moment require radical redistribution, persons ask only that three laws be in effect. (1) There would be agreed upon practices by which persons could acquire resources. (2) There would also be agreed upon practices by which resources would be transferred. And (3), there would be agreed upon practices to correct violations of (1) or (2). As long as all three laws were followed, unequal distribution could be accepted as a fair fact of life.

Of these two views, the 9 to 14 year olds sampled in our studies seemed to prefer the second approach. These children recognized individual differences and at the same time held that peers, in general, and friends, especially, deserved to be treated fairly. The composite conception which the data reveal is complex and should be analyzed according to its component parts. What is meant by individual differences? Children say that peers differ in terms of the following: material possessions, physical health, academic ability, social popularity, social skills, emotional stability, physical appearance, athletic talent, size, and a host of personality characteristics ranging from meanness to caring. To what are peers entitled? Children say that generally peers who recognize differences, and are in a position to respond to them, should act on one another's behalf. At any moment, the one able to assist the other should act. Over the long run, assistance ought to balance out so that one's talents and skills will be reciprocal with the other's.

Here is how children put it: *He is good in math . . . and [the other] is good in spelling; One is good in school and the other is good in sports.* Or, *Tim would help Bob get better in riding a bike and Bob would always help Tim at his homework.*

These descriptions, taken from the spontaneous qualifications in accounts of kindness, were completed by descriptions of how friends actually act and react in kind ways. When given a kindness, recipients said: *Well, now I owe you one; [I'll] try to pay them back. . . . If they're ever in the hospital, you may bring them a toy* (which is what the actor had done); *If you ever fall down, I'll help you too.* The conception is clarified in two protocols: *[Friends] exchange kindness for a long time, not just for a day.* And, *Try to do for them the things they did for me.*

Equal Treatment

From 9 years of age, children seem to recognize the fact that peers are different individuals. They believe that personality differences will lead to different sorts of contributions to interactions. For example, in describing reactions to offenses (study 10), children said: *If he's nice, he might just walk away. If he's nasty, he might pick a fight with him.* Or, *If the person had retaliated it, sometimes they'd continue teasing. If the person had ignored it, sometimes the whole thing is forgotten.* Children say that peers can take either type of option. But in describing friends, children believe that friends should adhere to the principle of equal treatment.

Emphasis is on equality of actions and not necessarily on the persons or results of actions. For instance: *A friend is a person who helps you do things . . . . You do the same for them.* And, *When I had problems, he helped me and when he had problems, I helped him.* The idea is straightforward in its expression. Peers have the power to assist one another: *A friend's there when you're down to get you up.* They might not, however, do so: *He leaves you there.* But in principle: *A friend can depend on you and [in turn] won't leave if you get in trouble.* The exchange is fair because it is based on a validated principle, not because it results in equal consequences: *Even though they can't help you, they'll sympathize.*

Equal treatment may be seen as a step in the process of adapting the method of direct reciprocity to cooperative ends. The advance involves adjusting cooperative procedures so that the persons let each other know that they agree to the arrangement. For example: *If someone is messing up in diagramming, instead of laughing, help him after class—help him as an equal and don't look down on them.* The case is made even more sharply by the following account:

> *If they're outside playing a game and [one is] not too good
> at it. You want to be on the winning team, so you don't pick
> her. You would say, "I don't want her because she can't
> throw or she can't catch."* (What would the offended girl
> do next?) *She wouldn't feel too good. If she were doing
> something you couldn't do, she would do it back; like not
> want you on a team or something.* (Then what would the
> first girl do the next day, the next time they met?) *Later
> that night it would probably bother me. I would apologize
> and say, "You can't do things I can do and I can't do things
> you can do. I'm sorry. Next time you can be on my team
> because games are just for fun."* (Then what does the other
> one say?) *She would probably say, "Don't worry about it.
> We're still friends." And we would be friends.*

This account contains all of the elements noted above.
The friends differ in ability and each girl recognizes this
fact. The difference at first leads one of them to put self-
interest ahead of concern for the other. The result is a
retaliation when the opportunity comes up. One of the
girls then thinks about the possibility that reciprocations
in a negative vein would emphasize differences and separate the friends further. An adjustment is immediately
made by asserting the principle that combines individual
differences with equality of treatment. The adjustment
is seen in the redefinition of games as not for winning but
for enjoyment. The second girl then accepts the principle
and attests to it by telling the first that she need not worry
and that they are friends as they were before.

Personhood   Sullivan and Piaget suggest that in the process of developing cooperative procedures, peers and friends begin to
discover their own and the other's personhood. This is a
difficult construct to deal with in light of traditional
theories in which personhood is taken for granted. Obviously, Sullivan and Piaget do not mean to say that younger
children are unware of their own individual being or think
that all peers are the same. What they mean is that conceptions of person have to be constructed and are not given.
Moreover, the construction is of a relative nature so that a
conception of self is dependent on the person's conception
of the other and vice versa. Sullivan and Piaget give peer

relations a special place in the construction process. They suggest that children need clear external reference points for comparisons with themselves. In relations with adults, children gain information about ways they differ from adults. But relations with peers allow both similarities and differences to be taken into account. Thus, children discover a differently articulated version of the self, and simultaneously of others, through their interactions with peers than they can through unilateral relations.

One sign of this development has already been mentioned several times throughout the studies. Children describe peers and friends as having different talents and being in different emotional states from time to time. A second piece of evidence appeared in study 9, which dealt with processes in the history of a friendship. Six to 8 year olds said that peers would become friends when they shared, played, talked, worked, or helped one another. From age 9 onward, children described these same activities not as the end but as leading to knowledge of one another as persons. They said: *They'll talk at first and get to know each other.* And, *They may have to work together on a project.... Then they know each other better.* Additional findings make it clear that by knowing each other as friends, children mean that friends find out that they are similar to one another. Children expressed the point as follows: *They might find out they like the same things; They would like each other's personalities.* And, *If they have something in common.* These statements of shared characteristics are reinforced by definitions of friendship in study 8. They included the following descriptions of friends: *Sharing interests with them; You have the same ideas; Someone who knows you and wants to be equal to you; Think the same feelings I do;* and, *They would believe in the same things and they would value the same things.*

The point is drawn out further by data on how children would not become friends. Children said that in interacting together peers might discover that: *They may have different opinions* [or] *attitudes; If they didn't have anything in common; They may not be each other's style.* And, *[They have] different personalities.* Unfortunately these data do not reveal the underlying meaning of these differences in behavioral terms. Nevertheless, descriptions such as these indicate that children realize that peers look to one another's personalities in a search for common characteristics, no doubt meaning that one's "style" of interacting reveals his or her person and serves as a basis for determining whether a friendship can be formed.

There is room for alternative interpretation to these findings. Children could be saying that characteristics inhere in persons, in which case their tasks are to identify and compare them. Or, they could be saying that common characteristics are constructed through interactive information and then imputed to conceptions of the persons. The former is the more conventional position, since it follows from the position that persons are by right existing, individual entities. In such a theory, each peer could assess the other's person and decide whether or not the characteristics a person possesses are likable.

The latter view is different. It is based on the premise that peers interact and in the process differentiate others with whom they can or cannot cooperatively form a reciprocal agreement. When children say that peers do not have similar opinions, they may mean that the peers cannot interact in cooperation so that when different opinions arise each insists on making his or her own position the only acceptable one. The possibility that characteristics may come from the test of actual procedures can be seen from two angles. One is younger children's descriptions of procedures which prevent friendship from starting. The other is older children's accounts of what makes for a "best" friendship. The procedures are by and large negative exchanges which by definition show the absence of mutual adaptation. The theme that dominates "best friends" is *getting along, sharing interest,* and *liking to do the same things.*

For Sullivan and Piaget, both persons bring characteristics of themselves to interactions. These characteristics give them styles of interacting which, for instance, determine how they will express anger as was seen in reactions to offenses. At the same time, what also determines how persons will be known is the way they interact together. In the case of peers, the relevant data refer to the ways peers adapt reciprocal exchanges to one another. To see one's commonality with others may then be equivalent to finding that one agrees to the same principles of interchange that the other does and therefore that the two can work out a level of reciprocal exchange which is satisfactory to each.

It would be fruitless to try to direct this discussion to a chicken-egg problem. The data do not identify which aspect of personhood comes first (i.e., person or relation). If anything, as further elaborated below in the section on mutuality, full self-revelation appears to progress with friendship and does not precede it so that it would be difficult to argue that friendship is a conjunction of two similar personalities. What the thesis adds that other theories overlook is the possibility that personal characteristics include such things as the ways persons participate in procedures and the degree to which they show allegiance to these procedures. For instance, children say that if they go to a friend with a problem and the friend helps and the friend does not brush them off or does not tell others about it, then the friend is *trustworthy*. What children seem to mean is that friends can depend on one another and that each can rely on the other to participate according to the norms of their reciprocal agreement. Trustworthiness is obviously a characteristic whose meaning is founded on children's knowledge of procedures. It is relevant to friendship because of the nature of the procedures which peers can use. A peer can reliably reciprocate or choose not to. Those who do the former merit trust.

Exploring this line of reasoning a step further, one can see why children choose to impute trust to friends and not to peers generally. It is a characteristic which implies a differentiation between those persons who act reliably and those who do not. It also implies choice. Therefore, if persons can opt to participate or not in reciprocal exchange, those who choose to do so are seen as persons upon whom one can depend. You can initiate interactions with them with knowledge of how they will react at the moment and assurance of what they will expect of you later on. You can trust their adherence to the same principles of relation you hold. Therefore as persons they are trustworthy.

Persons Also   It has already been pointed out that children recognize
Differy   individual differences among peers and friends. These
differences do not deter children from understanding
what friends share in common nor do they prevent children from working out procedures by which adjustments
are made for the sake of mutual benefit. Quite clearly,
children realize that friends with different talents can
combine their respective resources which, when put into a
reciprocal system, give friends more power than either
possesses alone. One's talents may lie in academic matters
and that friend can help another to do better in school,
while the other's talent may lie in areas of social skills and
then that friend can help the first get along with peers in
recreational activities. The contribution of pooled individual differences represents a gain to both parties. This
idea was expressed by several children specifically and
seems to signify a broader theme. Children seem to
understand that peers share a similar lot. The world of
peers is marked off as a societal enterprise involving such
domains as: doing well in school, enjoying peer activities,
and having material possessions. In addition, the world of
peers is made up of personal interests which include hob-
bies, games, sports, being happy, and getting along with
one's family. These are the general topics which recurred
in accounts and probably reflect the cultural-historical
background of the present samples of children.

If friends see one another as sharing membership in this
world, then children's ideas of combined resources and
equal treatment take on additional meaning. Faced with
the same tasks, friends are persons who recognize the
value of joining forces in meeting everyday requirements.
This recognition would enhance the sense of obligation
which is necessary if direct reciprocity is to be workable.
The nature of this method is such that one friend's assistance cannot coerce the other friend to make a return. Reciprocation will follow only if the other feels obliged to it.
Thus a sense of relationship based in part on feeling
bound within a common enterprise adds to the insurance
that friends will fulfill their respective roles within the
reciprocal system.

This factor helps to explain two aspects of the findings.

The first is the repetitive theme that friends are dependable. The theme at first appears to be obvious insofar as friends are those peers who actually help one another. But the obviousness is countered by the fact that children realize friends do not have to help and frequently do not. With increasing age, children become aware of the voluntariness upon which procedures rest. For instance, in describing why sharing was kind (study 3), older children stated: *Because you don't have to do it; He didn't have to give it up but he did;* and *She could have had it all for herself.* Sharing is a particularly clear case of the meeting of individual differences. One peer has something and the other does not have it. The former need not give it up and the latter has no inherent right to it. A comparison of responses in studies 3 and 5 shows that children know that some peers will share and that others will not. How then can children speak of dependability? For example, how do they know that someone will: *Not brush you off; Won't laugh at you; Doesn't just leave you there [in need];* or, *Won't walk away and ignore him?*

To depend on another's voluntary assistance when one knows that the other is free to act in self-interest implies a dialectical issue. One way to handle the problem is to attempt to build up a sense of obligation between the persons. This can be done by initiating those actions which supply others with what they need; letting them know that you want to join them in a reciprocal relation. One person can go only so far in the process. Ultimately it is up to the other to accept the obligation. If children say that friends are dependable they must mean, therefore, that friends share a sense of obligation which relegates their differences to the broader goal of cooperation (see Damon 1977).

The second set of results bearing on this point come from offenses (studies 10 and 11) which can be seen to be made up mainly of instances when individual differences exist and are taken advantage of. For example, recurring themes specify differences in terms of material possessions, school ability, social skills, popularity, and athletic talent. Children appeared to say that differences per se are not offensive but become so only when one of the friends takes advantage of the disparity between the persons. For instance: *Someone makes an out. The other kids hit him and pick on him.* Or, *When you're choosing sides, sometime the captain won't pick a person who's a lousy player.* The offense seems to consist in maximizing the difference instead of making adjustment to it.

The principle of equal treatment would entail that differences be handled with sensitivity rather than be ignored or maximized. Instead of stressing one's weakness or momentary position of vulnerability, friends would choose to adjust to it. For example, when someone makes an error, *You don't rub it in.* Or, if someone is not so talented, you do not exclude them, but, *let them in.* The conclusion would be that unfair treatment of individual differences constitutes offense. The acts themselves, in particular acts of omission, are neutral. They are offensive because they are violations of principle to which friends should consent.

One may now see better the reason for the high incidence of inequalities as a precondition for unkindness and offenses. Older children are sensitive to differences. Improper handling of them is judged unkind and breaches a relational agreement. It is now clear why most children spontaneously said that unkind exchanges would not continue in studies 7 and 10. To continue to retaliate would be to emphasize individual differences. Apologizing or refraining from reacting, on the other hand, would serve to put principle before personal interest. Friends differ but they can cooperate in using differences for mutual gain.

Finally, these data should be considered alongside those accounts in which friends in better positions took advantage of their power to hurt other friends. Some of the children pointed out the futility of recipients who did not have the power to retaliate. For example, one described a reaction to being excluded by three friends: *I'd be left standing there. I felt just awful. Sometimes I get in arguments. Sometimes I'd talk to my mom. Finally, I just stopped being friends with her.* After being teased by a group, a new student was described: *He wasn't big and he was afraid of the people. He would walk away. He got upset.* And, in another account, after a little boy was hung up on a hanger with his jacket on, *he started laughing but he must have been*

258 Transitions to Adolescence

embarrassed. In the majority of cases of inequalities such as these, the differences between the friends are bones of contention which did not get resolved. This is to say that children understand that friends do not have to abide by cooperative procedures. It is also to say, however, that if they continually fail to do so, the relation dissolves because the very procedures which define the relation are undermined (Gouldner 1960).

Mutual Understanding   According to the thesis, any person understands his or her own actions relative to the actions of another person. At a minimum, two persons know one another through the system of exchange in which they are participants. This allows each to anticipate the other's reaction and to plan initiatives accordingly. Since knowledge of the system is shared, the persons can be said to know each in similar terms. Nevertheless, Sullivan and Piaget propose that interpersonal understanding can be more or less mutual depending on the method and procedures by which two persons regularly interact. Reciprocity by complement deters mutuality because the persons generally do not construct opinions or viewpoints *together.* For example, adults tend to present views to which children are asked to conform. Children carry the burden of having to construct the matching view. Adults might help children by simplification, repetition, or encouragement. But unless adults were willing to compromise or abandon the views they hold and start to build new views based on interpersonal consensus, they would not be able to coconstruct along with children.

Peer relations should engender a high degree of mutuality. As previously shown, direct reciprocity allows two peers to present and hold different opinions, and therefore the method can easily lead to stalemates. When peers agree to use the method cooperatively, they have to develop procedures such as were outlined in the previous chapter. In general, these procedures may be summarized as ways of expressing one's own view while listening to the view of the other. Repeating these procedures over time, friends' ideas would be honed by mutual criticism and supported by mutual validation. Friends would have numerous opportunities to compare, contrast, and reach

compromises about reality in the process. These procedures thus describe what Sullivan and Piaget call cooperative or joint construction. Mutual understanding is its
logical product. The result is that each peer understands
the other much as the other understands him- or herself
and vice versa.

Additional data will now be considered in support of
this proposal. Consider first what children say about
mutual understanding. The most direct evidence in support of the procedural data appears in definitions of
friendship. One indication of mutuality was seen in
statements where children said that one friend filled in
understanding when the other did not understand something; for instance: *help you when you don't understand
something;* and, *If they don't know certain problems with
homework, you help them.* Accounts of this type represent
children's beliefs that friends learn from and teach each
other. Each friend exchanges knowledge he or she possesses with the other friend. As a consequence, over the
long run, both friends come to share similar understanding
of things. In contrast, in complementary procedures it is
more likely that adults provide knowledge for children
than that children provide knowledge for adults and consequently neither fully understands the other.

A second indication of mutuality was found in statements that friends shared feelings. Children said: *[When]
you're lonely and your friend on a bike joins you. You feel a lot
better because he joined you; He's there when you're down to
get you up. [You] have happy times together; Like if you're
sad, they'll help you feel better; [A friend] helps you when
you're in trouble and wants to come and talk about your problems; [Friends] think the same feelings I do; A person you
really can tell your feelings to; Someone you can share things
with and who shares things with you. Not material things.
Feelings. When you feel sad, she feels sad. They understand
you.* This form of mutuality may best be called *empathy,*
representing shared emotional existence where one's
feelings are shared and experienced by the other friend.

A third indication of mutuality refers to a broader and
shared knowledge between persons as persons: *They
would have the same personalities; You gotta know them and
they have to know you; A friend always understands your*

problems because they go through the same experiences; They understand you more than other people do; She understands you and knows how you feel; Friendship is being able to understand somebody. When these accounts are joined with descriptions of how peers become friends and best friends, an impressive point is made that friends share mutual understanding of personality which children apparently believe is close to being a shared identity.

Again a contrast is made with child-adult relations. Children say that: *Sometimes . . . you can't tell your parents, then you can go to your friend and he would know what to say; If I had a problem . . . I would probably go to my friend more than I could go to my parents because they might understand it more; A friend is somebody you can talk to and share your problems with. Like you can't talk to your parents because they have a one-track mind.* Older children appear to think that they and adults have different personalities and do not share experiences which would allow them to transmit clearly their deepest opinions or feelings. Such a barrier is absent between friends who: *Agree on the same things; You like their personality; Because you have the same ideas, you can talk more freely.* The block between child and adult also shows the ease with which opinions and feelings may be hidden in order to preserve one's authority and the other's need for approval.

Intimacy   In Sullivan's and Piaget's reasoning, intimacy is a logical outcome of the foregoing developmental steps. Sullivan describes it in terms of interpersonal sensitivity and love, which refer to mutual caring between friends who are concerned about one another's welfare as much as their own. Piaget describes it in terms of mutual respect which applies to valuing the principles friends stand for and consequently their personalities as well. For both Sullivan and Piaget the criteria for caring and respect are shared because friends have constructed them together and apply them with equal force to one another.

Intimacy, like mutual understanding is a construct which can be measured only approximately and with difficulty. Recently there have been attempts to assess it with statistical rigor (see Wish, Deutsch, and Kaplan 1976) through the use of multidimensional scaling. Intimacy or closeness has been found to be a reliable dimension which differentiates relations for adult respondents, friendship being a relation which appears high in the hierarchy along this dimension. Hinde (1978), using a logical argument, also concludes that intimacy or closeness should be made a component of peer relations. Hinde recognizes the measurement problem but suggests that leaving out this characteristic is an omission which leaves a gaping hole in a full description of this relation. Present findings contribute to a specification of intimacy by highlighting three possible components. The first is self-revelation; the second is trust or confidence; and the third is exclusivity of the relation.

Self-revelation   One sign of intimacy is openness in which two persons express themselves fully to each other. For Sullivan, this is essential to normal development since it allows other persons to give feedback to the self. Without such external criticism, there is risk that the self would build an illusory image which could be subjectively entrapping. Sullivan emphasizes that peer relations are a needed antidote to this possibility especially because complementary relations tend to induce children to hide opinions or feelings of which they think adults will not approve. Without the criticism of others it would be too easy to deny questionable parts of the self. Older children believe that friends are empathic and understand one another well at all levels of existence. They say that friends openly reveal themselves to each other. This means they not only judge what others are thinking or feeling, but friends also expect feedback when they openly express thoughts and feelings to others. Children in our studies said: *A friend is a person you can talk to, you know, show your feelings [and] he'll talk to you; You can talk more freely [to a friend]; Someone you can . . . tell your problems to and she can tell you her problems; They are open; You can tell [a friend] everything; A friend is a person you really can tell your feelings to; A person you can . . . confide in; Tell them what you feel and you can be yourself with them.*

Confidence and   These components, confidence and exclusivity, seem to go
Exclusivity   together in children's minds. Confidence pertains to the

assurance that a person feels that he or she will be helped in a relation and that self-revelation will not be used against him or her. Exclusivity pertains to one's knowing that revelations will be kept within the two-group and that it is only within this relation that one may achieve understanding. Sullivan points out that knowledge of a person necessarily involves recognition of assets and deficiencies. To reach normality persons must be able to admit both parts of themselves. If people hide their shortcomings, they are liable to create a distorted, self-serving conception of themselves. If persons expose their weaknesses, however, they risk not being accepted by others. For example, in complementary relations, they might not receive the approval necessary for the exchange. In friendship, the risk is lessened theoretically because exposure is mutual. When one is accepted with assets and deficiencies, it is possible to form an honest conception of self. The problem which might arise in friendship therefore is that what one has revealed will be let outside the relation. In order to prevent this from happening friends have to develop both trust and exclusivity, thus further fostering self-revelation in a circular manner.

The following observations demonstrate aspects of this reasoning in older children's own words: *Friends can keep [their] secrets together; They can trust you that you won't tell anybody; You . . . won't expect them to tell everybody else; You know she won't tell anybody anything; If you tell someone something, they won't use it to get revenge on you when you get in a fight.* These data are supplemented by the idea of exclusivity which was expressed as follows: *You talk about things you wouldn't tell other people; Friends would believe in . . . and value the same things; You can tell her everything; They understand you more than other people do; A friend is a person I trust and have faith in; You can believe in friends; They're even closer to you than a brother or sister.*

Transforming Child–Adult Relations   Results of studies 1 to 7 indicate that, between ages 9 and 14, children transform their conception of child-adult relations from one in which they play a complementary role to another in which they are more in a direct reciprocal position toward adults. Among other ways, children manifest this change by describing adults in deficient states, putting them more on a par with themselves and placing them in need of children's assistance. The change is no doubt complexly determined. Children may be motivated to reform conceptions as they become more instrumentally competent in activities which support family life. Simultaneously, parents and teachers undoubtedly assign older children increasingly responsible roles in the home and at school and in general treat them in more adult-like fashion. Given these and other possible bases for change, it would be simplistic to attribute the change solely to one factor, in particular to children's knowledge of other interpersonal relations. Nevertheless, young adolescents' descriptions of their relation to adults contain features which are similar to those which appear much earlier in friendship. It is therefore plausible to pursue the idea that some of the characteristics adolescents put into relations with adults come in part from their knowledge of interpersonal possibilities developed first within friendship.

Two general considerations suggest the reasonableness of this possibility. The first is that both relations already contain common elements. Neither relation is pure; child-adult relations must have moments when direct reciprocal exchange is enacted and children recognize that adults are making adjustments to children's needs and interests. The second is that the person who is developing can profitably be viewed as seeking unity in social experiences. This would imply that children search for common elements which might bridge relational differences and help in the construction of an integrated self. Several findings can be interpreted as congruent with this position. As children approach and enter adolescence, conceptions of friendship seem to be elaborations of characteristics which are found in younger children's conceptions of peers. Young adolescents' conceptions of relations with adults contain elements found at earlier ages, but they also show characteristics which come from friendship. Insofar as these conceptions imply development, the change has a direction, becoming more like friendship. Adolescents' conceptions of relations with adults have a mixed composition. Some features are old (conformity) while others are new characteristics which previously belonged to friendship.

The hallmark of the mixture is found in the seemingly contradictory phrase: *voluntary obedience*. In studies 3 and 5, and again in the data cited in chapter 8, many adolescents said that children's acts of conformity to adults' wishes could be judged only through children's freedom as agents. An overt act of obedience would be kind only if the actor did it out of free will. The same act would be unkind only if the actor were forced to do it or did it with a negative attitude toward the adult. These findings suggest a hypothesis that helps to unravel the paradox contained in voluntary obedience. The transformation in conceptions of child-adult relations may in part be due to young adolescents' understanding of the voluntary nature of interpersonal relations. Earlier the child-adult relation was best described as a *covenant*, as a transcendent bond which represents the universal order of things. Understanding through friendship that relations are based on agreement, adolescents may see themselves ambivalently with regard to adults. On the one hand, they consent to the relation but, on the other hand, the relation demands their conformity.

There are numerous signs in the data which support this hypothesis. In study 1, adolescents described adults' kindness to children in terms similar to those they used to describe kindness between friends. For example: *You're having trouble with friendship . . . . Grown-ups could give you hints on how to make friends better; Helping you with a problem. Talking it out and trying to solve it; Instead of calling the police [the man he stole from] gives him advice; The teacher didn't embarrass him in front of the class . . . . She talked to him afterwards.* These examples depict adolescents' ideas of how they think adults view them which obviously include procedures in which opinions or feelings are mutually exchanged rather than imposed unilaterally by adults. Additional examples were found in study 6 in which adults' kindness went beyond giving approval or material reward. For instance: *Her mother listened when she had problems; When they knew the girl was upset, the neighbor took time to talk to her and be friendly.* The reverse of this new relation was seen when children were kind to adults. For example: *When other kids were hassling the teacher, [a girl] showed her respect; He was considerate, went out of his way for an old man; It would be nice [for the girl] to make [her uncle] happier; make him higher in spirit.*

A similar picture was obtained from accounts of unkindness. Adolescents said that adults were unkind by not helping children when they asked or by not giving children opportunities to explain their behavior. Reverse instances included the following examples of unkindness from children: *You're too embarassed to be with [your parents]; The child is always degrading [the family's maid]; A lot of kids embarrass the teacher; The parents get things for the kid and he complains and takes them for granted; Make your parents worry about you by staying out late; Talking back to them when they tell you something.* The point is carried further by a few adolescents who described exchanges of unkindness in more symmetrical than unilateral terms. After children had failed to conform, adults reacted as follows: *Make an effort to see what they [themselves] did wrong.... Try to work it out; Her parents may be disappointed and hurt, not really angry; His mother would say, "Think about what you just said"; She'd feel hurt, but she'd punish them; Makes his parents feel bad.*

None of these accounts stand on their own as convincing cases, but as a whole they indicate the beginnings of a new sense in the relation. They show a focus on the persons and their feelings as well as a willingness to talk out difficult situations rather than demanding single-minded solutions. In this vein, it is interesting, therefore, that young adolescents were almost the exclusive users of talking back as a form of unkindness: *If they tell you to do something and you talk back; Talk back; Say he didn't do it; Like when they talk back; Talk back to his mother.* (See also table 7.) If talking back refers to expressing one's own opinion in the face of another's opinion, then this offense may be seen as a case of the same mixed conception described above. Young adolescents would be thinking of their relation to adults in terms of reciprocal procedures in which talking back and forth is normal. Peers talk back by presenting and listening to each other. Adults, on the other hand, may be thinking of it in complementary terms which demand adherence to their opinion. The result is an offense which young adolescents recognize but do not feel is reasonable. That is, they are punished for it but do not believe they were wrong.

The final piece of evidence for the hypothesis comes from findings obtained from several children which have not yet been cited. Some children in studies 1 and 6 were interviewed on additional questions about kindness. They were asked whether their ideas about kindness were the same as adults', whether they differed, and if so, how they differed. The findings indicated that up to about age 10 years, children said that their own ideas and adults' ideas were similar. For example:

(M,9)   *It doesn't differ. (Why?) Because adults know a lot and have taught me since I was little. So I take their word.*

(F,9)   *They're older. They studied more. They know more about it. (Can you say more?) Like if two adults are fighting. My mom tells me not to get in it when it's my business.*

(F,10) *Sometimes it's hard [to agree], like going to bed early or when you disobey and they won't allow you to watch TV (Yes?) You have to learn a lesson and going to bed early makes you feel good.*

(F,12) *Adults know more about if it's kind or unkind because they're older.*

In contrast, young adolescents showed a mixture in which they thought adults knew a lot but then they themselves knew much also. For instance:

(M,12) *Adults teach you what kindness is. When you're little, they say, this is what kindness is. You think your parents are perfect and hear what they say and do it. But you also meet other people's opinions, like friends and their parents and they come to be your own opinions.*

(F,12) *It's easier for adults to be kind . . . . They think in bigger terms, like helping the poor. Children think of little things, like sharing with friends.*

(M,13) *Basically their ideas are the same, but everybody thinks a little bit different. They may think it's kind not to associate with certain [peers], but you may think it's kind. (Where do you learn about it?) You pick it up from everybody here and there. When people do something to you, you do it back.*

(M,13) *Adults understand more and might know better. But sometimes*

you both don't understand each other because everybody has
a whole different mind. And they have different opinions.
(What do you mean?) *Like not being allowed to play with*
a friend because your parents have a bad impression of him.
They misunderstand him; the way he is.

These statements reflect the hypothesized transformation from the perspective of knowledge. In middle childhood, children attribute authority to parents and are
willing to accept parents' wisdom. Young adolescents continue to accept parental authority but recognize what parents say as opinions rather than unalterable facts. They see
themselves as also having opinions which come from
friends and other sources. Opinions are just viewpoints
which may differ from person to person. Neither person is
necessarily correct, and in the above citations young adolescents believe that their opinons are equally valid and on
a par with their parents'.

The protocols also show that the truth about kindness
always depends on interpersonal consensus. In these data,
the possibility for stalemate is evident, just as it is with
peers. When two peers confront each other with equally
sound views, they have to decide to separate or agree to
cooperate in reciprocal exchange. Young adolescents' assurance that their knowledge is valid—an understanding
which would come from validation by cooperating
friends—puts the complementary system in jeopardy.
This is especially true in the domain of interpersonal
knowledge where adolescents see themselves as experts
and able to create order. As experts they have the right to
assert their views in opposition to those of others and, from
prior experience with friends, this means that they and
adults will have to work out and come to an agreement on
the way they shall coexist in interpersonal relationship.

Present findings stop with early adolescence when apparently the child-adult relation has only begun to
undergo transformation. Very few instances of what
others have called rebellion or antagonism were observed.
This could be due to the samples or to its possible later
occurrence. Obviously there was no opportunity to observe either a resolved relationship in which adolescents
were fully equals to adults and comfortably positioned
with adults in symmetrical reciprocal procedures. It is not

possible to speculate on when or how precisely this further development occurs.

In any event, the changes observed imply the beginnings of such a transformation which breaks the covenant of complementariness and redirects the relationship toward the course of development which has been building from peer relations and friendship,. In any complex society, adults must respect and know how to deal with authority. This is not the authority of unilateral assertion of truth but, more reasonably, the authority based on some cooperation and mutual respect.

Concluding Remarks   During the age period 6 to 14 years, children's descriptions of friendship show increasing articulation of four characteristics. First, friends' interactions imply an agreement in which each is entitled to be treated as an equal. Each friend expects to be treated as he or she treats the other. Second, friends interact with continuing adjustment to one another's individual personality. They recognize the similarity of their persons and use their differences as persons to mutual gain. Third, as children progress in friendship, they reach increasing mutual understanding of one another and of the common outlook on social reality, which includes school, games, parents, social attitudes, and beliefs. Fourth, friends operate with a deep sense of intimacy. They care for one another's welfare, reveal themselves openly, act with assurance that their shortcomings will be accepted and not used against them, and take pride in the exclusiveness of their bond.

Each characteristic can be understood as a product of long-term participation in direct reciprocal procedures. The procedures worked out jointly by peers, involve the general method of direct reciprocity tempered by cooperation. The individuality of each person necessitates that the method be adapted to a cooperative venture or else peers would continue to run up against insurmountable differences. This pragmatic goal is eventually converted into an agreement in which friends voluntarily consent to cooperate. The agreement binds the friends through a sense of obligation to each other and their relation. Either person can break the agreement, and voluntary continuance in it is a risk with which friends are acquainted and learn to deal. Friendship is unique in children's interpersonal experiences. Other relations do not involve similar commitments, nor can they provide children opportunities to learn the full range of possibilities of relationship which friendship can. The two worlds of childhood are not just different. They teach children differently and result in qualitatively distinct types of social understanding. This includes conceptions of self, of other persons, and of relations which serve self and other's mutual existence.

At about early adolescence the two worlds begin to merge with child-adult relations taking on characteristics previously seen in friendship. It is reasonable to hypothesize that this deflection toward the method of peer relations represents a new insight into the parts played by those children who are in a position to give free consent to their complementary role with adults. An ambivalence is here implied and obviously not resolved fully during early adolescence. In fact, from about age 12 to 14, conceptions of the child-adult relation are mixtures that include elements from the friendship relation. How an adequate resolution and integration of the two social worlds is achieved remains open to empirical investigation.

Fourteen   A General Perspective on Development

The time from the beginning school years to adolescence has been typically considered a period of serenity. It has been called the "latency" period, when children take in societal information and become adherents of society's "law and rules." It is also recognized as a time when children first learn to get along in groups outside the family as they play games and join formal organizations, both of which are governed by rules. A social character is being built when children are able to listen to adults and are open to interesting ideas presented by peers. This picture, of course, changes with the advent of adolescence when serenity gives way to turbulence and acceptance is replaced by questioning.

Results of studies 1 through 11 suggest the usefulness of a different characterization of the child from early school age through preadolescence. Children are actually much less passive during this period and considerably more dynamic. The major stage for activity is peer relations in which children are working out ways to get along with each other. Continual adjustment is being made as a result of having to deal with direct reciprocity which is most apparent in a struggle between individual interests and mutual concerns. If children cannot, by natural right, dominate one another, then peers have to find the means to get their own way while they give in to the other. Procedures have to be evolved for bringing order out of the mixture of results which include positive outcomes, conflicts, and stalemates. Negotiation, compromise, and discussion become the focus of peer interactions. Relations with adults may contain hints of these procedures, but, behind them, children know that adults have a powerful world view which can be used to halt debate. While having to conform to this view, children are continually discovering alternatives which come from experiences with peers working together and adjusting to one another. The most important lesson which children learn with peers is that social business can be transacted smoothly only through a joint agreement to practice reciprocity for mutual ends.

In the working out of procedures which sustain this agreement, the fuller implications of direct reciprocity are found. In general, a new world of relations is structured. It is a world populated by individual personalities, having both common characteristics and differences. The main rule which is used to guide interactions involves equality of treatment. Within the confines of friendship, selected peers put these insights into practice. The world of peers takes new shape, and each advance in insight builds upon another. Common characteristics become grounds for a joint personality in which friends share an identity. Equality of treatment engenders a sense of dependency in which friends reveal themselves knowing the risk of exposure but trusting that it will not be used against them. Mutual understanding, exclusivity, and intimacy follow so that a relation is established which neither child has experienced before.

The foregoing description of results corresponds to Sullivan's and Piaget's account of development during the 6 to 14 year period. If this were all that could be concluded, however, we would be stopping short of seeing the deeper implications of their writings. In their original works, Sullivan 1953 and Piaget 1932 (1965) treat the period in question within the broader context of earlier and later social development. They offer insights regarding early parent-child relations and the general process of socialization. Having identified the importance of peer relations and friendship, they spell out the logical consequences which follow in the further growth of the personality and morality during adolescence and beyond. The goal of this chapter is to describe these points and present the thesis in its fuller context as a broad perspective on social development.

Parent-Child Relations

Sullivan

Sullivan (1953) offers an analysis of early development covering the conventional topics. He emphasizes the role of the mother in tasks such as feeding and toilet training. Following the formula that the development of the self is the development of interpersonal relations, however, Sullivan also provides an analysis of the mother-child relation. Of concern is its structure and the functions which follow from it. In this analysis Sullivan focuses on the relation as it might be shared by numerous parents and children rather than on the differences which distinguish particular parent-child dyads. Sullivan selects complementariness as a key characteristic which describes the composition of this relation. He depicts it in terms which are now familiar. The parent is an evaluating person who monitors children's acts, offering approval or withholding it in order to shape future acts. The role of evaluator is described as natural or normal given the role which most parents attribute to themselves. It is to help their offspring in the task of becoming socialized. To this end parents attempt to pass on what they know and have learned about society. Rather than letting children learn for themselves by trial and error from people in general, parents take the responsibility of teaching as their own right. They also control their offsprings' exposure to other people, by choosing babysitters or teachers, with an eye to their own goals in socialization.

Thus children gain, on the one hand, knowledge about particular actions and, on the other, knowledge that actions have interpersonal meaning. The latter is Sullivan's focus. Actions are approvable or not and this is true irrespective of the child's own motives or opinions. This lesson makes clear the interdependent nature of action and forces the child to take account of methods of interactions. Children have to ask: How will my actions affect the other? What will the other person do when I do something? What will happen if I fail to act in a particular way? If there is a nonsubmissive bent in young children, it is countered by the fact of parents' ever-present readiness to accept or reject what the child does. The role of evaluator serves the function of showing children that there is meaning beyond that which they alone might have for action.

Sullivan is aware that other theorists who studied the parent-child relation have described differences among parental evaluative techniques. Some parents tend to be punitive; others use love as a commodity; still others use multiple techniques and supplement them with verbal explanations. Aware that these differences are real and may have implications for the child's developing personality, Sullivan nevertheless emphasizes the common feature they all share. It is *control* or *constraint*, which, in whatever form it appears, remains a primary fact. Parents have definite ideas about actions. The ideas are imposed on children and parents expect children to accept them. Parents do not approve of everything that children do. Approval is selective. To be accepted, children have to conform to the scheme of approval which parents possess.

It should be noted that the term control has taken on negative connotation for many developmental theorists and the culture at large. It implies authoritarianism or rigidity and is frequently considered out of date with modern rearing techniques whereby children are given more initiative in discovering reality. Gadlin (1974 and 1978) clarifies the issue by pointing to the overlap among techniques which at their core represent control. Apart from extremes like over-punitiveness, there is a broad center ground in which parents, by whatever techniques they choose, clearly tell children that not all acts are unconditionally approvable. There may be less difference than psychologists believe between, for example, offering a sharp No, and telling a child, "When you do that, you make me unhappy." Neither instruction is necessarily authoritarian but both clearly lay out the lines of control (see also Baumrind 1975). As was pointed out earlier, Sullivan assumes that control may emanate from a healthy positive interest in the child's welfare. Parents believe that their knowledge of society is worth passing on. They want their children to be successful in this society and work to help them achieve it. By acting with this motive, parents cannot but be controlling and in the process establish the fact of interpersonal dependency of action. Therein lies the basis for reciprocity by complement in which children understand the exchange of their own conformity for the parent's approval, and the belief that parents are all-knowing people who care about them.

Sullivan pictures the result of early parent-child practices as follows. Upon entering school, children think of themselves as wise in the ways of the world. They have worked to figure out what parents have in their minds about social reality. They have tried to construct a corresponding view of society and, insofar as they have received approval, they believe that their ideas match their parents'. It is here that Sullivan introduces two terms which emphasize the limitations of the parent-child relation. He calls the children's belief an *illusion* and sees the version of reality which children have constructed as *narrow*. The illusory aspect refers to the lack of mutuality between parent's and children's ideas. Sullivan attributes this to both parties. Children cannot understand what adults hold because they lack the background to grasp ideas which adults have gained through their experiences. On the other hand, adults falter in their understanding of children because adults filter their perceptions through the distorting lens of social expectations. As Sullivan puts it, parents have difficulty treating the child as an individual in a here-and-now manner. Adults operate with a broad vision which includes how they wish other persons to react to their children and what they want their children to be like later in life. Consequently, such everyday matters as clothing, eating habits, and speech patterns may be treated from a social viewpoint that a young child could not possibly understand. A child may want to wear his red shirt, yellow pants, and blue tennis shoes to his first day at school. The boy's parents may have a different image of what appearance their son should have so they dress him in a manner in which he will be seen as a socially adept boy by others.

The narrowness of the child's view of society is primarily a product of children's own thinking. The parents' pervasive role as evaluator gives rise to children's belief that parents must know society well. Indeed, parents *are* society. In adopting their parents' views, children believe that they have entered this privileged view themselves. Their narrowness is not obvious and will not become apparent until children meet other viewpoints and are challenged to justify their own views and reach compromise with the new ones.

Piaget   Piaget's analysis of early parent-child relations squares with Sullivan's on most of the above major points. He identifies reciprocity by complement as the general method by which children find invariance, and therefore can order parent-child interactions. He sees acceptance of the method as forcing children to open their focus beyond just their own actions to seek sense in interpersonal interactions. He agrees further that the exchange system is seen by children as fair and engenders respect for adults whom children believe must have insight into the universal order of things. Piaget, like Sullivan, emphasizes the inherent limitation of a complementary system with regard to mutual understanding. He analyzes it differently from Sullivan, however. From Piaget's perspective, mutuality is limited whenever two persons do not construct ideas together or cannot transform their ideas into the other's and back again to their own. He therefore emphasizes the unilateral construction inherent in the process where children meet already established ideas of adults and then must try to match them. Piaget does not deny that adults attempt to simplify and break down their ideas so that they will be more understandable to children. He considers the effort generally ineffective because it partakes more of *adaptation* for the sake of communication than of *adjustment* where one person (the adult) would modify ideas in a true effort to reach modifications the other person (the child) has made.

One can see here the fuller meaning of unilateral constraint as Piaget uses it. Several theorists (e.g., Bell 1968) have pointed out that adults not only socialize children but that children also socialize adults. This is meant as a corrective to views that overly stress the one-way process of socialization from adult to child. Piaget's analysis of parent-child interactions in terms of exchange system necessarily includes the two-way flow which requires that adults adapt to children as well as the reverse. Nevertheless, in terms of constructing ideas, the burden falls to children to make unilateral adjustment. The alternative would require that adults be prepared to give up their ideas and present them tentatively to children, expecting in the process that a series of mutual adjustments would lead to a more valid set of ideas than that which they already possess. This is a remote possibility and applies at best to only a few domains of life. Adults may occasionally learn from children, but in the main it is difficult for them to be their children's students rather than teachers.

Conclusion   Sullivan's and Piaget's analysis of parent-child relations assumes the early establishment of an exchange system which forces children to see their own actions as interdependent upon the actions of adults and other persons more generally. Interdependency is established within the system of complementary exchange where conformity is traded for approval. The system describes the general method which is invariant and becomes the means for ordering subsequent interactions (see Hinde 1976 and 1978). Sullivan and Piaget suggest that children may view their relation to concerned adults as transcendent, with adults knowing all there is to know about society's inner workings. This gives the relation the character of a covenant. Insofar as children think that they have entered the mind of adults, they believe that they also come to know society in a privileged way. Factually, children's social knowledge is narrow and more like a private version of reality than a jointly constructed system. Children's ideas lack mutuality with adults' even though both parties may think otherwise. The disparity is possible because both work out ways of getting along and communicate well enough to sustain the illusion.

This analysis represents an approach to parent- or adult-child interactions in which emphasis is given to common features which hold across varying styles of child-rearing practices. The adult is assigned the role of evaluator or monitor and the child is given the role of seeking a positive evaluation. The relationship is marked by unilateral control in which adults are seen as authoritative, powerful, and benevolent. In this context children have to construct versions of what they think adults know. They respect adults for their wisdom and respect themselves for achieving corresponding ideas. They evaluate themselves negatively for not being able to match adults' ideas or for trying but failing to do so when adults signify it by withholding approval. That is why the first "original" idea, which occurs later with peers, is a developmental breakthrough. The product of living in this relation is a social self who believes that society is ordered by transcendent principles. These principles, which may be known as rules for interacting, exist outside the self but are known to adults. The child self can come to know them through adults, and, insofar as adults have given approval to children's ideas, opinions, and statements, school-age children can legitimately look on themselves as having learned much of what there is to know about how society works.

Socialization   Social scientists have generally looked at socialization from either of two points of view. In one, socialization stands for the child's internalization of adults' ideas and opinions. Adults are mature members of society who understand the way that society works. They communicate what society is by modeling actions, which children then imitate and, through verbal instruction, come to accept. This meaning makes socialization a synonym for development since the process of becoming a mature member of society, as adult members are, almost fully describes the progress from infancy to adulthood (see Goslin 1969 for examples of this general position). This model held sway in the field for several generations with little challenge until recently. The challenge came from theorists who describe the child as an active cognizing person rather than a faithful recorder of adult directions. Cognition refers to the child's handling of input from others. Most theorists who favor this view describe the child as acting on information to make it comprehensible. How children will interpret any input is said to be a function of the cognitive capacities and skills brought to the objective fact or event (see Kohlberg 1969).

The disparity between the conventional socialization model and the cognitive viewpoint is obvious. In the former, input which children internalize can be measured objectively. It is that which adults do or say. In the latter view, this is not true. When children act on input, they transform it into something they understand. This position breaks the direct line of transmission at a critical point which is the link between the adult's sending of a message and the child's recording of it. Other differences then become evident. In socialization theory, the child can be described at any moment as some composite summary of experiences which the child has had with society's members. For cognitive theory, experience alone is not telling of development. In order to understand how events have affected a child, one must know how the child has interpreted them. If cognitive development follows its own course of progress, then timing becomes important. The same event which occurs at two separate moments in this development is liable to be interpreted in entirely different ways.

These two models differ also on several other points, which may be traced to disparate philosophical stances (see Macmurray 1961). The present interest is in showing how Sullivan and Piaget treat socialization and cognition as compatible rather than distinct factors and offer a new integrative perspective. Systems of exchange which have been described previously have their basis in fact but also refer to children's cognitive understanding of the facts. For example, there are ways to know child-adult interactions other than by construing them in terms of the method of reciprocity by complement. To conceive of the method is a mental conclusion arrived at by children's seeking order in their interactions with adults. The achievement is a construction, a mental creation on the part of children. When the process of construction, as Sullivan and Piaget describe it, is inspected in detail, one sees a different type of cognition than is implied by the position cited above. The act of conceptualization is not a private event done by the individual child. But the process is really a two-person or social event. The conception is of the *exchange of actions* and includes the other person's as well as the child's contribution. The other's participation in the method is an undeniable determiner of the child's conception. The other represents the socializing influence which enters the child's own conception (Youniss 1977 and 1978a).

In Sullivan's and Piaget's analysis, cognition is not "social" simply because it refers to the content "person." It is social because persons in addition to the child have a direct hand in its making. In this analysis, social knowledge is the product of *dialogue* and not the result of the child's monologic construction of ideas in the privacy of mental contemplation (see also Riegel 1976). The other person does not fix the child's thought but is a codeterminer without whom thought would tend toward mere subjectivity and self-enhancement. The compatibility of socialization and cognition is more than a philosophical nicety. It is central to Sullivan's and Piaget's thinking. Thought which is privately constructed is neither social nor rational. It needs the influence of others and must be validated through mutual exposure and criticism from others. This is why Sullivan and Piaget distinguish between social knowledge which arises from reciprocity of complement and that which is achieved through cooperative procedures. The former puts the burden of construction unilaterally on the child, while the latter involves a continuing readjustment between two persons who construct knowledge jointly (Youniss 1978b).

Economic Determination   A second popular view held by social scientists is represented by the often-cited proposition attributed to Marx: Relations of persons to means of production determine relations of persons to one another. This proposition has been used to support the broader view of socialization in which individuals are said to be shaped by societal forces. Although the complete argument is complex, it may be represented simply through an example. Society exists as a set of economic relations which place persons in roles with regard to it and to one another. A person's labor is valued as it fits into the wider system of exchange. This institutional fact, in turn, determines how that person will value a spouse, children, and him- or herself. While persons may feel free and creative in establishing relations on the interpersonal level, the relations are in fact economically determined. Were this position taken literally, children's views of their relations to adults, peers, and friends would have to be considered illusory. Children believe that these relations are constructed by the parties and not simply imposed, and, at least in the case of friends, they think that relations exist by voluntary agreement. More importantly, children's conceptions of these relations change and are not fixed. There is no reason to suspect that the development observed from 6 to 14 years does not continue and lead to discoveries of other new possibilities for interpersonal existence.

The issue can be reduced to the question of whether there is room for interpersonal construction in a societal system where economic relations are given. The answer is yes if a more liberal view toward the Marxian proposition is adopted. Sayer (1975) has worked out the logic for this view in which the main proposition is rephrased so that there is reciprocity between societal and interpersonal relations. Means of production constrain but do not fully determine interpersonal relations. Sayer argues for a continuing interplay between the two levels and for good reason. Historical change is central to Marx's philosophy. But how could societies change if economic relations were fixed and persons simply lived out their determined roles within them? Change becomes less of a mystery if it can be initiated by persons who discover new possibilities of relations and confront the economic system with them. The free construction of interpersonal relations and the discovery of new possibilities for interpersonal existence is a potent fact of development. It is a force which has to be seen as logically reciprocal to the determining nature of economic systems.

To return to the previous example, a person's place in the sphere of production may have much to do with how he or she relates to fellow workers, neighbors, spouse, or children. But the reverse is equally true. Experiences gained at the interpersonal level need not be left in one's neighborhood or family residence. They may be brought to work and to those relations which are ordinarily seen as economic and institutional. One's interpersonal relations need not be suppressed when confronted with society any more than one interpersonal relation can be kept separate from some other interpersonal relation. If the person is a unity or seeks integration, then all of one's relations may be influential each to each and each as it acts on the whole (Riegel 1976).

Morality   Piaget (1965 and 1970) views morality as the logical outgrowth of social development. For Piaget, morality consists of systems of principles and the *respect* persons have for these principles. A good part of his 1932 (1965) book is spent explaining how the two types of interpersonal relations described in the present work lead to distinct moral viewpoints. He calls one a *heteronomous* morality in which rules and principles are thought to exist outside the individual in the fixed order of the world. This morality is engendered by relations of unilateral constraint in which persons in authority are seen as possessing privileged knowledge to which others must then adhere. He calls the second a morality of *autonomy* in which rules and principles are constructed by persons working together in the search for order. It follows logically from relations such as friendship in which persons as equals cooperate in defining reality. The premise that social relations are the bases of morality can be found in predecessors to Piaget's thinking, such as Simmel (1955), who originally postulated this in 1905. The idea is that morality is not an independent topic of thought but a conception about ways persons can and ought to form interpersonal relations. The question Piaget seeks to answer is how interpersonal experiences between particular individuals give rise to general principles which pertain to whole societies.

For various reasons, some interpreters of Piaget's work have put heteronomy and autonomy on a comparative scale, arguing that the former, which is found in early child-adult relations, is developmentally less mature than the latter. This interpretation is plausible but tends to detract from Piaget's effort to treat morality as a conceptual adaptation which is ultimately the product of persons' efforts to make sense out of social life as it is experienced and as it can be envisioned. If morality is such an adaptation, then a mature outlook would have to include principles found in both types of relations and be an integration of them. The characteristics of a heteronomous viewpoint include aspects of those features found in child-adult relations in younger children. In this view, order is preexistent and is known to the minds of authoritative persons. This order can be reached through adults' minds, and children have the duty to conform to it. The rules set forth by adults are legitimate and to be respected. The child's worth depends on conformity to the rules and the transcendent order they represent. The main principle of heteronomy is the method of unilateral constraint coupled with fair exchange. Respect for it implies a belief in the order behind it and the need to preserve it. This description does not mean that all authority relations reflect the naïveté of early childhood. Adults who consent to authority, represented by historical traditions, government, and the like, are not to be confused with young children whose everyday functioning is monitored and depends on caretaking parents. What Piaget suggests is that characteristics of adult-adult authority relations bear similarities to the earlier child-adult covenant. These relations have similar advantages (e.g., security in approval) and limitations (e.g., the risk of low mutuality). They also tend toward conservation of ideas rather than opening the persons to new discoveries.

But authority is not the whole of a mature moral position. Piaget traces the origins of autonomous morality to peer relations. Its hallmark is respect for those procedures with which persons cooperate in the search for order. Friendship is an obvious context wherein children begin to understand cooperation and jointly discover principles which serve mutual ends. Respect for these principles implies respect also for the persons who adhere to them. Here a new authority by consensus is engendered.

Autonomy Is Not Idiosyncracy   In a democratic society adults have to find a balance between authority which is unilateral and authority which is shared by equals. In some psychological theorists' minds, the former is considered the less mature, and the latter is interpreted as incompatible with the epitome of human existence, which is individuality (see Sampson 1977; E. V. Sullivan 1977 for a fuller analysis). Some developmental theorists have adopted this model and gone on to propose that autonomy is a progression toward self-assurance in one's moral posture. This has tended to yield depictions of the mature moral person as "one who stands alone on principle" and "one who resists conformity." These are complex constructs which defy simple analysis since they partake of philosophical controversy and are part of a cultural ideology. Nevertheless, it is worth sorting out where Piaget (1965) stands on these matters and to show what he means by autonomy as well as how he describes its origins. Autonomy is not a synonym for individuality, in the sense of a self-assured idiosyncrasy. The autonomous person submits to principles which have been validated through interchange with others (p. 95). It is "the opposite of ego" (p. 96).

Autonomy arises from cooperation and respect for the method by which persons as equals verify one another's ideas and feelings (p. 97). As mentioned previously, this is the method of cooperative reciprocity which includes procedures of discussion, compromise, and negotiation. The basis for autonomy may be found in friendship where the procedures themselves are constructed jointly and thus are based on interpersonal verification. Respect for the persons who follow these procedures comes from the mutual agreement to submit one's own ideas to the test these procedures involve (pp. 98–99). For Piaget, moral autonomy is not individualism but is relational in origin as well as composition. At least two people are required for its existence. The autonomous person is not acting alone on a self-constructed vision. The very principles autonomous persons believe in are those which constitute relationship with others.

An example of such a principle is found in the data reported here on friendship as seen by young adolescents. Their accounts of friendship attest to the principle of equal treatment. Friends are described as following procedures which are mutually beneficial. Each friend's ideas are listened to. Feelings which are expressed openly will be respected and kept secret. Disputes will be talked out. And if a procedure is violated, the violator will correct the error. Descriptions such as these are congruent with other views on morality and, in particular, correspond closely with Nozick's (1974) theory of entitlement. In this theory, morality is based on consent among persons to follow fair interpersonal transactions. This type of theory contrasts with those which emphasize the results of moral actions (Kohlberg 1969; Rawls 1971). Young adolescents know that not all persons are equal in all domains. They seem more concerned about procedures and seem willing to let procedures have their natural consequences. They go even further in admitting that the procedures are enacted by free agents, and therefore they can tolerate breaches of agreement as a realistic possibility.

Piaget's view adds an element to Nozick's theory which leads back to one of the original issues faced by moral theorists. Nozick describes transactions as if rules had preexistence and consent to them were a matter of individual will (Coleman 1976; Lieberson 1978). Nozick's mature person fits the model of free enterprise where individuals compete and agree to follow rules primarily to preserve self-interest. For Piaget, the rules themselves are jointly constructed for mutual interest. When practiced in friendship, the persons who practice the rules develop an intimacy where one's interests and even one's personality is scarcely distinguishable from the other's. If friendship in the social domain leads to a moral viewpoint which is developed later in life, then this morality should be based on the knowledge of one's own existence in relation *with* others. The base is cooperation, not competition.

The Personality or Self   For Sullivan and Piaget the classic breakdown between "self" and "other" as independent entities by right is changed to an analysis in which self-and-other is an indissociable unit. Interpersonal relationship describes the unit, and development of the self proceeds from development of this unit. In Macmurray's (1961) terminology, the self's existence is constituted through relation with the other. The "I" in psychological formulas becomes the *I with respect to you*. There is no empirical proof for this revision. It is a theoretical starting point which can be judged only through its fruitfulness in explaining persons' conceptions of social reality. Part of the effort in this book has centered on showing the implications of the relational starting point. Again, as with morality, this is a difficult issue because the convention in the field of developmental studies has been to posit individuality and then explain how the individual child becomes socially influenced and takes on social membership with increasing age.

Sampson (1977) contrasts the relational view with the more familiar "individualism" of most developmental theories. It pays to make the distinction even clearer. In his book, *Two Worlds of Childhood*, Bronfenbrenner (1973) contrasts children reared in the United States with those reared in the USSR. He argues that the former think of society in individualistic terms. For example, he contrasts children's responses to a situation in which a classmate was seen to cheat on an exam. Soviet children expressed the belief that cheating would be wrong because it violated a group rule. They also said they would talk to the violator and point out the reasons for not cheating. Children reared in an individualistic culture were more concerned about being caught and were three times more willing to tell on the cheater by going to an adult. Bronfenbrenner argues from data like these that the United States culture promotes individualism in contrast to a deep sense of community found in Soviet children. He ends his book with an essay on the waning of community in our society and the accompanying breakdown of moral responsibility. Among those specific factors are the abdication of adult responsibility and the increase in negative influences from peers (see also Lasch 1979). "There is evidence already cited from our own researches that the peer group has quite different effects in the Soviet Union and in the United States. In the former it operates to reinforce adult-approved patterns of conduct, whereas, in our country, it intensifies antisocial tendencies" (Bronfenbrenner 1973, p. 112).

Bronfenbrenner appears to represent a school of thought in which parents and peers play two contrasting roles in social development: parents teach children how to control their individualistic impulses for the sake of other persons; peers feed into these impulses and fan the fires of individualism. For this kind of theory, peers represent a risk. When children begin to instruct one another, the teaching of parents and teachers is endangered. Thus, Bronfenbrenner recommends a form of adult intervention into peer activities which maximizes peer imitation of adult norms and converts it from its natural tendency for disorder to a more socially adaptive promotion of community.

The data presented in this book do not sustain Bronfenbrenner's argument or support his fears. The children in our studies came from typical middle-class suburban homes in the United States. Some young adolescents did indeed say, like those cited by Bronfenbrenner, that in times of trouble they would more likely turn to peers rather than parents for help and advice. But in their turning to friends, these adolescents were not seeking nurture for self-indulgence, but rather sustenance in a deeply felt interpersonal bond. The closer one looks at the present data, the clearer it becomes that friendship during the school years contains the essential elements for putting the self in communion with other persons. The principles of friendship which children spontaneously expressed appear to be those upon which true community can be founded. It was not individualism which friendship engendered but instead a clear sense of responsibility to one's part in relationship with another. If nothing else, friends view their individual personalities in terms of characteristics shared in common and with a sensitivity to differences that demands empathy rather than self-aggrandizement.

Bronfenbrenner's fear may be traced to the model of the person he has chosen to follow. The model fits conventional premises in the social sciences. It includes the following: The child is "idiosyncratic"; parents counter this with social instruction. Children who meet as peers lack "sufficient internalization of societal values" to be trusted to act in a spirit of community. Around school age, children act as law-abiding persons, but when "adolescent rebellion" begins, peers stimulate one another to act against parental training. The "normal" adolescent outgrows this negative attitude and returns to positive values as a new individual ready to accept social duties. The more mature adult goes even further in developing moral values and is not afraid to step outside convention to assert his individuality.

This mixture of ideological premises conflicts sharply with the Sullivan-Piaget perspective. It is not the content of social instruction that makes children social but the interdependency they first learn from adults who interact consistently with them. When peers meet in school, they do not necessarily pose a threat to earlier socialization. In the first place, the parent-child relation is not a completed product but will undergo further transformations, one of these clearly occurring around early adolescence. To see peers as counteracting early parental training is to believe that early training fixes the personality while implicitly denying the continuing changes of self which later development will bring. In the second place, the view that peers compete with parents ignores the prospect that children's social conceptions are attempts at integration of experience. Again, the focus is too often on content in the sense that parents may say one thing while peers say another. If the child were a mere recipient of information, differences would pose a problem. But if the child were attempting to integrate input, then competing messages would be an opportunity to seek synthesis with the result not having to be either this or that but some new position which reconciles the two.

A third point, the position that peers enhance individualism, is to misunderstand the opportunities peer relations offer that early parent-child relations cannot. Friendship relations provide children with a view of self where for the first time the self can be seen as a free and equal agent. The practice of direct reciprocity gives children a full range of the consequences of pursuing individual interests unabashedly; these include, continually reaching stalemate, competing, and entering a struggle in which either the more powerful holds sway or else neither can control the other. It is no wonder that peers come to discover cooperation. To miss the nature of cooperation which peer relations can engender is to bypass the most important meaning of friendship. For the children interviewed, the principle of equal treatment, the common personhood between individuals, and the need for intimacy appeared originally in friendship and only later began to enter relations with adults around early adolescence. These children did indeed see peers differently from adults, but not in the sense which Bronfenbrenner speculates. Peers do not have to tear down what parents have built. Peers and friends provide entry to new possibilities of social existence where community is grounded on the need to adjust one's individuality to another's rather than on conformity based on the child's naïve awe of parental perfection. Parents are persons with imperfections, and until children can relate their own individuality to their parents' personhood, mutual understanding with them is an illusion.

Two Worlds   The contrasting data derived from children reared in a socialistic milieu and children reared in a capitalist society must be seen as tentative at the present time. No doubt economic-political forces influence relations on the interpersonal level. But when these abstract forces are reduced to methods of reciprocity, a new form of analysis becomes possible. Despite the labels one might use, any political system may be seen in practice to lie at some point on the continuum where complementariness is one extreme and cooperation is the other extreme. And within any cultural system, children probably experience relations based on both methods as well as in-between forms.

My view, which corresponds with Sullivan's and Piaget's proposal, is that complementariness leads to interpersonal relations that are different from those engendered by the cooperative use of direct reciprocity. These methods are the grounds for two relations in which the self takes distinctive roles with respect to others. The self is constituted through systems of exchange. If individuality is the issue, then persons partaking of both systems are bound to check their individuality and be checked by the other persons in the systems. The question then becomes a matter of how the reciprocal dependency affects the self. Present findings suggest that control of self-interest can be more or less based on mutual understanding. The "more" applies to relations based on direct reciprocity and the "less" is found in relations of reciprocity by complement. Insofar as, in childhood, these relations correspond generally to peers and adults, respectively, they can be said not just to differ but to engender two selves, two types of individuality, both social in nature. However, it is the world of direct reciprocal exchange which ironically offers the most individual freedom and which appears to lead to the deepest form of communal existence, where self and other merge into a relational *we*.

If the present findings are reliable and the conclusions plausible, the call for more adult intervention into peer relations is precipitous and perhaps wrongly directed. Adults' intervention into children's lives is legitimate and fulfilling of a natural motive. But there is just so much adults can do for children's social development. According to the present analysis, the structure of children's relations with adults puts limitations on mutuality. Peer relations on their own have different limitations; most notably they contain an ambiguity which can lead as easily to competition as to cooperation. But children do not need adults to instruct them on the contradiction inherent in direct reciprocity. They need friends, peers who are their equals with whom they can discover the relational possibilities of cooperation.

This analysis in no way demeans the place of adult-child relations in social development. The present data cover a relatively brief period of time and say nothing of these relations beyond early adolescence. Emphasis was given to young adolescents' new understanding of agreement in relations with adults. Realistically speaking, parents, teachers, and other significant adults in adolescents' lives undoubtedly also make corresponding transformations in their conceptions. The logical possibilities for subsequent development of the relation are obvious. The adolescent self and the redefined parent are no longer the same persons who exchanged conformity for approval a decade or so earlier. These persons have new opportunities for mutuality which were not possible previously and the result may be intimacy which can be nurtured for the remainder of their life-spans.

For Sullivan and Piaget, the normal personality may be seen in an adult who understands the two forms of interpersonal existence and can act with a consciousness of the implications of these relations. In any relation, there will be submission of the self in conjunction with the other, with the person being able to take a position in relations based on unilateral constraint as well as cooperation. Knowing the implications does not mean that the self will act consistently in keeping with relational principles because the self understands its own as well as the other's free agency. It does mean, however, that the self can control its individuality in cooperation with another and consciously seek intimacy with all that it entails.

A Perspective   In recent years there has been dissatisfaction with conventional approaches to the study of social development. Contemporary theorists have begun to look at cognition and affectivity in counterpoint to socialization models. Theorists have also begun to look at peer relations, in part, to balance the selective focus and overemphasis on early parent-child relations. While it may be said of any time that a field is in transition, the present state of the study of social development is alive with new approaches, each offering interesting insights into one or more aspect, issue, or phenomenon. The approach to development through the study of interpersonal relations is old but relatively unexplored. Theorists have over the years picked up on Piaget's (1965) or Sullivan's (1953) ideas but have not adopted their underlying rationale or worked with the integration of the two. The present work is a step in creating this theoretical synthesis. The data, presented for illustrative support, are also preliminary, being based on loosely controlled procedures and being descriptive in nature. The discussions offered after each study and in the last three chapters are equally tentative.

Nevertheless, the present work offers a general perspective toward social development which others might find useful for generating empirical studies and clarifying theoretical constructs. The perspective rests on sound philosophical grounds that existence is constituted in interpersonal relationship (Macmurray 1957 and 1961). It offers a means of analysis through treatment of interactions as methods which describe relational structures and their functions (Hinde 1976 and 1978). It promises to give clarity to the study of parent-child relations (Damon 1977; Gadlin 1976 and 1978) and to redefine peer relations and friendship as positive contributors to the development of the self (Youniss and Volpe 1978b; Youniss 1978b). More broadly, the perspective treats socialization and cognition as compatible forces (Youniss 1977 and 1978a) and holds promise for a synthesis among cognition, affectivity, and action (Riegel 1976; Youniss 1975 and 1978b).

The elements of Sullivan's and Piaget's proposal are the very constructs which empirical researchers have called "soft" and "fuzzy." The proposition that "self and other" comprise a basic unit of analysis, which is *interpersonal relation*, is an obvious example. One could immediately ask: "But how can relations with all their psychological depth be quantified?" This book is addressed to those who would rather ask: "If the thesis and its perspective are reasonable, how might we ask better questions about the nature and processes of interpersonal development?" This book, rather than answering the question, is meant to raise new questions clearly so that others will be encouraged to pursue the relational perspective and all that it implies.

References

Ainsworth, M. D. S. 1969. Object relations, dependency, and attachment: A theoretical review of the infant-mother relationship. *Child Development* 40:969–1025.

Baumrind, D. 1968. Authoritarian vs. authoritative control. *Adolescence* 3:255–72.

———. 1975. Early socialization and adolescent competence. In S. E. Dragastin and G. H. Elder, Jr., eds. *Adolescence in the life cycle*, pp. 117–43. New York: Halsted Press.

Bell, R. Q. 1968. A reinterpretation of the direction of effects in studies of socialization. *Psychological Review* 75:81–95.

Bell, S. M., and Ainsworth, M. D. S. 1972. Infant crying and maternal responsiveness. *Child Development* 43:1171–90.

Bronfenbrenner, U. 1973. *Two worlds of childhood: U.S. and U.S.S.R.* New York: Simon and Schuster, Pocket Books.

Chapman, A. H. 1976. *Harry Stack Sullivan: His life and his work.* New York: G. B. Putnam's Sons.

Coleman, J. S. 1976. Individual rights and the state: A review essay. *American Journal of Sociology* 82:428–42.

Damon, W. 1977. *The social world of the child.* San Francisco: Jossey-Bass.

Elder, G. H., Jr. 1975. Adolescence in the life cycle: An introduction. In S. E. Dragastin and G. H. Elder, Jr., eds. *Adolescence in the life cycle*, pp. 1–22. New York: Halsted Press.

Escalona, S. K. 1968. *The roots of individuality.* Chicago: Aldine.

Furth, H. G. 1969. *Piaget and knowledge.* Englewood Cliffs, N.J.: Prentice-Hall.

Gadlin, H. 1976. Spare the rod: Disguising control in American childrearing. Paper presented at the meeting of the American Association for the Advancement of Science, Boston, February 1976.

293

————. 1978. Child discipline and the pursuit of self: An historical perspective. In H. W. Reese and L. P. Lipsitt, eds. *Advances in child development and behavior*, 12:231–65. New York: Academic Press.

Gillis, J. R. 1974. *Youth and history*. New York: Academic Press.

Goslin, D. A., ed. 1969. *Handbook of socialization theory and research*. Chicago: Rand McNally.

Gouldner, A. W. 1960. The norm of reciprocity: A preliminary statement. *American Sociological Review* 25:161–78.

Hinde, R. A. 1976. On describing relationships. *Journal of Child Psychology and Psychiatry* 17:1–19.

————. 1978. Interpersonal relations: In quest of a science. *Psychological Medicine* 8:373–86.

Kett, J. F. 1977. *Rites of passage*. New York: Basic Books.

Kohlberg, L. 1969. Stage and sequence: The cognitive-developmental approach to socialization. In D. A. Goslin, ed. *Handbook of socialization theory and research*, pp. 347–480. Chicago: Rand McNally.

Lamb, M. E., ed. 1976. *The role of the father in child development*. New York: John Wiley.

Lamb, M. E. 1977. A re-examination of the infant social world. *Human Development* 20:65–85.

Lasch, C. 1979. *Haven in a heartless world*. New York: Basic Books.

Lewis, M., and Brooks, J. 1975. Infants' social perception: A constructivist view. In Cohen and Salapatek, eds. *Infant perception: From sensation to cognition*, 2:102–43. New York: Academic Press

Lewis, M., and Rosenblum, L. A., eds. 1975. *Friendship and peer relations*. New York: John Wiley.

Lieberson, J. 1978. Harvard's Nozick: Philosopher of the new right. *New York Times Magazine*, December 17.

Macmurray, J. 1957. *The self as agent*. London: Faber and Faber.

————. 1961. *Persons in relation*. London: Faber and Faber.

Nozick, R. 1974. *Anarchy, state, and utopia*. New York: Basic Books.

Piaget, J. 1965. *The moral judgment of the child*. New York: Free Press. Original publication in English in 1932 by Routledge and Kegan Paul, London.

————. 1970. Piaget's theory. In P. Mussen, ed. *Carmichael's manual of child psychology*, pp. 703–32. New York: John Wiley.

Rawls, J. 1971. *A theory of justice*. Cambridge, Mass.: Harvard University Press.

Riegel, K. F. 1976. The dialectics of human development. *American Psychologist* 31:689–700.

Sahlins, M. D. 1965. On the sociology of primitive exchange. In

M. Banton, ed., *Relevance of models of social anthropology.* pp. 139–238. New York: Praeger Press.

Sampson, E. E. 1977. Psychology and the American ideal. *Journal of Personality and Social Psychology* 35:767–82.

Sayer, D. 1975. Method and dogma in historical materialism. *Sociological Review* 23:779–810.

Shorter, E. 1975. *The making of the modern family.* New York: Basic Books.

Simmel, G. 1955. A contribution to the sociology of religion. *American Journal of Sociology* 60:1–18. Originally published in 1905.

Sullivan, E. V. 1977. A study of Kohlberg's structural theory of moral development: A critique of liberal social science ideology. *Human Development* 20:352–76.

Sullivan, H. S. 1953. *The interpersonal theory of psychiatry.* New York: Norton.

Watzlawick, P.; Beavin, J. H.; and Jackson, D. D. 1967. *Pragmatics of human communication.* New York: Norton.

Weinraub, M.; Brooks, J.; and Lewis, M. 1977. The social network: A reconsideration of the concept of attachment. *Human Development* 20:31–47.

Wish, M.; Deutsch, M.; and Kaplan, S. J. 1976. Perceived dimensions of interpersonal relations. *Journal of Personality and Social Psychology* 33:409–20.

Youniss, J. 1975. Another perspective on social cognition. In A. Pick, ed. *Minnesota symposia on child development,* 9:173–93. Minneapolis: University of Minnesota Press.

————. 1977. Socialization and social knowledge. In R. Silbereisen, ed. *Soziale Kognition,* pp. C3–22. Berlin: Technische Universität Berlin.

————. 1978a. Dialectical theory and Piaget on social knowledge. *Human Development* 21:234–47.

————. 1978b. The nature of social development: A conceptual discussion of cognition. In H. McGurk, ed. *Issues in childhood social development,* pp. 203–27. London: Methuen.

———— and Volpe, J. 1978. A relational analysis of friendship. In W. Damon, ed. *Social cognition,* pp. 1–22. San Francisco: Jossey-Bass.

Index